Unearthing Gender

Unearthing Gender

Folksongs of North India

Smita Tewari Jassal

DUKE UNIVERSITY PRESS

Durham & London 2012

© 2012 Duke University Press
All rights reserved
Printed in the United States of America
on acid-free paper ∞
Typeset in Adobe Garamond Pro by
Keystone Typesetting, Inc.
Library of Congress Cataloging-in-Publication Data
appear on the last printed page of this book.

Hear the bells ring
the notes of a chime
when our words may not
the worlds will rhyme.

FROM "TEMPLE BELLS,"
RAMINDER SINGH JASSAL

To the memory of my father
JAGDISH NARAIN TEWARI (1925–1990)
and for RAMINDER (1952–2011)
who made life a song.

When, during my research in Uttar Pradesh, I introduced myself to an informant, B. K. Dubey, in preparation for a structured interview, I first had to quell his curiosity about my interest in the songs of the region. The explanation I offered—that the inquiry was prompted both by my desire to pay homage to the memory of my deceased father and by the opportunity this provided for "reclaiming" the language of my ancestors—so satisfied him that he warmed to me instantly. He found it entirely appropriate for a daughter, especially one married outside the community, to repay her debts in this manner. I encountered such responses repeatedly during fieldwork. Ironically, however, in discharging this particular debt, I invariably incurred others over the many years I spent in different academic environments. It is therefore a great pleasure to finally thank all those without whom this book would not have been possible.

The knowledge and vision of several individuals have impacted this project in countless ways. I could never have imagined writing such a book had Arun Kumar, in the late 1990s, not infected me with his enthusiasm for documenting songs that are fast disappearing, his lyrical Bhojpuri providing the impetus for my first tentative translations. Our shared project and research for a documentary film, "Land of Memories" revealed the scope and potential of my inquiry. In Israel, my conversations with David Shulman, and in New York, with Lila Abu-Lughod, encouraged me to explore the scholarly potential of my growing archive of songs, especially its implications for gender. I am also grateful to David for offering me the chance of a lifetime, in the spring of 2004, to sit in at the Sanskrit *kavya* symposia of world-renowned Sanskrit scholars at the Hebrew University of Jerusalem. That unique experience had a major influence on the contours of this book. Since the beginning of my writing process in 2005, Narayana Rao, Kirin Narayan, and Eyal Ben-Ari have been wonderful sources of inspiration and ideas.

Many individuals have generously read and commented on different stages of this manuscript. I warmly thank Eyal Ben-Ari, Carla Borden, Dipankar Gupta, Saul Sosnowski, Lila Abu-Lughod, Philip Lutgendorf, Sarah Lamb, Ann Grodzins Gold, Melanie Braverman, Patricia Uberoi, Nandini Sundar, Aftab Jassal, and the anonymous readers at Duke University Press for their insightful comments. I am indebted to Bharati Ray, Adam Jones, and Namita Gokhale for publishing earlier versions and sections of these chapters in volumes they edited. I thank the *Journal of Peasant Studies* and *Contributions to Indian Sociology* for permission to republish large sections of chapters 1 and 6.

I completed this book during my tenure as the Madeleine Haas Russell Visiting Professor in the department of Anthropology at Brandeis University in 2008–09. I am grateful to Wendy Tarlow Kaplan and Shula Reinharz for this remarkable opportunity and to Sarah Lamb, Harleen Singh, my colleagues at Brandeis, and Naseem Hines for their friendship and support during that wonderful year. For their support in early 2005 in Washington, D.C., where I conceived and wrote most of the book, I thank Sunil Khilnani at SAIS, Johns Hopkins University, and Dean Goodman and Shalini Venturelli of American University, along with Sonalde Desai and Aseema Sinha. The perspectives of Israel's Nirit Singers, Barbara Johnson and Skaria Zacharia, experts on songs of Israel's Cochin Jews, helped strengthen my own arguments. Ruth Freed, Manjula Kumar, Dakshita Das, and M. J. Akbar deserve warm thanks for directing me to sources of songs, and Ali Kucukler, for supplying Devnagari fonts. I sorely miss the energy and support of the anthropologist Ruth Cernea, who as my walking companion in Bethesda shared the highs and the lows of the writing process but, alas, is no longer with us to celebrate the final product.

I am grateful to Jaunpur's Ajay Kumar Singh and his friends for engaging me in fascinating conversations about music and for introducing me to folk musicians in Chachakpur village and musical experts in Jaunpur city. Through Daulat Ram of Bharatiya Jan Sewa Ashram, Badlapur, and Munnilal of Barsara, I was able to contact a number of village communities, including those of Sauraiyan and Barsara, whose songs are captured in these pages. I thank Brahm Deo Upadhyaya for his assistance during the many field trips I made in Jaunpur district. In Misraulia, Chhapra, Ajay Mishra and his family generously shared their musical treasures. Thanks to him, the sessions I attended at the village temple at Misraulia will remain forever etched in my memory. Avinash Chaudhury and Radhey Shyam Nishad introduced me to singers in Sadiapur, Allahabad, and Rakesh Pandey, to singing communities in and around Benaras. Nirmal and Ajay Pandey, Rajeev Singh, and Momita Mukhopadhyay were particularly helpful in directing me to Sita songs circulating in Ballia, Ghazipur, and Chandauli. I thank Muniza Khan for introducing me to the Dalit and Muslim communities of Katesar village near Ramnagar, Benaras. I thank Shubhra Nagalia for introducing me to the singers of Kala Commune and to other folk music enthusiasts in Benaras, including Vidya Niwas Mishra. I relied on Shyam Lal Nishad for all manner of information in Benaras, and through Arun Mishra, I was able to contact folk singers in Robertsganj, and Dankinganj, Mirzapur.

Ashok Choudhary, Hazari Singh Pankaj, Roma, Bharati, and many others of the U.P. Abhiyān Samitī deserve my warm thanks for facilitating my earliest recordings at the various workshops across Uttar Pradesh. I made many of the recordings while working on research projects at New Delhi's Centre For Women's Development Studies. I thank my colleagues and the librarians and staff at the Centre, especially Priyanka, who ably translated my early recordings.

The singers whose songs are immortalized in these pages are too numerous to mention by name. However, I do wish to extend my heartfelt thanks to Auntie Shanti Tewari and her friends and neighbors in Jaunpur's Atara district. Munraji and Subhavati of Barsara, along with their friends, held musical sessions and wakes especially for my benefit. The repertoire of Khatun of Jaunpur city, and the songs of Bhagirathi Devi

and Urmila Maurya of Chachakpur invariably surpassed all of my musical expectations. The villagers of Sauraiyan, especially Usha, Sushila,
Kamala, and Ishraji Devi, adopted me and treated me to their songs and
stories on numerous occasions. In Sadiapur, Allahabad, my thanks go to
Sitara Devi and her companions not only for their songs but also for their
wonderful spirit. In Misraulia, I thank Meena Devi for generously sharing her extensive repertoire with me. The team of extraordinary Dalit
singers in Misraulia showed me just how much is conveyed through
music. In Benaras, I was privileged to learn about musical traditions from
the *biraha* maestros Hira Lal Yadav and Laxmi Narayan Yadav. I am indebted to them as well as singers near Ramnagar, particularly Badru-
nissa, Shama, Aarti, and Savita Devi. I thank them all for generously
sharing their heritage with me and for enabling me to claim it, too.

Several sections of this book were first presented at conferences and
seminars, and the feedback I received at these events has proved invaluable. The arguments I make in chapter 2 were first presented at the
Special Anthropology Talk series on 18 September 2008 at Brandeis University. I presented sections of the introduction on 6–7 April 2008 at a
series of symposia held in Washington, D.C. on "The Women Who Kept
the Songs: From India to Israel—The Musical Heritage of Cochin," at the
University of Maryland, the Library of Congress, and in the Goldman
Theater at the D.C. Jewish Community Center (DCJCC). I thank Stephen
Stern and Gail Shirazi for their insights and interest in these programs. I
first presented the ideas developed in chapters 3 and 4 at the "Gender and
Development: Perspectives From India" conference held at the Center for
South Asia, University of Wisconsin, Madison, on 18 October 2007.
Selected themes from the book were also presented at the "Indian Art in
the Contemporary Art World: Women Artists of India Transforming
Culture" symposium, held at Brandeis University's Women's Studies Re-
search Center on 3 October 2007. I presented songs from the book at the
workshop "New Directions in the Social and Cultural Study of Sleep" at
the University of Vienna, Austria, on 8 June 2007 and at the Richard H.
Foster Lecture in Idaho on March 1, 2007, at the 36th annual Frank
Church Symposium. I cited many of the songs relating to land rights in a
talk I gave on 5 December 2006 on Women, Land, and Development in
India at the Sigur Center for Asian Studies, Elliott School of International Affairs at George Washington University. I presented the de-

velopment aspects of this book at the Gandhi Center in Maryland as part of the panel "India, U.N. and the Challenges of Development" in September 2006.

My students of South Asia at Columbia and Brandeis Universities were often the first to hear about the ideas I develop in this book. Their curiosity and questions helped me toward clarity in subsequent presentations. I take this opportunity to thank Mark Dellelo and the students of Brandies University's Getz Lab for their assistance with digitizing the songs. Ilona Yuhaev, Tom Hawk, Zach, Harry Wolf, Laine Kaplan, Andrew Riker, Evan Gluckman, Anthony Seibelli, and Muhammed Kundos deserve special thanks for their patience with this process between 2008 and 2009. I thank the librarians and staff of the Harry S. Truman Research Institute for the Advancement of Peace at the Hebrew University of Jerusalem; Mason Library at SAIS, Washington, D.C.; McKeldin Library at the University of Maryland; University Library at American University; Butler Library at Columbia University; and Goldfarb Library at Brandeis University.

I would like to thank Valerie Millholland and the editorial team at Duke University Press. It was a pleasure working with Gisela Fosado. I am especially grateful to Neal McTighe, for ably steering the book through the many stages of production.

Other details and updates are available on the Facebook page for this book. A small selection of representative field recordings used in the book may be heard here.

Finally, the hardest task of all—acknowledging the boundless generosity, extraordinary humanity, poetic sensibility, and fantastic sense of humor with which Raminder, my partner and life companion, infused every page of this work. With his passing away in the last stages of the book's publication, the joy of the final product is considerably diminished. Wherever he is, I hope this book is a source of delight and pride for him. May the journey that his soul has now embarked upon be as beautiful and joyful as our time together.

SMITA TEWARI JASSAL

ANKARA, TURKEY

21 APRIL 2011

To minimize the use of diacritics, I have not included proper names in the transliteration scheme, such as the commonly used Sita, and caste names, such as Chamar. I have also dropped the default vowels from the system of Sanskrit transliteration at the end of words like Rama, such that the word appears as 'Ram'. For Hindi and Bhojpuri speakers, I have followed Roman Sanskrit Serif. To retain the oral pronunciation, I have transcribed the sounds phonetically, rather than standardize the spellings:

c is pronounced as *ch* in *church*
ī is pronounced as *e in carefree*
ā is pronounced as *a in father*
The spellings *ke* and *kai* produce variations in pronunciation from song to song.

For phonetics, I have relied on tables on page xvii of the 1993 edition of R. S. McGregor's *The Oxford Hindi-English Dictionary*.

⇥ The Unsung Sing

What is the question here, as I have already said, is the ability to "hear"
that which we have not heard before, and to transgress in situating the
text or the "fragment" differently.

PANDEY, "VOICES FROM THE EDGE," 285

At wedding festivities across rural and urban north
India, just as the groom and members of the *barāt*
(groom's party) prepare to depart with the bride, the family of the bride, the "wife-givers," belt out playfully abusive songs calculated to assault the ears of the "wife-
takers." Veiled animosity toward the extended family for
taking away a beloved daughter pours forth in finely orchestrated ritual abuse. This genre, known as *gālī* or *gārī*
(abusive songs), is but one of many types of songs that
might be heard during a wedding ceremony. At numerous wedding rituals, blessings loaded with symbolism
and advice are customarily sung.

Wedding songs, of course, constitute only a small proportion of song repertoires that range from congratulatory birth songs and those marking other rites of passage
to songs associated with festivals and seasons. Such songs
are quite distinct from the songs that punctuate women's
labor while grinding grain or transplanting rice, for ex-

ample. Dominant and recurring themes in folksongs are humor and subversion, especially at the spring festival of Holi, brother-sister affection, the separation and pathos of lovers, and the struggles of Sita, the heroine of the epic Rāmāyanā. Easily recognized through their rhythms and melodies, women's song genres are vastly different in mood and style of performance from those of men. As the very hum of life, folksongs offer much more than just the right mood. In rural contexts, their appeal is comparable to the potent points of identification offered by Bollywood films. Just as urban Indians often narrate their lives in reference to Bollywood characters and heroes, rural Indians have long articulated the human condition by aligning with the messages and moods of folksongs, their own scripts of reference.

Making sense of the ubiquity of this song culture in all its bewildering variety, with a song for every occasion, is by far the most compelling and rewarding aspect of conducting anthropological fieldwork in the Purabiya and Bhojpuri-speaking countryside of northern India, namely, eastern Uttar Pradesh and western Bihar. Since songs are also pedagogical, critical, and interrogative, they offer abundantly rich source material for anthropological inquiry.

This study focuses its investigation on the way songs, as a people's oral traditions, illuminate the social construction of gender through which overarching caste and gender ideologies are transmitted and reproduced. Because the kinds of relations that obtain between men and women are not merely determined by the biological givens but also are products of social and cultural processes (Ortner and Whitehead 1981, ix), songs make it possible for us to understand the organization of maleness and femaleness in relation to a particular society. As the same songs suggest how dominant ideologies are not merely complied with, accommodated, and reinforced but also resisted and interrogated, they also enable us to address the question of agency. Since songs are integral to people's lives in rural settings, the light they shed on caste, kinship and marriage, work cultures, gender, power, sexuality, family life, patriarchy, and the forms of agency and constraint operating within the same framework turns them into a resource for anthropological research.

Additionally, since songs "provide a medium for expressing emotions that are taboo topics in everyday conversations," (Narayan 1986, 56) subjecting these texts to close scrutiny allows us a glimpse of people's intimate worlds. In cultures that do not openly discuss inner emotional states, songs are the shared tradition through which emotions are expressed, thus providing a medium for the expression of what might be taboo in everyday conversation (ibid). For instance, in the emotionally charged fragment below, about a visiting brother's dismay at his sister's unhappiness, we also learn that women are prone to conceal details about ill treatment in their marital homes, so as not to alarm their natal kin.

Sonvā t jarai bahinī sonarā dukaniyā
Bahinī jarthīn sasurariyā ho Ram
Loharā t jarai bahinī loharā dukaniyā
Bahinī jarthīn sasurariyā ho Ram
E dukh jani kahiyā bhaiyā Bābā ke agvā
Sabhavā baithī pactaihen ho Ram
E dukh jani kahiyā Maiyā ke agavā
Chatiyā pīti mari jaihen ho Ram.

Gold melts at the goldsmith's.
Sister burns away at her in-laws.
Iron smelts at the ironsmith's.
Sister wastes away at her in-laws.
Brother, don't speak of this grief to father.
In the assembly, he'll be filled with remorse.
Brother, don't speak of this to mother.
Beating her breast, she'll die of grief.

URMILA MAURYA AND FRIENDS, CHACHAKPUR, JAUNPUR

In north India, from the nineteenth century onward, forms of women's entertainment attracted the attention of "social reformers, urban intellectuals, emerging middle classes and caste associations," each intending to initiate changes in the social and customary behavior of women and lower castes (Gupta 2001, 90). In response to the colonial state's attempts to place castes on a hierarchical grid, caste organizations aiming at upward mobility and keen to secure for themselves a high position in the census schedules were quick to crack down on women's practices that reformers had looked at with disfavor. They were eager to restrain women from the practice of singing abusive and obscene songs both at weddings and, for example, at the annual festival of Holi, where role reversals are common. This eagerness to censor hints at the often provocative nature of women's songs. In the nineteenth century, the *gālī* genre, for instance, generated a great deal of embarrassment among social reformers. High on their list were several genres of folksongs that were considered unworthy of being sung by "chaste" Hindu women. The reformers argued that gālīs promoted women's confrontational behavior and aggression and prompted women to transgress boundaries and challenge familial relationships (Gupta 2001, 93). This reasoning completely overlooked the logic and place of people's oral traditions within the society.

Since the reformers' objectives were to be accomplished by targeting women's songs and patriarchy was to be refurbished by silencing women, forms of women's cultural expression, such as their folk and oral traditions, require urgent attention. This anxiety about folksongs went hand in hand with the alarm generated about women's use of public spaces and the need to restrict women's access to these spaces in the so-called interest of protecting women. The reformers' platform was dictated in part by their desire to efface the erotic from women's lives and to suppress women's sexuality in the interest of conjugal harmony.

This book addresses how conventional understandings of caste, gender, labor, agrarian relations, and the complex workings of power may be strengthened, questioned, and fine-tuned through the study of folksongs. The power of these songs also lies in their ability to hint at and suggest, rather than directly address, social themes. The aim here is to identify those areas of the social enterprise, including political-economic organizations, that directly impact cultural constructions of gender (Ortner and Whitehead 1981, 10). In foregrounding the songs and their significance to those who sing them, the book also seeks to refine our understandings of the interplay between caste, class, and gender.

The significance of the texts analyzed here is heightened by the fact that they embody the voices of the marginalized, those who rarely have been the focus of systematic analytical inquiry. Indeed, the search for women's agency in biographies, diaries, poems, and other forms of written expression by individual women, largely of the elite or middle-classes, has obscured the value to be found in the voices of unlettered women, who comprise the vast majority. Drawn from laboring castes and classes, peasant milieus, or groups otherwise marginalized, these songs, like the one below, largely reflect women's "subaltern consciousness."

Kahiyā bidāyi dihalā
Buxar me dhāhi dihalā
Gaiyā niyare pagahā dharavalā, ho Bābujī
Pahilā me budhā baravā
Dūsar garīb ho gharavā
Tīsar me jadūgaravā khojalā, ho Bābujī

Why did you get me married?
Dumped me here in Buxar.
Handed me like a cow, to be tied up, why did you, O Father?
First, a groom so aged.
Then, a home impoverished.
Third, a magician you found for me, why did you, O Father?
DALIT STREET MUSICIANS, BUXAR FAIR, 14 JANUARY 2000

The concerns and worlds of Dalit and subaltern women have largely remained obscure, not only because of upper-caste men and women's distance from Dalit struggles but also because of the latter's lack of integration into mainstream knowledge, academic disciplines, and even the middle-class women's movement. While, like the rural and urban worlds, the worlds of marginalized or Dalit women and those of women of the upper castes remain distinct, hints at how these worlds have been sometimes bridged can be found in the songs.

If women's early literary expressions were aimed at greater visibility, the opposite tendency of anonymity emerges as the dominant feature here. Songs have allowed women (and men) through the ages to articulate, acknowledge, and affirm shared impressions. Hence their validity for large collectivities, especially those of women, offering precisely the kind of anonymity that facilitated the fleshing-out and articulation of shared experiences.

Songs constitute the spaces wherein the collective voice of women may be said to have evolved. Since repertoires largely associated with agricultural tasks are being steadily eclipsed with the mechanization of farming, the urgent need to document them cannot be overstated. Further, Indians' simultaneous distancing of themselves from folksongs as representative of the "old" ways or their modifications and reworkings of these songs to address contemporary concerns offer other compelling rationales for this investigation.

Indeed how folksongs respond to social change, including urbanization and mechanization, is a promising area of research (Blackburn and Ramanujan 1986; Narayan 1993, 177–204). Narayan suggests that we must think of the material as a dynamic making and remaking of folklore in response to changing conditions, rather than, as has been the tendency since colonial times, to equate folklore with "bounded, authentic and unchanging materials" (Narayan 1993, 197). Hence the utility of viewing songs in situated contexts to gauge their relevance for the individuals who perform and interpret them (ibid). Today, for instance, the young and upwardly mobile residents of north Indian villages strive to distance themselves from these traditions. This distancing also derives from the association between these songs and certain kinds of labor and, along with the general devaluation of manual labor, this labor has served to indicate a lower status in the caste system (Jassal 2001, 46–48).

Women's repertoires, in particular, are eclipsed and modified partly as a result of the wider appeal and reach of the Bollywood music industry and partly due to a thriving industry of musical cassette production, themes I discuss in chapter 6. While classical musical traditions have drawn heavily on women's field songs, this incorporation of women's genres into the world of classical music has invariably eclipsed the association of these songs in public consciousness with "women's voice," a dimension I return to in chapter 2.

Despite the richly layered possibilities women's songs offer, it is not true that only women's articulations are worthy of attention. Masculine song traditions are both rich and vibrant and, while they represent distinct worlds and social concerns, they offer equally significant insights into gender relations. Unlike women's song traditions, male *gāthā* (ballad) traditions retain their vitality not only because they are largely performative and remembered by village bards but also because they are periodically renewed through all-night celebrations and festivities. In contrast, women's songs, while also integral to ceremonies and rites of passage, tend to accompany agricultural work or other forms of productive activity. However, it is useful to remember that, in addition to classical musicians, folk singers and bards received the patronage of upper-caste elites and landlords, thereby reproducing the existing inequities of caste and class.

UNEARTHING GENDER

Songs as Forms of Communication

What can the songs tell us about caste, gender, and class that cannot be learned in other ways? What do the songs convey that might otherwise be obscured by merely observing social interaction in the field or by deploying more conventional anthropological tools such as participant observation? Elucidating their special quality, Paul Friedrich argues that through poetry and songs, "one is often given the gist of the culture in a way that would be difficult or impossible to infer. These insights and intuitions are of singular value because they characteristically deal with and involve the emotions, the cultural experience as felt in addition to as understood—that is, in psychological terms, the phenomena of intention, identification, motivation, and affect that are often neglected in cultural analysis, including much of the recent research that combines an ideology of emotionality with practices that feature analytical instruments and objectivized data" (Friedrich 1996, 39).

What Friedrich claims for poetry, we can claim for the texts of songs: "Poetry is a constituent as well as a vehicle of the culture. . . . Poetry in this sense is at once 'data' for analysis and itself a body of generalizations about life that are at least as subtle as what the social scientist normally comes up with" (39).

Significantly, like good poems, folksongs exist in the memories and voices of living individuals (see Rao and Shulman 1998). They are primarily a means of social communication among those who share common bodies of knowledge, value systems, and ideologies. Constituting people's oral traditions, the remembrance and recollection of songs in particular contexts also invoke a variety of interconnections with other contexts. They are therefore loaded with meaning precisely because of the interplay of intertextual resonances wherein each seemingly isolated song may in fact be related to others, which often represent competing viewpoints and voices within the given folksong tradition. These strong intertextual connections and interactive relationships between the songs of a region are what make them so effective as forms of social communication. The fact that folksongs are sung again and again and passed down through generations also indicates the high degree of acceptability of the ideas, moods, and messages they contain.

Gender as Socially Constructed

Songs can be regarded as a reserve pool of folk resources and wisdom that people may draw upon to reflect on, and understand and struggle with, their own realities. A central concern of this book is to investigate how women's work songs become vehicles for the construction and reproduction of gender identity. While interviews with individual women and participant observation offer anthropologists and ethnographers one, often conventional, sort of fieldwork data, songs, as existing cultural codes of approved behavior and norms, provide another window into women's shared insights. These codes appear to equip women to maneuver and negotiate conditions that are often inherently disempowering. If the act of singing imparts psychological strength to individual women and to women's collectivities, then the underlying messages these songs transmit should offer us a range of clues about how the feminine gender is constructed.

Chapter 2, for instance, investigates how songs as cultural codes can take us one step further toward understanding the daily negotiations of power within households. The ironic song below shows how women both internalize and question male control.

Nibi kaurī laharedār o balamuā
Jab nibi kaurī jāman lāge
Sasuru mero rakhvār, o bālumā
Nibi kaurī laharedār, o bālumā
Jab nibi kaurī pharan lāge
Bhasaru mero rakhvār, o bālumā
Jab nibi kaurī pākan lāge
Devaru mero rakhvār, o bālumā
Nibi kaurī laharedār o bālumā
Jab nibi kaurī jharan lāge
Balmā mero rakhvār o bālumā

This Neem seed was a spirited one, beloved.
When the Neem seed began to grow,
Father-in-law was my protector.
When the Neem seed began to fruit,
Senior brother-in-law became my caretaker.
When the Neem seed began to ripen,

Younger brother-in-law took charge.
When the Neem seed was ready to drop,
Husband dear took control.

FIELD RECORDING, ROBERTSGANJ, 2002

The articulation and transmission of ideologies such that gender is socially constructed may, at first glance, suggest that women are simply victims of their society's customs and traditions. Numerous elaborations of alternative femininities, however, raise questions about the potential of songs to serve as spaces for the emergence of women's critical consciousness. The multilayered and varied texts, such as the song below, which offers a glimpse of a forceful femininity, encourage readings that refute unidimensional understandings.

Hamrā bālam eik diliyā ke naukar, diliya ke chākar
Diliyā se ākar cale jāye re sakhī re
Āye, cale jāye re sakhī re
Jab cala āve
Pahariyā mai dākalun
Dantava se katālun janjīr mor sakhī re

My lover is the servant of his will, heart's slave.
At will he comes, then goes back, my friend.
Comes and goes.
But when he comes,
I could jump across the highest mountains.
With my teeth, I'd bite off the chains, my friend.

SITARA NISHAD AND MALLAH WOMEN, ALLAHABAD

Such songs offer startling commentary on women's lives in contexts that otherwise seem, in various ways, to have silenced women, or at least made them invisible, especially in public discourses. One drawback of feminist writings hitherto has been the unconscious privileging of the upper-caste point of view. In tracing the history of the women's question at the end of the nineteenth and beginning of the twentieth centuries, we find that it is the upper caste woman, the "*bhadramahilā*," who is most written about and it is women from this class we come to know through their first literary expressions. The bhadramahilā, this new woman, was crafted through a series of dichotomies that differentiated her from the "coarse," "common," or "peasant" woman devoid of refinement (Chatterjee 1990). The latter category is the subject of this book.

This book takes as its source material the oral articulations of generations of women who were not only traditionally deprived of access to the written word but who may also have internalized this exclusion as normative. In this sense the songs invoke the perspectives of women who have been silenced, perhaps simply because what they have to say was not of interest to the privileged. These perspectives of laboring women also largely predate the conscious or politically articulate viewpoints that are now emerging as a consequence of the Dalit women's movement in several pockets of Uttar Pradesh, Maharashtra, and other regions of India.

Songs as Cultural Capital

Taking oral narratives as our lens also allows us to unravel caste, as an ongoing system of inequality reproduced in current modernity, in its complex interaction with class and gender (Dirks 2001). While anthropology has examined how women are embedded in relations of production, relatively unexplored are the cultural dimensions of women's work, the history of women's entry into the work force, the hidden nature of women's labor, women's access to and control over productive resources, and the dimension of women's consciousness, especially as it evolves during work processes. Mary Douglas's understanding of the mix of subcultures that would ideally lead to "the joint production of meaning" through intercultural dialogue within constituent elements engaged in a continuous process of "contestation, coordination and collaboration" (Rao and Walton 2004, 21) could well describe the multiplicity of cultural codes embedded in the songs this book examines. Hence, the meaning that these narratives hold for their singers is both essentially variable and made more so as a function of context.

Therefore it should come as no surprise that when the social reformers of the nineteenth century sought to regulate and sanitize certain kinds of women's songs, they also sought to urgently replace them with "proper" and "correct" alternatives. Songs considered corrupting and indecent were thus to be expunged from the repertoires of the new Hindu woman the social reformers hoped to shape. The emerging compilations and anthologies produced by men seeking to replace women's so-called trivial

songs with inspiring *ādarsh gīt* (idealistic songs) in the service of the
nation signaled this new trend:

Dekho lajjā ke darpan me tum mukhrā
Pativratā kī orho cunariyā,
shīl ka nainon me ho kajrā

See your face in the mirror of modesty,
Wear the veil of chastity,
Mark your eyes with the kohl of decency.

Na nācnā uchit na nacvāna,
Na byāhon me gālī gānā.
Kabhī mat dekho sajnī rās,
Krishan sakhiyon kā vividh vilās.

It is inappropriate to dance and get others dancing
Or to sing galis at weddings.
Girlfriends! Refrain from watching dramas
About the playful frolics of Krishna with the milkmaids.

GUPTA 2001, 95–96

Similar concerns to those Gupta points out in Uttar Pradesh were
voiced in Bengal as early as 1855. By the turn of the twentieth century, a
range of independent song forms practiced by women had disappeared,
unable to withstand the multipronged attack by Christian missionaries,
colonial administrators, and the Bengali *bhadralok* (Banerjee 1989, 160).

The new sense of morality the bhadralok represented rejected the
Radha-Krishna motif in plays and dances, especially in terms of human
passions, sensuality, and eroticism. Banerjee explores the impact of these
new attitudes, which regarded all native customs and habits as obscene,
including the form and content of performances, despite the fact that
recitals by women Vaishnavite *kathākatās*, or storytellers, were an important source of religious knowledge for women (Banerjee 1989, 151).
Krishna's erotic dalliances, metaphorically understood as the locking together in total involvement of the body and the mind, suddenly appeared, under colonial influence, to threaten domestic stability. Moreover, in this context, the erotic is envisioned entirely from the woman's
perspective, and the excitement of erotic love unites with ideas about the

crossing of given sexual boundaries. It is this explosive mix that appears to have threatened caste patriarchies. Banerjee cites a bhadralok writer who complained that it was impossible for uneducated young women to remain unexcited during the narration of the Krishna Lila. He therefore proposed: "Since it (kathakata) has become a source of so much evil, it is not advisable for bhadraloks to encourage it. Those who allow their ladies to go to kathakata performances should be careful. . . . If, during kathakata performances women stay at home and are provided with opportunities to listen to good instructions, discussions on good books and to train themselves in artistic occupations, their religious sense will improve and their souls will become pure and they will be suitable for domestic work" (Somaprakash cited in Banerjee 1989, 151–52).

Another aim of this book is to understand women's emotions, which are best approached through the language of the songs discussed in chapter 3. In this sense the songs are "inescapably and fundamentally social" (Abu-Lughod and Lutz 1990, 10). Trawick, through the analysis of a hymn sung by an untouchable woman about caste pollution, reveals the singer's concern with problems of inclusion and exclusion. Abu-Lughod and Lutz argue that "the singer's artistic technique, which involves deviating from the code of grammar as well as the social code, is a strategy for challenging that which has cast her out" (10). Close readings of some of the songs indeed point to similar strategies.

Folk genres exist in the public domain and have always constituted the common heritage of the rural communities in particular regions. The innumerable variations in content that the same song can undergo in different regions, and sometimes even from one village to the next, testifies to the prevalence of several versions of the songs. This variation also explains why there is no such thing as an "authentic" version of these songs. The masculine ballad, Lorikāyan, also known as Chandaini in the Chhattisgarhi region, is a case in point. The Lorikāyan of the Bhojpuri region, which is the subject of chapter 5, is a masculine ballad claimed by the Yadava caste. Yet its enormous appeal for a range of middle and lower castes makes it equally a part of the socialization processes of these caste groups.

What kinds of messages do these songs transmit, and how do notions of inequality, including gender inequality, become internalized? I seek answers to such questions, which are begged by the song's narratives themselves, at several points in this book. For instance, while certain well-known Sita songs, the subject of chapter 4, may be claimed by all castes, the plurality of voices they represent embody a range of meanings and divergent viewpoints. Their singular appeal to the women who sing them appears to derive from the fact that Sita songs mirror peasant women's own existential struggles with their socially constructed roles.

Jab re Sita dei Tulsi hāthe lihalī, Tulsi gailī sukhāi ai
Aisen purukhvā ke muh nahin dekhabī
Jini Ram dehlen banvās ai
Phāti jaiti dhartī alop hoi jaiti re, ab na dekhabī sansār ai

When Sita Devi touched the Tulsi, it dried up.
"Such a being I never wish to set eyes on again.
That Rama who exiled me to the forest,
Let the earth part, let me disappear in it."
UPADHYAYA 1990B, 169

Agency in Women's Songs

Many of the songs presented in this book articulate particular interests and agendas that are clearly inimical to those of women. Saba Mahmood broadens the notion of agency beyond that of Judith Butler, who defines it as the capacity to subvert norms (Mahmood 2005). Mahmood's arguments against reducing the heterogeneity of life to a flat narrative of either succumbing to or resisting relations of domination are useful in the context of women's songs. She cautions against equating values such as humility, shyness, or modesty with passivity and inaction simply because they do not "buttress the autonomy of the individual" (206–22). Again, limiting the notion of agency to the actions taken by individuals obscures how structures of gender, class, caste, and race shape or affect the possibilities for agency.

Limited views of agency in western feminist discourses fail to account for the lives of women shaped by nonliberal traditions. Such discourses seldom problematize women's desire to resist. Moreover, their assumption that women's actions emerge from their own free will, rather than from the dictates of custom, tradition, or direct coercion, is one that has been naturalized in the scholarship on gender (208). Instead of simply taking this for granted, it might be more useful to determine different situations wherein women would want freedom from subordination and structures of male domination. In their efforts to achieve greater piety, women in Egypt's mosque movement, for instance, strive to become more shy, modest, persevering, and humble—attributes that have hitherto also secured their subordination. While men control and produce Islam, women's practices may be understood as spaces for subordinate discourse that cultivates women's consciousness. Women's insistence on their dynamic complementarity with men may be identified through their various women-only ceremonies and practices. Since women's ritual practices are separate from those of, and exclude, men, they serve in themselves as a "means of resisting and setting limits to domination" (206).

Thus, where social protest and economic necessity are hegemonized, other motivations, like divinity, virtue, morality, female modesty, or piety, receive scant attention. Clearly, since the binary terms "resistance" and "subordination" cannot capture the range of goals women have, attending to different forms of personhood, knowledge, and experience, in addition to inquiring about those spaces that are free from the influence of men and their coercive presence, might be a more productive approach.

Abu-Lughod has also cautioned against the tendency both to romanticize resistance and to treat agency as a synonym for resistance. As women always play active parts in accepting, accommodating, ignoring, resisting, or protesting—sometimes all at the same time (Abu-Lughod 1990a, 41–55)—one might take for granted that "resistances, of whatever form, signal sites of struggle" (47). Instead, she suggests that we learn more about the types of power women are up against. Further, in assuming that some types of power are more significant than others, we may be hampered from exploring how these forms operate simultaneously, either in concert or at cross-purposes (48). For instance, in the case of the songs I discuss in chapter 2, the same lighthearted ones that offer humorous lessons on how to negotiate visits to natal homes (a euphemism for a "break" from chores), underlining the need for such cajoling and negotiation in the first place, also reveal the extent of the power and control husbands exercise over their wives and their labor. Broadly, these songs also indicate women's contribution to their peasant "household" economy, as well as the uncompensated and unrecognized nature of this contribution.

Focusing on the terms that people use to organize their lives and that might be "constitutive of different forms of personhood, knowledge and experience" (16) allows for conceptualizing agency "not simply as a synonym for resistance to relations of domination, but as a capacity for action that specific relations of *subordination* create and enable" (18). The songs suggest not only that women are influenced by the larger social and political structures but also that their actions, in turn, impact these structures. As Sherry Ortner has argued, "human beings make society just as society makes them." Yet if, in the process of reproducing society, society is also transformed, a notion of agency that is socially, linguistically, and culturally constrained is a more effective one when trying to understand how women are sometimes complicit with, while also making accommodations for or reinforcing, the status quo—often all at the same time (Ahearn 2000, 12–15).

In defining agency as the socio-culturally mediated capacity to act, Laura Ahearn suggests that instead of passively taking in the songs, we might also fruitfully look for how the kinds of meanings that might emerge are constrained, that is, how these meanings are socially mediated and "intertextually situated within a bounded universe of discourse" (Ahearn 2001, 111). Since singing communities have their own beliefs, values, ways of talking, and even power relations that emerge over the course of their mutual endeavors, the term "communities of practice" as "aggregates of people who come together around mutual engagement," a processual yet structural unit may be identified, one that is both constitutive of and constituted by its participants. The extent, then, to which the following songs broaden our understanding of women's agency remains a core question of this inquiry.

FIELDWORK

I collected the songs on which this book is based intermittently during innumerable field visits stretched out over a five-year period. I carried out my intensive fieldwork in Uttar Pradesh in the Atara, Barsara and Sauraiyan villages in the Badlapur block of Jaunpur district; Chachakpur village near Jaunpur city; the rural neighborhoods around the city of Varanasi and in village Sadiapur near Allahabad. My collections were greatly enriched in village Misraulia in Bihar's Chhapra district during

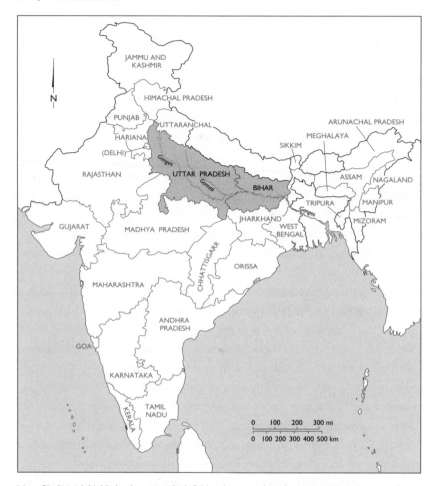

1 Map of India with highlighted areas in which fieldwork was conducted

my research for a documentary film on the song traditions of the Bhojpuri-speaking region. During this period, I also attended the Buxar *melā* (fair) where I met itinerant singers, whose songs have enriched this collection.

Along with my fieldwork villages in Chhapra district of Bihar, the Jaunpur and Benaras districts in Uttar Pradesh constitute a large chunk of the hinterland that, since the days of the East India Company, provided the workforce for the growing port city of Calcutta and, subsequently, migrant labor to the sugar colonies of the Caribbean, Fiji, and Mauritius. Folksongs provide a rich source for understanding how migration shaped the consciousness of the region. As my song collection grew, the links

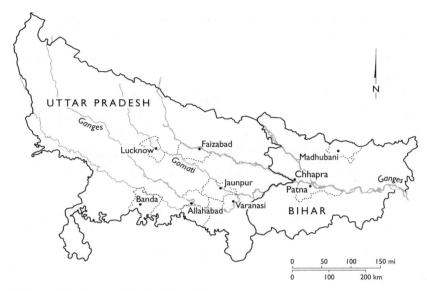

2 Fieldwork districts in eastern Uttar Pradesh and Bihar

between the agrarian structure, patriarchal ideology, social control, and women's lack of power were thrown into sharp relief.

Today Jaunpur is one of the most prosperous districts in eastern Uttar Pradesh. In recent years, this prosperity has accompanied a growing commercial agriculture, with the increased mechanization of farm activities, including the replacement of labor-intensive irrigation with motor-driven tube wells, tractors for ploughing, electrical threshers for harvesting, and flour mills for milling. As a result of these processes, a number of song genres that accompany women's labor, particularly songs of the millstone, are on the decline.

Here, medium-sized holdings predominate as a result of the post-Independence emphasis on the Zamindari Abolition, the breakup of large landed estates and the power of the landed gentry, the *zamindars*. Since the 1950s, a strong and resourceful middle peasantry has emerged and small-scale intensive agriculture has become the norm. The pre-Independence landlords of Jaunpur district, predominantly of the Thakur and Rajput caste of warrior nobility, are today petty commodity producers, relying largely on family supervision and agricultural labor. Further, owing to the intergenerational partition of lands, many of the large holdings have decreased in size, with each landlord owning an average of five acres of land, worked both by family and hired labor. The financial stability of this class of former landholders has enabled substantial investment in threshers, tube wells, and tractor rentals. The small-scale nature of agriculture has produced a corresponding decrease in the dependence on hired labor. Benefiting from the break-up of large land-holdings were the former sharecroppers and tenants belonging to the middle caste of Yadavas, who thereby secured ownership and control over land and today constitute the majority of small landholders. Women from intermediate castes are skillful and industrious agriculturists, and their economic contributions have, in no small measure, contributed to the recent prosperity of castes such as the Yadavas, Kurmis, and Koeris. Chamars, the Dalit (downtrodden) caste in the region who occupy the bottom rungs of caste and class hierarchies, remain landless.

Women's Land Rights

My initial impetus for recording songs grew from my research on women's land rights. During my fieldwork on this subject, my discussions with groups of women usually ended in extended and enthusiastic song sessions, where women's problematic relationship to land ownership emerged with striking clarity. I recorded many of the texts included in this book, as in them I observed the nature of the relationships between women and their employers in the field. Sometimes women who were otherwise reluctant informants proved eager participants in the song sessions and were even transformed by them. In fact, as singing is so much a part of the voice of women in the countryside here, it would be hard to imagine conducting any insightful fieldwork on women's issues without referencing these song sessions. Both the rich narrative content of the songs and the willingness of female informants from the entire range of caste and class backgrounds to share these songs with outsiders made this discourse an accessible point of entry during fieldwork.

Between 1997 and 2000, I regularly participated in grass-roots workshops organized by the "U.P. Bhūmi Sudhār aur Shyam Adhikāri Abhiyān Samitī," the Movement for Uttar Pradesh Land Reforms and Labor Rights, a loose coalition of approximately thirty NGOs that came together in 1997 to work on agrarian issues in several districts of Uttar Pradesh. The discussions generated at these village- and district-level meetings, where participants ranged from activists, administrators, academics, and legal experts to small and marginal farmers, tenants, and agricultural laborers, sharpened my research questions. These song collections owe a tremendous amount to the monthly sessions of the Abhiyān Samitī.

During my years of fieldwork I have found that women, despite being silenced in other spheres and contexts and reluctant to volunteer information on contested issues such as the nature of rights and entitlements to land or to share their points of view even when coaxed to do so, nevertheless participate in song sessions with great enthusiasm and lack of inhibition. On many occasions, asking women to sing individually or collectively was infinitely more rewarding than asking them to elaborate on a particular theme through a series of questions or in focus-group discussions. Over time, as the collections and genres evolved and revealed their treasures, it became clear that many issues on which women were otherwise reluctant or unable to voice an opinion were in fact explored in the various song genres. Rarely, for instance, did I elicit responses on the theme of women's rights to land, largely because this theme constituted a different discourse for them. Women were often unable to connect the culture of disinheritance with the immediate marginality they were experiencing. The political explosiveness of the subject also hindered frank expression. In this setting, marked by the systematic denial of women's rights to land, marriage songs wherein brides claim their shares from fathers spoke volumes. The song below is a stunning example, spelling out the sleight of hand by which women are denied rights in natal properties. We hear both smugness and relief in the father's tone as he evokes the bride's vermilion, the symbol of matrimony that will eliminate the threat to the property of the patrilineage that unmarried daughters pose.

Je kuch arajihe e bābā, adhiyā hamār
Adhiyā adhiyā jini kara betī
Sabhe dhan tohār
Cutki bhar sindurvā e betī
Tu ta jayebu kaunā pār

In all you earn, Father, I stake a claim for half.
"Insist not on half your share, daughter,
This entire wealth is yours, after all.

Just a pinch of vermilion,[1] daughter,
Before long, far and away you'll be gone."
JASSAL 2001, DEDICATION

Because of my status as an outsider, women's sexuality was another theme that was not easily broached. However, the singing of *kajlī* (a song genre associated with the rainy season and women's work in the fields), the subject of chapter 2, and other songs of intimacy that are light-hearted, ironic, and humorous often provided points of entry into discussions on otherwise taboo subjects. I found myself returning to the singers for clarifications sometimes months and even years after the initial recording was made. The very informality of the process of song recordings thus offered me the richest insights into the culture and allowed me to resume and maintain contact with the most interesting singers. Though the songs themselves were not initially the subject of my research but only the vehicle for comprehending cultural complexities, they ultimately helped me to remain connected with the field well beyond the specific research questions I was investigating at the time.

A feature of my fieldwork was that I was seldom left alone with a single woman for any length of time, unless I specifically requested it for the purposes of the study. When not attending to immediate household chores, women were invariably surrounded by other kinswomen, neighbors, friends, or caste women. This community proved a most fertile ground for facilitating wide-ranging discussion and debates. Women's collective participation in my interview sessions and informal singing sessions created the ideal atmosphere for sharing ideas. Women were most relaxed during song sessions and therefore most likely to respond thoughtfully to my questions. I soon adopted the singing of folksongs as a research strategy for putting my informants at ease.

When Women's Songs Pack a Punch

It was a common practice for upper caste village women to invite a few agricultural laboring women to their homes to entertain them with their songs. During these afternoon sessions, songs that explored tensions between the conjugal and natal homes were hot favorites, both in terms of listeners' requests and singers' repertoires. During a particular pre-arranged recording session in 2003, of women's laboring songs with six

Dalit women, I soon had misgivings about the recording session's location, a spacious hall in one of three sprawling dwellings belonging to the Brahmin landlord and his extended family for whom the women worked as daily wage laborers. The setting was far from neutral, even if it did provide soothing shelter from the oppressive noonday sun. This lack of neutrality became apparent as soon as the Dalit women, some of them veiled, arrived and seated themselves on the floor.

As I had commonly experienced during fieldwork, recording invariably attracted inquisitive youngsters. On this occasion, too, sundry adolescent youths from the extended Brahmin household entered and sprawled themselves on a divan at the far end of the large room. Middle-aged Brahmin women and girls stood outside, peeping in through the windows. Led by a senior Dalit woman in her sixties, the singers began the session, while one among them, sat sideways and heavily veiled, her singing barely audible. At first it appeared that, despite the unequal social relations the context underlined, a mood of cozy familiarity was building, with easy banter exchanged between the youths and the senior singer. The singers sang:

Dhīre re dhīre devā baris gailen
Ab anganā me lāgal bāre kāi re, man dhīre re dhīre
Anganā me chalali ho bahinī
Ab tangvā gailen bichhlāi re man dhīre re dhīre
Dhāval dhūpal, alien unke bhaiyā
Godiyā me lihalī bator re man dhīre.
"Are bahinā kaunā gatar lāgal chot re man"...
"Ānjar choro bhaiyā, pānjar choro
Ab sirvā me lāgal bāre cot re man dhīre re dhīre
Ab undā davaiyā batlāva re man dhire"...
"Lal mirīciyā re, olvā ke tusvā re
Ghasi ke lagāva ohi thaiyān re man dhīre re dhīre.

Pitter-patter fell the rain.
Now the courtyard is slippery, pitter-patter.
Into the courtyard stepped that girl.
Then her foot slipped, pitter-patter.
Panting and puffing, arrived her brother.
Took her in his arms, pitter-patter.

"O sister, where are you hurt?"
"It's not my sides and hips, brother.
It's my head that's hurt.
Give me a potent curative concoction."
"Take some red hot chillies, the fruit of the oel.
Grind them well and apply on that very spot, pitter-patter."
DALIT SINGERS, MISRAULIA CHHAPRA

The song's mischievous punch is packed in the last two lines where, in response to his sister's request for a "cooling" ointment for her bruise, the brother playfully suggests a "hot" remedy—a concoction of chilies and *oel* fruit. As the singers completed the song, women of the surrounding Brahmin households had taken positions around the hall and were even encouraging the singers with song suggestions. By then the singers were looking increasing uncomfortable with the overwhelming male presence in the room. The source of their discomfort was the male gaze from the exclusively male, though youthful, audience sprawled on the divan, a setting that evoked traditional gender and caste hierarchies. Just as I was about to interrupt the session and exercise my researcher's privilege to request the impromptu audience to leave, the women sang a lewd version of the same song!

In the second version, the women substituted the names of the sister and brother with the names of two young siblings from the Brahmin household, thus casting the most offensive youth on the divan as the incestuous brother of the song. The sister was first named and then referred to throughout the remainder of the song as the "slut." In place of the medical remedy suggested, the women made up and sang out an improbably funny concoction, detailing various anatomical parts of donkeys and pigs, to be rubbed on the sister's forehead. The allusion to sibling incest and the obvious vulgarity and derision worked as a signal for upper caste males to leave or to be prepared for further insults and name-calling. The youths wisely chose the former. The women had succeeded in forcing the youths sprawled on the divan to leave the hall in embarrassment.

Where the honor of women is the real indicator of status, playfully insulting the women of the Brahmin household, through the otherwise nonthreatening medium of song, proved effective, evoking for me the genre of galīs (insulting wedding songs). The incident powerfully brought home the fact that songs have constituted one of the few spaces for resistance traditionally available to lower caste women. As soon as the men left, the tension lifted, the young Dalit woman revealed her beautiful face, and as her veil slipped away wonderful full-throated singing emerged from the room and hovered over the village all afternoon.

Abu-Lughod's notion of "resistance as a diagnostic of power" offers one way to understand the Dalit women's response to the unequal power relations. While many of the songs indeed reflect a reality, they also create that reality with important socio-cultural implications, thereby demonstrating the intertwining of language and power as well as the importance of both text and context.

Masculine Song Traditions

My fieldwork in masculine musical traditions always required a great deal of planning, and contacts in the cities, especially in Benaras and Jaunpur, have been essential for tracking upcoming performances and artists. Perhaps because of these performances' very inaccessibility to women—women are not routinely accepted into these well-defined and guarded male spaces—my memories of these performances are either of being debarred from attending them or of never enjoying them fully. I always had to insist that I be included and frequently faced polite but firm denial couched in concerns for my safety. The over-protective and shielding environment created by my relatives, friends, and informants in the field, was, alas, sometimes the greatest hindrance to my getting to know masculine traditions as I would have liked. For a long time I regarded the songs as only a secondary interest in my fieldwork, and I regret that, as a result, I was not forceful enough in gaining access, which has lead to a rather uneven collection. However, the experience did teach me a great deal about the concrete ways in which the cultural worlds of men and women remain separated and, as such, how the gender of the researcher determines the kinds of data accessed.

The nature of the masculine singing traditions, from which women are excluded, hit home in a stark and striking way. Despite my participation and involvement in the festivities associated with a wedding in a village near Chhapra, western Bihar, I was discouraged from attending the all-night entertainment for the groom's party that the bride's family had arranged. My hosts' rationale was that proceedings could become rowdy or violent and women may be unsafe, but I suspect that since women are not to be seen at such events, they were being protective. Reluctantly, I was forced to hear the entire performance throughout the night, as it was broadcast on loudspeakers, and could only watch the proceedings captured on video the next day. Accordingly, I am unable to record my impression of the audience and its response.

The stirring Launda-nāch[2] performance was given by a rural Dalit traveling theatre and musical company consisting of eight seasoned actors, impersonators, singers, and musicians who held the packed rural audience spellbound until dawn. The show that began with bawdy and humorous singing around midnight had, within the space of a few hours, transformed into something elevated and profound. The tenor of the singing in the wee hours—at once melodious, inspired, and haunting—was interspersed with appeals to social justice. As in the best traditions of such rural performances, the most compelling feature of this performance was the artful and skillful assumption of female personae by an all-male cast (see Hansen 1992). I later found out that the actors and musicians in the company were landless laborers and marginal farmers who adopted this performance as a supplementary source of livelihood during the wedding season. Indeed, when traveling through the rural countryside during the festive season of Dusshera in October and during the wedding season in May and June, I saw numerous makeshift colorful tents erected for all-night performances. The more remote the villages, and the further their locations from towns, the larger the number of makeshift performance tents, testifying to the persistence of this form of entertainment in remote areas.

Not all masculine musical communities are purely performative, however, in the sense of a clear relationship between the performers and their audiences. Folk singers also often converge at temples, village shrines, or to commemorate folk bards. Where singers and musicians meet for the sheer pleasure of it, an easy informality and by the blurring of caste distinctions characterize the sessions. At village Misraulia, Chhapra district, a community of folk singers has emerged around the memory of the nineteenth century bard, Mahender Misir, whose compositions are popular across the countryside. In this village, Thursday and Sunday afternoons are set aside for folk singers and accompanists to meet informally for impromptu musical sessions outside the village goddess temple.

1   Mixed caste devotional singing in Misraulia.

2   Sādhū (holy man) sings in Misraulia. Ajay Mishra accompanies on harmonium.

3   Preparing for a singing session at the goddess temple in Misraulia, Chhapra.

4   Dalit singer, second from left, sings songs of the bard Bhikhari Thakur in Misraulia, Chhapra.

5 Ajay Mishra sings songs of the bard Mahender Misir, his ancestor, in Misraulia.

6 Ecstatic devotional singing in Misraulia, Chhapra.

7   A singer of the Sorthi genre, Misraulia, Chhapra.

The atmosphere at these gatherings is suffused with spirituality, but the unique caste-inclusive male camaraderie, with the *chillum* (pipe) passed around and shared, was even more surprising in a setting here, where caste distinctions can be otherwise restrictive. The repertoire usually includes songs that are not overtly *bhajans* (spiritual songs), though they may explore *nirgūn* themes, wherein the idea of the divine is formless. Many of the *sagūn* songs, in which the divine takes a form, were about Radha's agony of separation when Krishna left the idyllic Brindavan of his youth and childhood with its lovely *gopīs* (cowherdesses) to become king in the city of Dwarka. Conveyed through their messenger Udho, the songs detail the yearnings of the gopīs, which serve as a metaphor for the human soul's craving for union with Krishna. The feminization of the masculine in relation to the Divine was a recurrent motif at these "masculine" gatherings, as in this Kabir song heard in the bard Mahender Misir's household, though here it is death's inevitability in the midst of joy that is highlighted.

Kaun thagavā nagariyā lūtal ho
Chandan kāth ke banan khatolnā
Tāpar dūlahin sūtal ho

Utho re sakhī mor māng sanvāro[3]
Dulahā mo se rūsal ho
Āye jamrāj palang carhī baithe
Nainan ānsū tūtal ho
Cāri jane mili khāt uthāin
Carhūn dis dhū dhū uthal ho.

Which deceiver looted the city?
Of sandalwood, the bedpost,
On that lies the bride.
"Rise, my friend, arrange my coiffeur
For the bridegroom remains estranged."
Comes the lord of death, seating himself on the bed.
Tears break from the eyes.
Four people assemble to lift the hearse.
In all four directions, wails and cries arise.

AJAY MISRA AND COMPANIONS, MISRAULIA, CHHPARA

As Joyce Burkhalter Fleuckiger found in Chhattisgarh, men would often "appropriate a particular female genre to displace its defiant voice," thus confounding gender roles in much the same way as women sometimes challenged or defied upper caste, masculine expectations of gender (Fleuckiger 1996, 3). One such example is to be found among a branch of Ramanandi sadhus of Ayodhya, the *rasiks,* who by dressing as females "attempt to bring about a radical transformation of their masculinity in the ritual theatre of temple worship" (Van der Veer 1987, 691). Cross-dressing by male performers who portrayed women in the all-night dramas, the *laundā-nāch* and *nautanki,* often with sensitivity and aplomb, suggested this masculine world's desire to understand the feminine psyche and to connect with it.

Among the villages in which I conducted my fieldwork, Misraulia is a favorite for its enthralling music, performed by teams of singers and percussionists. On one occasion, an upper caste *sādhū* (religious ascetic) concluded a particularly stirring session with a philosophical song about river-crossings, "*naiyā tū lagaibo kaune pār re sanvaliyā,*" which likens life to a boat buffeted on a stormy sea with no shore in sight. The powerful rendition, accompanied by at least five percussionists playing different kinds of *dhols* (single oblong shaped drum played with both hands), *pakhawaj* (a variety of drum), and a range of *majīrās* (cymbals), displayed the sort of virtuosity and abandon that is rare even for the most sought after musical venues in the country. At the end of this most satisfying of musical treats, which concluded with the stanza below, it appeared that half the village had gathered and as the sun set people only reluctantly dispersed.

Ab naiyā tū lagaibo kaune pār re sanvaliyā
Bīch bhavar me
Ek nadī duī ghatiyā re bālam
Kaun ghatiya, kahi jaihā
Ho bālam
Ek gali duī rahiyā re bālam
Kaun rahiyā, kahi jaiha ho bālam
Naiyā bahut purāni hai
Purje purje alag hūe hain
Barā jor ka pāni hai
Mālum dela sab dhokhe ke ghāt ho sanvaliyā
Ab naiyā tū lagaibā kaune ghāt o sanvaliyā

Now, at which bank will the boat come to rest, my love?
It's the middle of the stream.
One river two banks, my love.
Which bank is it going to be?
One river, two banks, which bank?
One road, two paths, my love.
Which path will you take, my love?
The boat is very old,
Weather beaten and coming apart,
While the water gushes with force.
Now the shores seem deceptively false, beloved.
At which shore will the boat come to rest, beloved?

AT TEMPLE IN MISRAULIA, CHHAPRA

The following morning while passing through the neighboring town, I saw one of the pakhawaj players from the previous evening mending shoes by the wayside. Still bubbling with enthusiasm about the night before, our research team could hardly keep from complimenting him on his mastery of the instrument. Pointing to his tools and anvil by the roadside and his makeshift cobbler's post, he quietly said, "It is this which is my art."

Throughout India, drums have traditionally been played by leather workers, since it was only through their expertise that the tonal qualities of skins, so essential in the crafting of highly evolved percussion instruments, was discovered. While the scene evoked the poet saints of the Bhakti era, such as Raidas who was himself a leather-worker, reconciling this drummer's virtuosity with the profession of shoemaking, considered among the lowliest in the caste hierarchy, was nevertheless a challenge. So ingrained are these categories that even experienced anthropologists, who know that music is usually but a secondary occupation of agricultural laborers or specialists of various kinds, are likely to be ill-prepared for actually confronting such everyday contradictions. This moment is merely one example of the myriad subtle and everyday realizations that I encountered in the field and that enriched my understanding of caste as a form of social inequality and of its ramifications in the countryside, which for me were further brought home through my own positioning in the caste and class hierarchies.

On Translation

For every song cited in this book, I reluctantly had to leave out several others from every occasion that were equally illuminating or illustrative. A major determining factor in my choice of songs became my ability to adequately translate the rich local idiom into modern English. Capturing the flavor of the local idiom was both challenging and rewarding. Transcriptions of the original songs, as I recorded them, are also available for Hindi and Bhojpuri and Purabiya speakers. I have retained these original texts along with their translations, since they allow us to see the material not just as texts to be analyzed, but as songs with a unique structure, flow, rhythmic quality, prefixes and suffixes, and extraordinary lyricism. In translating them, I attempt, not always successfully, to capture the rhythm I heard in the original sung versions along with the element of surprise and emotion that often accompanied the listening. On rare occasions, and particularly when my own recordings were garbled or inadequate, I have resorted to few existing authoritative anthologies of

Bhojpuri folksongs, but owing to this book's grounding in fieldwork, I have kept such selections to a minimum.

The process of translating the songs also proved to be an invaluable exercise in translating an entire culture and way of thinking into a language that may lack corresponding categories. In addition to Bhojpuri, I represent in these selections other dialects spoken in the villages where I conducted my fieldwork, such as Awadhi and Purabiya. As songs form the core of my research, my analysis of the culture and society is pegged entirely upon these articulations. Hence, each song provides an anchor for the interpretative exercise that follows, including the associations and cultural interconnections each inspires. As songs are cultural discourses on emotion, my challenge often lay in translating the meanings as they related to emotions. I have attempted to convey something of the meaning-and-feeling system under study, since the cultural meaning systems are socially and publicly produced through song. In the words of Lutz and White, this effort also entailed a "translation of emotion concepts and the social processes surrounding their use" (Lutz and White 1986, 407–8).

This book is divided into six chapters. Chapter 1 is concerned with songs of the millstone, the long ballads that women sing while grinding grain and spices. In chapter 2, our attention shifts from the courtyard to the field, exploring songs women sing when involved in productive labor in the fields. Chapter 3 takes as its subject songs associated with marriage as a rite of passage, and chapter 4 songs about the chaste Sita, the mythical heroine from the epic Ramāyanā. Chapter 5 investigates gender dimensions in a masculine ballad, the Lorikāyan, and chapter 6 addresses cassette recordings and the impact of technology on folksongs sung at the festival of Holi. The conclusion highlights some of the significant issues this book raises and the themes it explores.

CHAPTER ONE

⇻ The Daily Grind

People woke up to the sound of the *jāta* as just before sunrise, one home after another seemed to come alive with the hum of this most basic of women's activities, the refrains of the *jatsār* along with the trundle of the stones against each other, being taken up as if in relay from one household to the next.

FIELDNOTES, HARICHARAN MAURYA, CHACHAK VILLAGE, 2002

Haricharan Maurya's glowing account of the atmosphere in his village in eastern Uttar Pradesh when women were grinding grain and spices on millstones—a practice discontinued twenty or thirty years ago—captures the essence of women's productive labor in villages across rural north India and its ability to cut cross caste divides. Perhaps because the work of processing the food crucial for daily existence is so time-consuming and demanding, the most diverse of women's oral ballads have evolved to accompany these tasks. Maurya remembers waking up to jatsār songs every morning and to his ears "the rumble of the grinding stone combined with the words of the song, remains the sweetest and most comforting of sounds." During my fieldwork, Maurya could barely contain his enthusiasm as the women began a song, often joining in the chorus. While Maurya's pride in his wife's repertoire was not always shared by others, given that men's musical worlds are distinct from those of women, his observations are relevant to the questions this chapter raises, particularly those regarding women's consciousness in the genre of grinding songs.

This chapter, then, is concerned with the construction and reproduction of gender identity in the work songs known as *jatsār*, which traditionally accompanied women's daily grinding of grain and spices. The songs also serve a pedagogical purpose, transmitting societal values from older to younger women, serving to warn and prepare women for the hardships of married life, and spelling out the limits of transgression, the nature of punishments, and the rewards for compliance. By delineating family relationships that might be threatening and antagonistic, and by outlining codes of honor and conduct, the songs indicate the extent to which women internalize society's values and strictures. The chapter examines songs with diverse narratives and investigates their underlying messages for the women who sing them. A related question is the extent to which lessons learned through the jatsār inform female subordination, or the lack thereof, in the sphere of agricultural production, particularly in women's relations with their employers in the field.

As this genre represents only one of the region's many varieties of work songs, it offers only a partial picture of what women sing about when working. Sung within the confines of the household in the inner court-yards of homes, these songs are part of a much wider range of songs associated with women's work, both in homes and fields.[1] Unlike the performance of male ballads, women's work songs match their rhythm to the rhythm of repetitive tasks. While the jatsār or ballads of the millstone are not caste-specific but are sung by women of all castes, they are most often heard in upper or middle-caste homes. This shared aspect of the songs tends in some instances to blur caste distinctions and hierarchy.

Grinding grains and spices requires considerable effort, and women sit on the courtyard floor with the *jāta* (grinding stone) held between their legs. The physical act of grinding also resonates with the grind of daily life for village women. One may surmise that in cases where women sing the same kinds of song day after day, they indeed absorb the lessons imparted in the course of this activity. In short, the apparently benign and empowering practice of women singing the songs of the millstone enables

8 Small version of the type of grinding
stone still in use in Barsara village,
Jaunpur.

wider social and gender-specific lessons, about both power and powerlessness, to be most effectively learned.

In south India, for instance, in the seventeenth and early eighteenth
centuries, Sufi mystics used grindstone songs to disseminate ideas about
Sufism. At least in Bijapur, a number of short poems in Dakani employed
indigenous themes and imagery for the propagation of mystical doctrines. Preserved in the oral traditions of Dakani speaking villagers of the
Deccan plateau, this folk poetry appears to have been sung by village
women engaged in various household chores, especially while grinding
grains and spices at the *chakkī* (stone grinding mill) and while spinning
thread at the *charkhā* (the spinning wheel). For women the genre's appeal
lay not only in the fact that it accompanied their household tasks but also
"because it was permeated with imagery especially meaningful to them"
(Eaton 2002, 192). Thus, "what the Sufis did was to adapt the simplest
elements of Sufi doctrine to the already existing vehicles of folk poetry
and to substitute vernacular Dakkani for vernacular Marathi or Kan-

nada" (192). The works of the mystic Burhan al-Din Janam are associated with the *chakkī-nāmā*, a major development in the cultural history of the Deccan. These songs recognized that the power that turns the wheel is witness to the light and thereby to the essence of God (Eaton 2002, 194). The songs appear to have ontologically linked God, the Prophet, and the *pīr* (mystic) with the woman at the grindstone.

Phule and other lower caste radicals also attempted to project a new identity for Maharashtra's lower castes by drawing on symbols from warrior and agricultural traditions and giving them powerful new meanings, revealing their sophisticated understanding of processes of identity formation (O'Hanlon 1985, 8). The dissemination of new ideologies and worldviews through women's work songs appears to have been an effective way of reaching people.

These ballads of the millstone as a way of "speaking bitterness" that is gender-specific are by no means unique to India, and a similar process is found in Africa, where women's working songs serve as a way of expressing grievances. The absence of colonial government documentation about the impact of the Malawi famine of 1949 on rural communities, for example, led Megan Vaughan (1987) to utilize women's pounding songs—sung by rural women pounding maize in the central courtyard area, where the songs' content would have had the maximum social impact—as a rich source of gender-specific oral testimony concerning events that occurred forty years before.[2] Unlike these songs, however, whose principal function appears to have been forcing appropriate kin and caste norms on young women, those in Malawi were designed to upbraid male kin for not adhering to kinship obligations, for example, providing food for the women of the household in times of scarcity.[3]

FORM, CONTENT, AND METHOD

A striking aspect of the jatsār is their duration; they can be very long, lasting the time it takes a woman to grind the 5 kilos of grain or flour necessary to prepare a meal for an extended family. Another is their distinctive rhythm, which not only accompanies but also mimics the trundling of the two millstones (one on top of the other) that completes a full circle.[4] Yet another is their social context; because the singing makes the task of grinding easier, usually two women—one old, one young—sing the jatsār together. This arrangement facilitates the process of ideological transmission, in that the social values (anxieties, concerns, negative/positive behaviors) familiar to the older woman are conveyed to the younger. In such circumstances, it is the voice not just of experience but also of female authority (i.e., one's mother-in-law) that instructs the subordinate female (i.e., the daughter-in-law).[5]

The punishments accorded for transgression and resistance is an important theme of these songs, the narratives of which fall into three broad categories.[6] First are songs that describe women's daily lives in their conjugal homes, along with the bleakness of their situation. Second are songs about conflict within families and close kin and how this conflict is (or is not) to be resolved. Family relationships in these narratives are characterized as potentially, in many cases actually, antagonistic, reflecting the turbulence experienced by inmarrying daughters-in-law. Third are songs that narrate, in some detail, the consequences for women who transgress a variety of behavioral norms, such as breaking caste boundaries, violating codes of honor, and so on.

JATSĀR SINGERS

How the women who remember and sing these ballads relate to them became an important question for me, one unearthed through the wide-ranging conversations I had with the singers during recording sessions. Here I follow Narayan's insights from an article published in 1995 about Dundes's suggestion back in 1966 that while a focus on context is important to ascertaining the meaning of folksongs, in order to reflect on how the genres are indigenously conceived the researcher must also actively elicit the meaning of the folklore from the folk themselves (Narayan 1993, 178). The differences between versions of the same song may serve to highlight minor distinctions between the song repertoires of the upper and lower castes.

Meena Devi, a young Brahmin woman from village Misraulia, Chhapra district, in Bihar, who has memorized hundreds of songs, says that senior female members of her family sang jatsārs every day, so she was raised on a rich diet of songs in her natal home. In her marital home the tradition of morning singing to the accompaniment of the jāta has continued and enriched her repertoire. Due to her vast and varied repertoire, Meena

9 Meena Devi (Brahmin) in Misraulia, Chhapra.

Devi could often sing for hours at a stretch without pause. Once when a group of Dalit singers in the same village sang a lewd version of a song to embarrass the upper caste males, an incident I describe in the fieldwork section of the introduction to this volume, Meena Devi was quick to distance herself from the Dalit version, emphasizing that her songs were "not like that," that is, as outspoken, challenging, or subversive as those sung by the lower castes.

Shanti Tewari, another Brahmin woman of village Atara in Jaunpur, says that whenever there is a wedding in the family the food preparations stretch out over several months, and the grain and spices required for the feasts must be prepared in advance. Shanti says, "Only intense concentrated activity and collaboration between several close and distant kin in the village makes it possible to get these tasks completed in time. Kinswomen must lend a hand." When kinswomen come together in these task teams, assisted by the village women of other castes, they also get to hear and learn new songs.

In Atara village, a Rajput (Thakur) woman confided to me that she regretted forgetting whole stanzas of many of the jāta songs she had once known as she now no longer engages in grinding activity. However, by mimicking the semi-circular motion of the hands across the grinding

10a Shanti Tewari and friend enjoy an afternoon singing session with their Kahar helper, Tengra (on floor).

10b Shanti Tewari (foreground) with upper-caste singing companions.

11   Shanti Tewari and singers at Shanti's doorway, Atara village, Jaunpur.

stone (jāta), the woman was able to remember the words of some of these
songs from her youth. Often during recording sessions, when groups of
women sang jatsārs as a team, the genre's ponderous narrative style generated plenty of discussion among the singers about their own lives and
struggles. During one of these recording sessions in Sadiapur, Sitara Devi
remarked: "You're hearing us laugh so much and we're having so much
fun now, but Dīdī, these songs are the saddest songs ever! You know,
sometimes we have tears streaming down our eyes, as we sing. Tears will
be streaming down your face too, when you really think about the tragedy
in the song." Regarding the air of tragedy in these narratives and the
desperation that leads the protagonists of the songs to commit suicide,
Malti Devi explained, "In the songs, women always protect their honor,
that's because they are great satīs [formidably chaste women]."

    For my recordings of this and other genres, I relied on Munraji of
village Barsara, a woman in possession of a rich and varied repertoire. A
Mallah by caste, Munraji is marginalized by virtue of belonging to one of
the so-called backward castes in the region, situated on the lowest rungs
of agrarian and caste hierarchies. Munraji became blind as a result of an
attack of chickenpox when she was barely seven years old. As she explains

12 Rajput singer in Atara trying to remember grinding songs.

it, it was the year of the great flood when *mātā* (the chickenpox deity) took away her eyes ("*jis sāl barā būrā āyā rahā*"). Perhaps to compensate for her lack of this critical faculty, Munraji developed a sharp memory and a keen sense of touch that enables her to live independently. She was married very young and, despite the handicap, has raised four children, all of them now adults. Two of her sons are married and live in separate household units in the village.

Munraji clearly appreciates her neighbors' helpful gestures, though I have always marveled at her remarkable self-sufficiency, cultivating greens and *arhar* pulse in the land adjoining her backyard. She also has a couple of goats that she grazes in the tall grasses along the river at the edge of village Barsara. She cooks simple meals efficiently, and often I have seen her borrow one of her neighbors' fires, once they have lighted their hearths for the evening meal. It could be said that she is the memory-keeper of this village. Munraji is much respected, both because of her age but also because of her self-sufficiency, her fair and clear thinking, and her integrative approach in dealing with village and caste matters. As she remembers hundreds of songs from a range of genres, she is the natural lead singer at collective gatherings.

13　Munraji, Barsara village's memory-keeper, stands outside her hut
with Subhavati and her grandchildren.

　　Subhavati of the Kahar (water-carriers) caste, also of Barsara village
and Munraji's friend, is in her forties and, unlike other women in her
community, has only one teenage daughter. She and her husband are
both vegetable vendors. Her skills lead to her recent unanimous nomina-
tion by the village women as leader of the newly formed group-lending
society. Subhavati starts her day by going to the wholesale market where
she purchases the basket of vegetables she will sell that day. She then sits
at a busy intersection at the edge of Khutahan town, close to Jaunpur.
She usually manages by the end of the day to sell everything, but if some
vegetables remain unsold, she walks through the village calling out her
wares. Subhavati is a successful vendor and although her husband sells his
vegetables by bicycle over a wider distance, Subhavati manages to make
more profits. She explains her strategy as follows: "I have a number of
permanent clients who only buy vegetables from me because I am willing
to give loans and often advance them goods even if they may not have
the amount to make the purchases. My clients know that they can always
pay me later if they are short of cash. I also try to add (*cungī*) a small
token free gift for an accompanying child, such as a tomato or radish. It
makes mothers and children happy and then they always come back to

14   Subhavati in Barsara village, Jaunpur.

me. I am good at calculation and remember to make a mental note of all the loans."

Owing to her highly practical and enthusiastic approach, Subhavati is recognized as a keen businesswoman. Her hard work is admired, and she is a role model for many, partly because of her ability to hold her own in the male world. She is keen to give her daughter a good education. Yet, despite her obvious pragmatism and solid common sense, our exchange revealed another side to her personality:

"I intend to expand my business once I am free of the demons that visit me," said Subhavati.

"What demons?" I asked.

"You know, the ones that possess you and will not leave. My entire body is getting very weak because of this. I think my bones are turning watery. That's why I go every Thursday to Ghaus Pir to exorcise them."

Ghaus Pir, located in Khutahan near Jaunpur, is the revered shrine of a medieval Sufi saint and is visited by both Hindus and Muslims. Munraji and Subhavati of Barsara often sing together and are familiar with each

15   The aged Bhagirathi Devi sings jatsàr with her friend, Asha, in Chachakpur village.

other's repertoires, encouraging, prompting, and completing each other's songs. Bhagirathi Devi and Urmila Maurya of Chachakpur village form another such pair, whose repertoires and tonal qualities complement each other, making the recording of songs a scintillating experience. In their explanations of the songs' lyrics, women often compare these narratives with their own lives, remarking, for instance, "see my husband left me when I was so young," or "I too had such a problem when I was married."

Munraji, when asked about the meaning of a particular song has often playfully remarked, "You are a Professor and yet you do not know this simple thing!" before launching into a detailed explanation of the song.

WORK SONGS

The recordings presented here allow us to discern patterns and themes in women's preoccupations. I recorded the following song during a session with Bhagirathi Devi and Urmila Maurya. They belong to the Maurya caste of vegetable growers and market gardeners in Chachak village on the outskirts of Jaunpur. Chachakpur, one of the more prosperous villages in the region, is known for the commercial cultivation of flowers, and its relative prosperity is due in part to its proximity to Jaunpur city, which facilitates access to urban markets. When the recording was made in 2003, Bhagirathi Devi, a small farmer, was well over seventy years old and Urmila was in her fifties. The song they sang provides a good introduction to the jatsār. Haricharan Maurya, with whose observations I began this chapter, himself took up its refrain, citing it as the most representative of the genre.

I

BROTHER DON'T TELL THEM

Sāsu birnā jo ailen pahunariyā ho na
Sasu kahu banāv jevanravā ho na?
Kothilā mein bāti bahuta sarlī kodaiyā ho na
Bahuvā retvā mein chakvāre ka sagvā ho na
Sāsu kāhu banau jevanravā ho na?
Sāsu sathiyā puthiyā rinhbai bhatvā ho na
Sāsu mungiyā dariyā rinhbai partī ho na
Àva jevahin je baithe sār bahnoiyā ho na
Are Rama bhaiyā ke dhurkin hain āsuiyā ho na
Bahini re bipat tohre upra bāti ho na
Bahini bari re bipat jevanravā ho na
Hamri bipat bhaiyā māī āge jinni kahyo ho na
Māī maciyā baithlī carkhā katain ho na
Māī carkhā pataki lagiyain rovain ho na
Hamri bipat bhaiyā bahinī āge jin kahiyo ho na
Bhaiyā bipati sunahi bahini sasure na jaihain ho na
Hamri bipat bhaiyā bhaujī āge jinni kahyo na
Bhaujī bipati sunei lagihain rovai ho na

Mother-in-law, when my brother comes visiting, you know,
Mother-in-law, what shall I cook for the meal?
"There's plenty of spoilt kodon grain in the loft,
Daughter-in law, some salad leaves in the sandy field."
Mother-in-law, what shall I cook for the meal?
Mother-in-law, coarse rice I'll cook
And ground Moong dāl.
When husband and brother-in-law sat together, you know,
O Rama, brother's tears started to roll.
"Sister dear, such hardship has befallen you.

Sister, your life is so difficult."
"My hardships, brother, to our mother don't tell.
Mother seated on the cot spinning, you know,
Tossing aside the spinning wheel, will burst into tears, you know.
Brother, don't tell of my hardships to sister.
Brother! hearing of my hardships, sister will refuse to go to her conjugal home.
Brother, don't tell of my hardships to sister-in-law.
On hearing them, sister-in-law will start to weep."

The bleak reality young women face in their conjugal homes is the poignant theme of this song. The relative indifference of the mother-in-law to the respect that should be accorded a bride's brother, along with her suggestions for the items to be prepared, compounds the bride's misery. As we will see in chapter 3, the song hints at cultural sanctions against visits by members of the bride's natal family. The withdrawal of hospitality appropriate to a visiting guest emerges as but one of the mechanisms conjugal families deploy to discourage periodic visits from brides' natal family members, thus isolating brides in their marital homes. The song serves as a warning to the brothers of brides that even they can never be sure of the treatment they will receive in the *sasurāl* of their sisters. The song provokes its listeners and singers to reflect on the bride's state of mind after her conjugal household snubs her brother, greeting his ritual visit with calculated indifference.

The song appears to illustrate the rationale for *anuloma*, or hypergamy, the preferred north Indian form of marriage, in which daughters ideally move from lower to upper echelons of caste hierarchies. I explore the implications of this principle in chapter 3. Some scholarly consensus does exist about the preference for this norm, and indeed the rule appears to have been devised to support women in adapting to their new homes and to spare them the pangs of deprivation as seen here. The folklore, however, is replete with tales that violate this norm, despite its apparently preferred status.

The following tale describes societal expectations that require married women to furnish proofs of fidelity and chastity and legitimate the rights of members of the patrilineage to demand them. The narrative indicates the stringent controls brides face within their conjugal homes. While this particular song was sung by a large group of Dalit women, the values of chastity and morality, and indeed the motif of testing women's chastity, has long been associated with upper-caste women as in Sita's trial by fire.

2

SHIMMERING NECKLACE AND SIMMERING VAT

Sātahu Bhaiyā ke Satmal Bahiniyā ho na
Bahinī tohen lāibe surujū harauvā ho na
Barah barisvā laute pardesiyā ho na
Satmal tinhi letu suruju harauvā ho na
Paehari orhi gaili govanvā ho na
Unke sasurū mangaitin pāni datuan ho na
Paniyā dhulkat jhalkat suruju harauvā ho na
Kahān paiayu suruju harauvā ho na
Nata bhaiyā ke Satmal bahiniyā ho na
Sasuru Bhaiyā dinhi suruju harauvā ho na
Paehri orhi gaili gavanvā ho na
Unke jethau mangaitin pāni datuan ho na
Unke devar
Unke samiyā mangaitin datuan pāni
Paniyā urail jhalkat surujū harauvā ho na
Dhanā kahān pāiu suruju harauvā
Satahi bahiniyā
Parabhu Bhaiyā dihin suruju harauvā ho na
Ham nāhi manbai Dhanā tohari baciniyā ho na
Dhana ham lebe dharami karahiyā ho na
Morai pānco barvā Bhaiyā mitvā ho na
Nauva baba āge khabarvā janāvau ho na
Nai kahe hamre Babāji ke agavā ho na
Ramā tohrī betī bhabe bahi karihavā ho na
Āri āri baithahin gānv ke logavā ho na
Rama bicavān me dharamī karhaiyā ho na
Āva rove bhaiyā Bābā ho na
Betī āj jau sanaca thārahu
Betī tohein jake dalvā khanaibe ho na
Tuhi galat
Beti jiya the khan ke garaibe ho na
Bicva ho

Rama carhī gain dharamī karahiyā ho na
Khaulat telvā mein Satmal kudein ho na
Dhadhakī aginiyā bujhi gailī ho na
Are mere satilī raniyā chuti gailī ho na

Seven brothers have a sister, Satmal, you know.

"For you, sister, a shimmering necklace we'll bring."

Twelve years later return the travellers, you know.

"Sister, are you there, a shimmering necklace we brought, you know."

Mother says, "Brothers! It's only her laughter that is left behind.

All dressed up, Satmal was sent off to her marital home."

Her father-in-law says, "Fetch the neem brush and water."

In the water he sees the necklace reflected.

"Where did you get that necklace?" he asks, you know.

"Sister of seven brothers, Satmal am I.

Father-in-law, my brothers gave me the shimmering necklace, you know."

All dressed up, Satmal for her marital home departed!

Elder brother-in-law asks for the neem brush and water.

Younger brother-in-law asks for the neem brush and water.

"Whence came you by that necklace, wife?"

"Lord, my brothers bought me this shimmering necklace."

"Wife, your words cannot be believed.

A test of truth from you I want with the simmering vat."

My seven brothers are friends.

Barber, you must inform my father.

"Your daughter is to be tested with the heated oil vat."

On the sides are seated the village folk.

In the center the vat of truth is ready.

Brothers and father, come crying.

"Daughter, we'll bury you right here with our own hands.

If indeed you are found not to be true."

In the center the vat of truth is ready.

Into the flames, Satmal leaps.

Into the piping hot oil, Satmal leaps.

The raging flames are immediately extinguished.

"O my true Rani, she left me, alas!"

DALIT SINGERS, SAURAIYAN, JAUNPUR

The homelessness of the woman is poignantly underlined in the unexpected last stanza, where her brothers and father, rather than confirm that the jewel was indeed a gift from them, proceed to endorse her need to furnish the required proof. The statement that they will bury her should she be proved untrue serves as a chilling reminder to all women of the folly of relying on long-term support from their natal homes. Thus a woman's inherent lack of security in both her natal and conjugal homes serves as a powerful weapon of control for ensuring her conformity with established norms and behavioral expectations. Hence, even the abundant filial affection women blessed with as many as seven brothers may enjoy is likely to be quickly withdrawn. Since it is a family's women that represent the honor of its lineage, we see how male members of both the natal and conjugal households are equally concerned about upholding the woman's chastity. The song alerts women to the reality that tests of fidelity, while certainly more stringent for newlyweds, are likely to remain a continuous feature of their married lives.

FAMILY CONFLICTS AND THEIR RESOLUTION

This section focuses on songs that attempt to resolve the tensions inherent in the family unit and in the several dyads the family structure comprises. As we will see, the resolutions are violent, leaving almost no room for ambiguity or compromise. The songs depict various scenarios that capture the threatening nature of these relationships and of related problems such as incest, positing in the process extraordinary solutions. Embedded in these solutions are forms of resistance and, very occasionally, clues about how one might subvert existing relations of power.

3

PREGNANT SOLUTIONS: DISGUISE

Phūl lorhe gaīl re Rama, malin phūlvariā, nu re ki
Are phūlva lorhat re Nando, are rahelā garabhiyā, nu re ki
Piyā pardes e Nando, are devarū larakivā nu re ki
Iho garabhiyā e Nando, kekre sire dharab nu re ki
Hajipur hatiyā re Bhaujo, Bhaiyā ham dekhnī nu re ki
Malini ke sangavā e Bhaujo, dhūinyan le ramāvale nu re ki
Kholi da chunariyā e Bhaujo, re panhelī lugariyā nu re ki

Hathvā ke lehalu e Bhaujo, bāns ke chabeliyā nu re ki
Netuin bhes dharahī e ai Bhaujo,Bhaiyā khojī ail nu re ki
Eik galī gaīl e Ram, ki duī galī gaīl nu re ki
ūncī re jharokhvā me carhī, nirkhlelan Bhaiyā nu re ki
Godnā ke godavle e Netuin, Kāī lebū danvā nu re ki ?
Bahiyan bharī godlī e Ram, kehuniyā bhar godalī nu re ki
Tīsar godan godlī e Ram, tuhūn chīnhal nu re ki
Deh tore thakau e Raja ji, bahiyān lāge ghunvā nu re ki
Tohre kāranva e Ram, Netūin bhes dhailī nu re ki.

Scented blossoms, O Rama! in the gardener's garden.
The heavy scent caused, O sister-in-law! conception in the womb.
My husband abroad, sister-in-law! and brother-in-law, barely a child.
This pregnancy, O sister-in-law! at whose head, to attribute?
At the Hajipur market, O brother's wife! I spotted my brother.
With the gardener's daughter, O sister-in-law! in a smokescreen enveloped.
"Undo your fancy saree brother's wife, put on the threadbare garment.
In your hands, pick up, O brother's wife! a bamboo basket.
Disguised as a Netuin, O brother's wife! Go seek out elder brother."
The first street, went she, the second street, she went.
From a window, looking out, brother she spied.
"To make the tattoo, hey Netuin! how much will you charge?"
An armful she tattooed, O Ram! until the elbows, she did.
On the third tattoo she was recognized.
"May your body rot and your arms disintegrate
Only because of you, O Ram! this Netuin[7] disguise I adopted."

MEENA DEVI MISRAULIA, CHHAPRA

This jatsār provides an ingenious solution to an illegitimate pregnancy, and thus pushes against many societal norms. In this sense it echoes the so-called bedtrick tales common to several cultures (Doniger 2000). First, here it is none other than the brother's own sister who finds the solution, pointing to a shared and secret understanding between these kinswomen, who are traditionally portrayed as antagonists. The plan and its successful execution depend on the resourcefulness of the sister-in-law, and the fact that the absent brother is himself spied in town in an alliance with the gardener's daughter somehow mitigates the enormity of the subterfuge. Here, when the disguised pregnant woman is recognized by her husband, her trick backfires, and the option to prove the "legitimacy" of her pregnancy is now closed. Instead, her curses suggest that having discovered her husband's infidelity, she can claim that it was the need to uncover his dalliance that led her to adopt the disguise. The lower-caste Netuin's disguise and the art of tattooing clearly made for greater geographical mobility and appear to have been available to women in distress.

The song is easily recognized as a jatsār through its typical line endings of "O Ram," which along with "Nu re ki" and "Arai Rama" are common in this genre. These line endings impart a rhythmic quality to the song and coincide with the circular hand motions of the singers.

4

SISTER-IN-LAW FOR A TATTOO

Are āni are āni Sasujī, ghūmne tūi aniyā nu re ki
Are kām kar le āyi Sasujī, godaitī godhanvā Sasujī
Are godhnā ke godainī Netuī, are mānge lāgin danvā nu re ki
Toharā ke debai Netui, Dāl bhar sonavā nu re ki
Dāl bhar rūpavā nu re ki, godhanā ke godainī Netuī
Ihe debau danvā nu re ki, āgi to lagāibe Sanvariyā
Are Dāl bhar sonavā nu re ki, are Dāl bhar rupavā nu re ki
Are chotkī nanadiyā Sanvariyā, ihe dayei de danvā nu re ki
Chotki nanadiyā Sanvariyā, are dei dailī danvā nu re ki
Har phari āile Saudagar, kudariyā phāri āyele nu re ki
Are oriyā kar baithat Saudagar, nīchā mūri gārile nu re ki
Sabh kehu lauke Dhaniyā, anganā se dūarā nu re ki
Are chotki bahiniyā Dhaniyā, kahan u diāyulī nu re ki
Purba se āndhi āule, are pachimā se barkhā nu re ki
Are ahi me āve Svāmijī, are bahinī udhī āili nu re ki
Pīsū pīsū āve Dhaniyā, are jiyavā se satuiyā nu re ki
Are hamahū to jayene he Rama, are Bahinī ka udesvā nu re ki
Ek kos gaile Bhaiyā, are dūī kos gailen nu re ki
Are netuā ke sirikiyā ho dhāīle, Didiyā bari khar nu re ki
Calu calu āhe didiyā, are āpan ū desvā nu re ki
Are purvā se āndhī ho āīle, pachim se barkhā nu re ki
Are ohī me āye u Netuā, are didiyā udhī āvalī nu re ki
Khāilā mai Netuvā ke bhatvā, are godiyā paisi sutlī nu re ki
Are Bhaujī godailī godanvā, uhe dailī danvā nu re ki

"Oh! look who comes, mother-in-law roaming around, who comes.
Work done, mother-in-law, allow me to get tattooed."
Oh! Netuin, the tattooer of tattoos, began to ask for her fee.
"To you I'll give Netuin a basketful of gold, a basketful of silver.
To the tattooer of tattoos, the Netuin, this is what I'll give as fee."
"To hell with your fee, young one, the basketful of gold and basketful of silver.
Your husband's younger sister, O young one. It's her I demand as my fee."
So the sister was given away as fee.
After ploughing the husband returned, having wielded the sickle, he returned.
On the porch he sat, the husband, head hanging down, he sat.
"Everyone I can see, wife, from the courtyard to the door.
Younger sister, O wife, oh where did you send her away?"
"In the east rose a storm, in the west, lashed the rain.
In that disappeared the sister-in-law."
"Grind and pack for me, wife, some nourishing sattu food.
Oh, I must go on a journey for the purpose of finding my sister."
Two miles went the brother, four miles went the brother.
Holding a stick at Netua's place, the sister stands.
"Come on sister, let's go, let's return to our land."
In the east rose a storm, in the west lashed the rain.
In that O Netua, my sister disappeared.
Oh, but the sister, she refused to return.
"I have shared the Netua's rice and slept in his lap.
Your wife, O brother, got herself tattooed and for that, she gave me away."

MEENA DEVI, MISRAULIA, CHHAPRA

While the opposition between a husband's wife and his sister remains the subtext in this song, this opposition is expressed in an unusual way as the wife gives away her sister-in-law to the tattooer, thus permanently eliminating her presence from the household without actually killing her. The tension inherent in this relationship and its perceived worthlessness to the wife appears as the fulfillment of the unexpressed wish of wives in general. Commensal and conjugal relations, once entered into, are irreversible, and the narrative powerfully underlines this fact. That the Netuin household of itinerant tattooers, where the sister has taken residence, numbers among the lowest of the lower castes, with its polluting overtones, doubly underscores the permanency of the sister's fall in status.

An acceptance of her fate, as ordained by the brother's wife, resolves the tension, but the last stanza also provides an interesting twist, for as the mean wife prepares the worst fate possible for her sister-in-law, the sister accepts it with unexpected aplomb. In refusing to return to her former world she subverts the system in an unexpected way so that the shoe is now on the other foot. By shaming her brother's wife in willingly acquiescing to her fate in the Netuin's home, the sister also registers her resistance to established caste norms.

If, on the other hand, the wife had connived to give away her sister-in-law at the sister's own behest, the above scenario would be cast in an entirely different light. In this case, the wife would appear as her sister-in-law's abettor and would be complicit in her elopement, given that no other alternatives to her union were available. Indeed, an individual's ingenious resolution of such problems, with minimal disturbance to the established social order and patriarchal controls, remains the motivating force behind these narratives.[8]

5

MOTHER-IN-LAW'S POISON

Ghar līpe goilī Rama, sāsū ki irikhīā nu re Ram,
Gorvā tari parle e Sāsujī gahuvan sarapvā nu re Ram.
Morā khātir āho Bahuā saurā machariā nu re Ram.
Mūriyā se pūncchvā e Sāsu duarā bigī āilu nu e Ram,
Bīce ke guriavā e Sāsujī hardī lagāilī re Ram.
Sabh din dihalu e Sāsu hudiyā ke bhātava nu e Ram,
Tutahi bhariavā nu e Ram, āju kāhe dihalu e Sāsu,jī
Phulahā thāriavā nu e Ram, dhānava ke bhātva nu e Ram?
Sabh din dihalu e Sāsu, mūriyā se pūnchvā nu e Ram,
Āju kāhe dihalu e Sāsujī, bīc ke guriavā nu e Ram?
Khāt pīat e Sāsujī, bari nik lāgale nu e Ram.
Āncve ke beriā e Sāsujī, ghūrme la kaparvā nu e Ram.
Sūti rah āle he bahuā, sasur ke sejiyavā nu e Ram.
Har phāri āile saudāgar, kudariā phāri āile nu e Ram.
Oriā tar baithat saudagar nīcha mūri gārle nu e Ram.
Sabh kehū lauke e āmā, āngnā se dūarā nu e Ram.
Patarī tiriavā e āmā, kahān rūsi gailī nu e Ram?
Patarī tiriavā e Babuā, jariye ke bigaral e Ram,

Sutalī bāri āho e Babuā, sasur ke sejiyavā nu e Ram.
Ek sont marle saudagar, duī sont marle nu e Ram.
Ânkh se na taklī sanvariyā, mukh se na bolali nu e Ram.
Javne mahuriā e āmā, dhaniyā ke dihanī nu e Ram,
Âhe re mahuriā e āmā, ham ke khilaitu nu e Ram.
Dhaniko mualake e āmā, Ganga dahvāib nu e Ram,
Candan gāch katvaib nu e Ram.
Tohare mualke e āmā, gādh me dabaibū nu e Ram.
Dhanike mualke e āmā, bābhnā nevat bu nu e Ram
Tohre mualke e āmā, kagavā nevat bu ne Ram

Went to mop the floor and faced mother-in-law's bitterness.
Under the feet, O mother-in-law, I see the poisonous cobra.
For you, O daughter-in-law, the cobra, for me the Saur pond fish.[9]
The head and tail, O mother-in-law, I went and threw out.
The middle portion, O mother-in-law, I wrapped in turmeric.
Everyday you gave me, mother-in-law, the kodon gruel,
Served in a broken platter, then why today, mother-in-law,
The precious metal dinner plate and the rare rice meal?
Everyday you gave me, mother-in-law, the fish head or tail,
then why today, mother-in-law, the tender middle portion?
The meal, mother-in-law, tasted so good.
When washing up after the meal, mother-in-law, the head began to spin.
"Go sleep, daughter-in-law, on the bed of father-in-law."
Having ploughed, returned the son, wielding the sickle he returned.
On the porch he seated himself, head sunk low.
"Everyone, O mother, I see, from the courtyard to the door.
My slim wife, O mother, where is she hiding, in pique?"
"Your slim wife, my son, a born slut!
There she sleeps, O son, on the bed of her father-in-law."
One blow he dealt her, then the second blow.
Not an eye did she raise, the beauty, nor a word did she speak.
"The very poison, O mother, you gave to my wife,
The same poison, O mother, feed it to me.
My wife's remains, O mother, into the Ganga I'll consign, sandalwood trees I'll
     get cut.
Your remains, O mother, under the earth will be buried.

At my wife's funeral, O mother, Brahmins I'll invite to feast.
On your funeral, O mother, black crows I'll invite."
MEENA DEVI, MISRAULIA, CHHAPRA

In this macabre tale, the simmering antagonism between mothers-in-law and daughters-in-law, an integral part of north Indian folklore, reaches extreme proportions, with the senior woman plotting and successfully poisoning her daughter-in-law while also attempting to prove her guilty of incest with her father-in-law. In a patriarchal context that reveres the mothers of sons, the ending of this song comes as something of a surprise, for here the son actually acknowledges his mother's brutality. The son's resolve not to carry out his mother's last rites in accordance with scriptural norms, namely, with fragrant sandalwood for the funeral pyre and the feeding of Brahmins, is especially interesting. The last lines allude to the son preference in Indian society, which is largely predicated on the ritual responsibility of sons to ensure the parental soul's proper transition to the next world.

The song also follows the recognizable formula characteristic of jatsārs. For instance, to build the tension, the singer underlines again and again how this particular day is different from other days. Again, when the husbands of these songs return, invariably after ploughing, they ominously wield a sickle or an axe. They see "everyone from the courtyard to the door," except their "slim" wives. This is the cue for the big troubles in store for the *patari tiriyavā* (slim wife)! The husbands of these tales are quick to inflict violence on their wives at the instigation of their mothers and only repent when it is too late.

6

THE TRAVELER'S BENGALIN

Tuhūn to jaibā rāur Muniya, se hamrā ke kā le aiya re Muniya?
Toharā ke laiba Muniya, kasmas re choliyā, se apana ke purbī Bengālin rāur
  Muniya
Jab hun Bengālin goyrā bīc āile, se ūnce re mandiliyā nīc bhail ho re
Jab ho Bengālin dūarva bīc āilī, ki sasur ke pagariyā nīc bhail ho
Jab ho Bengālin dūarva bīc gailī, ho sāsu ki akiliyā nāhin cale re
Maciyā baithal raurā sāsu barhaita, se eik hi akilyā batlaitī.
Pisiyā me gehuān pakiehā me pūriya, se parīc parīc māhurī dariyā.
Pahile je pūriya Bengālini ke dihā, se tab khaihen kul parivār rāur Muniya

Khāt pīat Muniya barni nibhan lāgele, āncve ke beriyā bāthe kapār rāur Muniya
Se sūti rahā sasur ke sejiyā rāur Muniya,
Se sab din dihalu sāsu tutī khatiavā, se āj kāhe sasur ke sejiyā?
Har phāri aile Sāmi kudariyā phāri aile, se oriyā to nīcha muh garli
Sab kahu lauke angnā se duarā, se pūrbi Bengālin kahān gailī rāur Muniya
Pūrbi Bengālin Babua jāri eik bigral, Se sutal bāri sasur ke sejihvā
Kānc ke katlin Sāmi cirkī banaulin, se māre lagre sobaran satakvā
Ānkh se na taklī Muniya, Muh se na bolalī
Se kaun mahuriā ā dihil rāur Muniya?

"When you go on your journey, pray, what will you bring for me?"

"For you I'll get a form-fitting blouse, for myself, an eastern Bengalin."[10]

When the Bengalin arrived in our midst, the imposing temple just diminished in size.

When the Bengalin came to the door, Father-in-law's turban was lowered.

When that Bengalin went through the door, Mother-in-law's senses stopped functioning.

From her perch on the cot, mother-in-law, just one piece of advice, she gave.

"In the flour you grind to bake the bread, in that flour, add poison.

The first bread, serve to the Bengalin, then serve the other family members."

She ate and drank and then the headache came, "Go sleep on father-in-law's bed."

"Everyday you gave me mother-in-law, a broken cot, why today, father-in-law's bed?"

Returning from the field kudar in hand, husband sat on the porch with bowed head.

"Everyone is visible from the courtyard to the door, Bengalin, where did she disappear?"

"That eastern Bengalin from birth, a slut, sleeps on father-in-law's bed."

Of the kachnar tree, husband fashioned a stick, then rained down blows on her, he did.

With her eyes she did not see, she uttered nothing.

What kind of poison was given to her?

MEENA DEVI, MISRAULIA, CHHAPRA

The anxieties of the wife who must stay behind while her husband migrates to far-off lands is the subject of this narrative. Calcutta, home to the Bengalin of this tale, has long been the favored destination of migrant workers from the Bhojpuri-speaking belt. Since the days of the East India Company, and throughout the history of industrialization, the region drew its workforce from eastern Uttar Pradesh and Bihar. The songs richly document the absence of male family members, who went away for years during which time they invariably entered into second marriages and alliances with local women. Folksongs recount how men succumbed to the charms of the women of Bengal and in the process lost the urge to return. Back home the trauma of separation and the break up of family life was devastating, and its impact has yet to be adequately understood.

In this song, the absent son's return with his new wife from Bengal causes so much alarm, sadness, and loss of face within the village community that the only solution appears to be to murder her. In these songs, aggrieved women redress the wrongs they perceive their migrant husbands have done them. Again, we encounter the plotting and devious mother-in-law, who offers the fatal suggestion about sleeping on the father-in-law's bed, calculated to trigger her son's murderous response.

7

SATI FOR A BROTHER-IN-LAW

Apanā osarvā e Tikuli are jhāre lāgi kesiyā nu re ki
Are parai to gaile Rama, are bhasur ke najariyā nu re ki
Gharī rāt bitale ho Rama, paharī rāt bitale nu re ki
Are ādhi rāt āve Rama, are bhasur tāti phāre lāge nu re ki
Are piyavā pardesiyā nu re ki, hamrā biyehuā oh Rama
Are larrikā nadanavā nu re ki, are eihon to hoihe Rama
Are bhasurjī hamare nu re ki, tohrā biyehuā ke Tikuli
Are belā tāl mārlā nu re ki, are chandanā lakariyā ai Tikuli
Are cirwhā sajaulī nu re ki, Gor to lāgi bhasurjī
Are kari le minattiyā nu re ki, Are tani aisā āve bhasurjī
Are sāmī dekh leutī nu re ki, lāli lāli doliyā ai Rama
Are sabujī oharavā nu re ki, are laggi uh te gaile ho Rama
Are batison kaharavā nu re ki
Eki kos gailī ho Tikuli, are duī kos gailī nu re ki
tīsar kos āiele ho Rama, are chilhiyā nu re ki
Gor tore lāgi bhasurjī, are karilā minatiyā nu re ki
tani aisa karihā bhasurjī, are agiyā ani dihatī nu re ki

Are sāmī mukh tārtī nu re ki, jab le ke āve bhasurjī

Are agiyā āni gaiylā nu re ki are tab le ke āve Tikuli

Are kari minitiyā nu re ki sat ke tū hoibai sāmī

Are hamrī biyehuvā nu re ki, are aggiyā ūthi jaitā nu re ki

Sat ke to haile sāmi are ghar ke biyehuva nu re ki

Āncre se agiyā he ūthle Sāmī mukh tarle nu re ki

Jo ham janatī e Tikuli aisan chal karatiu nu re ki aisan dhokhā karitī nu re ki

On her porch, Tikuli started brushing her tresses.

Oh was cast on her, the glance of elder brother-in-law.

The night hour drew near and its first phase passed.

When midnight came, elder brother-in-law began banging the door.

"My husband, O Ram! but an adolescent

and this, O Ram, my respected elder brother-in-law"

"Your husband Tikuli, lies dead under the Bel tree.

With sandalwood, Tikuli, I have prepared the pyre."

"I fall at your feet, brother-in-law, entreat you, brother-in-law

if just for a moment, brother-in-law I could see him."

Red palanquins readied, with green canopies.

Already in attendance are thirty-two palanquin carriers.

One kos[11] she went, Tikuli, and the next she went.

On the third kos came the funeral pyre.

"Fall at your feet, elder brother-in-law, entreat you, brother-in-law,

Please fetch the light for the pyre."

"If indeed I'm a chaste and faithful wife,

Then let the fire rise from my bosom."

"If indeed I am a chaste and wedded wife

Then from my bosom cloth should rise

The fire offered to the husband's pyre."

And the fire leapt from her bosom.

"Alas, had I known, Tikuli, this deception you would play on me!"

MEENA DEVI, MISRAULIA, CHHAPRA

This song elaborates one of the many *sati* narratives[12] that celebrate the chastity of married women and their attempts to protect their honor in the face of threats from even their closest of kin, including their husbands' brothers. In this song, which takes place in a region where reverence and respect for an elder brother-in-law is expressed by maintaining one's distance and by avoiding close encounters as one would with one's father-in-law, the practice of sati is endorsed by the wife's preference for death over an incestuous relationship with her brother-in-law. In north Indian folklore, it is through sati that chaste women establish their honor and successfully restore and even elevate their own status, along with that of their conjugal families.

Ironically, while the offending brother-in-law appears to remain blameless for succumbing to the attraction, the woman of his attentions must die for the social order to be restored. Through the act of death staged in the trial by fire, women not only avert the misfortune of a threatening or illicit relationship but also secure for themselves an elevated status that is denied to them in their quotidian lives. This recurrent theme confirms the presence of social tensions, particularly where the threat is so close to home, with veiling and the minimizing of contact between women and their elder brothers-in-law being two ways the social order has sought to manage and contain such tensions. The horror that attends suspected incest with one's father-in-law, for which the women in the above songs pay with their lives, here extends to elder brothers-in-law.

TRANSGRESSION

These songs confirm that potential contradictions exist in the discourse about gender. It is clear, for example, that following a woman's abduction (and rape), the only way for her to redeem the honor of her clan and caste is by taking her own life. How does this gender-specific code (of honor) accord with the predation of high-caste males against low-caste females? If a high-caste woman is dishonored in this manner, and if the code applies to women generally, what happens when women in poor peasant households are harassed or raped by males from rich peasant or landlord families? Are they subject to the same code, or does it not apply to them? If not, then this would suggest that the code of female honor applies only where the honor of upper-caste women from landowning families is in question. A related question is the degree to which the patriarchal ideology reproduced in the jatsār songs also licenses control over women-as-workers.

8

ELOPING WITH A DUSADH

Pānī ke piyasal saudagar, ghorā daurāvale re ki
Paniyā hi piyat saudagar, dantavā jhalkale nu re ki
Aisan man kare saudagar, toharā sanghe chalti nu re ki.
Hamrā sanghe calbū Sānwariyo, Urahari kahaibu nu re ki
Babā ghare rahbū e hario, Babunī kahaibu nu re ki
Pāni ke piyasal saudagar, ghorā baithāwal nu re ki
Ūnci atariyā ho carhī, Dhaniyā nirekhali nu re ki
Ghora daurāval e Parbhu, Urahar le āve re ki
Uraharī le aib e Parbhu, kaunā ghare rakhab nu re ki
Chunari tu khol e Sanwaro, lugarī pahir nu re ki
Hathavā le chhariā e Sanwaro, suarī charāv nu re ki
Jāhu ham janatin e Ram, are jāt ke tū Dusādh nu re ki
Babā ghare rahatin e Ram, Babunī kahaitin nu re ki.

Thirsty for a drink, the traveler, riding a horse came by.
Just as his thirst he quenched, his teeth flashed.
In my heart arose the desire, O traveler, to take off with you.
If you go with me, fair one, Urahari, the Eloper, you'll be called.
In your father's house, if you stay, Babuni, "beloved daughter," you'll be.
Then the thirsty traveler, seating her on his horse, left.
From her high perch, his wife, in the distance she saw.
"Riding a horse, O god! Urahari, the eloper, he's brought!
Urahari, he's brought, O god!" Where to keep her, which room?
"Undo your fancy sari, fair one, put on the torn one.
Take this stick in your hand, fair one, go graze the swine."
"Had I known, O Ram, that by caste you're Dusadh,
I would not have left father's home, would have stayed Babuni forever."

MEENA DEVI, MISRAULIA, CHHAPRA

This tale about the repercussions of transgression, the price one pays for acting on impulse without thought to the consequences, and the trauma that results from unseemly alliances, mostly with lower caste men however compelling their attractions, states its moral clearly and unequivocally. An interesting dichotomy is set up between the woman who elopes and the ideal daughter worthy of a father's affections, since it is with the transgression of this moral code that daughters forever forfeit their fathers' love as well as their natal homes. There is no fate worse than grazing, raising, and trading in pigs, the occupation of the Dusadh, the lowliest of castes. That the errant woman is lured away without first ascertaining the caste of her seducer reinforces the importance of establishing such social relationships before engaging in romance. The narrative packs fear of the lowborn and of pollution through association with lower castes, and projects the latent threat to the established caste order that the actions of low-caste men represent.

The perspective this song reflects must be viewed in light of the Dusadh caste's political activism in recent years. Within the Dalit movement, Dusadhs have been systematically claiming and forging a separate cultural identity linked to a self-contained counter-public sphere (Beth 2005, 397–410). They have also sought recognition within mainstream national consciousness. The Dusadh folk hero Chuharmal, who has a festival named after him and is celebrated locally in areas of Bihar, is a case in point (Narayan 2001). This Dalit caste, next only to the Chamars in number, has raised its profile in the village Mor, in Bihar, by organizing large-scale cultural festivals, which in 1976 were attended by between 8,000 and 9,000 members. By 1981, the Chuharmal *melā* had increased in popularity with 100,000 participants, by 1998, with 300,000. How the caste, in its efforts to redefine a powerful identity, view songs like the above is a question worth investigating. That the caste seeks visibility, a sign of power, through festivals and melas adds an interesting contemporary twist on the discussion in chapter 5 of this volume on women's exclusion from festivals and public spaces. The women who sing these songs appear to punish themselves most harshly for adultery and elopement.

To suggest travel over a great distance, jatsārs invariably adopt the formula of crossing one forest, then another and another, or a couple of miles (*kos*), then another kos and another kos as the case may be. Further, after their long journeys, the eloping heroines of jatsārs invariably end up devastated by the new conditions they encounter. They must confront loss of face and status, which, of course, fills them with remorse.

9

AT THE BANGLEMAN'S ABODE

Eik ban gailī Raniyā, duī ban gailī ho na
Are Rama tīsre me churiyā maraiyā ho na

Bhītrai bātiu ki bāhire maraiyā ho na
Māi patari patohiyā paricchā ho na
Sāsu leī aile rere kai musarvā ho na
Sāsu leī ailīn bāns ke supaliyā ho na
Sāsu le ailīn palarī me bhatvā ho na
Bahuvā latvā se marlinī bhatvā ho na
Bahuvā latvā se budhiyā dhakelin ho na
Bahuvā ulti-palti tākin maraiyā ho na
Cunarī utārī Rani lugari pahinā ho na
Hamre māi sanga suarī carāva ho na
Raniyā bahut rovai le curilā ke gohanavā ho na
Curilā nāhin janli jāti ke Khatikvā ho na
Curli chhor dihalu āpan rājdhaniyā ho na
Chorrhi dihalun godī ke balakvā ho na

She went into one forest, Rani, then into the next.
O Rama, in the third was the hut of the bangle-seller.
Are you within mother? Come out.
Welcome the slim daughter-in-law.
Mother-in-law brought the pestle for the ritual welcome.
Mother-in-law brought the bamboo grain-tosser.
She brought cooked rice, in a bowl.
Daughter-in-law kicked aside the rice dish.
She pushed the old woman with her foot.
Daughter-in-law stared at the hut in anger.
"Undo your fine sari, Rani, put on the torn one.
With my mother, go graze the pigs."
Rani cried and cried and cursed the bangle-seller.
"Bangle-seller, I did not know your caste is Khatik.
Oh, why did I leave my palace of comfort?
My infant son, I left for the bangle-seller!"

URMILA MAURYA AND FRIENDS, CHACHAKPUR

Suffused with regret and traumatized at discovering that her impulsive act has brought her to the humble bangle-seller's abode, where she must graze pigs, the highborn eloper of this tale is disconsolate to the point of lashing out at her mother-in-law, who stands ready to give her a ritual welcome with the grain tosser and rice. This scene, possibly an excerpt from a longer tale, focuses on the horrifying consequences of the eloper's actions and the self-pity that results. This song tells the tale from the perspective of the eloping woman rather than the judgmental eyes of society (as in earlier tales and songs). The punishing remorse the act evokes in the eloping woman makes the tale's cautionary message even more effective.

IO

ABDUCTION AND SUICIDE

Ghorvā carhī āile sipahiyā re, u jo Laichi par najariyā parri gaīl re
Toharā ke debai Kuttni kān du thai sonā, hamrā Laichi se milanavā ho karrai diha na
Hathva ke le lihu Kuttni, cheapri goyeithā to agiyā āni na
Gaī Laichi ānganva to agiyā āni na.
In mahinavā ke lāgal ba tīrathavā ho
So calahū Laichi na Gangasagar asnanvā to calahū Laichi na
Ek ori āyo Aditsingh, ho karai dātunvā ho ek oriyā na
Laichi karai asnanvā ho se ek oriyā na
Bīr karo dhīre karu dhīre karu asnanvā, ho ki parī re jaihai na
Mora dehiyā par chittakavā, ho se pari jaihai na
Tora niya Laicchi ho dehiyā par chittakavā ho se mora lekhā na
Jaise chandan abharanavā ho se mora lekhā na
Aisā na boli kāhai, bolela sipahiyā ho ki toharā aisa na
Hamrā baba ke nokaravā ho ki toharā aisa na, aisa na boli kāhe
Bolelu tu Laichi ho ki tohrā aisā na, rakhni, randī kasminiyā ho ki tohrā aisā na
Ek kos gailī Laichi, duī kos gailī ho se lagri gailī na
Ho se madhurī piyasiyā, ho se lagri gailī na
Jab le ke Adit Singh, tab le ke na, Laichi khila lī patalvā
Ho se tab le ke na, hāth le jali mukhe khalī panavā
Ho se tīn kulavā na, rakhlī Laichi bahiniyā ho se tīn kulavā na.

On horseback arrived the soldier, his glance fell on the maiden, Laichi.
To you Kutni, I'll give gold earrings, if you introduce me to beautiful Laichi.
For your hands, bracelets, Kutni.
Kutni went to Laichi's courtyard to borrow the hearthfire.
"This month starts the holy fair. Come with me Laichi, to the fair let's go.
To the Gangasagar holy dip, come let's go."
On one side came the soldier, Aditsingh, rinsing with the neem brush,

on the other bathed, Laichi.

"Please bathe carefully,

for drops may fall on my body, careful, not to spray this way."

"On your body, Laichi the spray from me is like sandalwood, according to me."

"Why do you speak thus?" "Because like you soldier,

are servants in my father's employ, just like you" "Why do you speak thus?"

"And, Laichi, like you, are whores and fallen women, just like you."

And he made off with her.

She went one kos, Laichi, and another kos she went.

Then she felt arise a great wonderful thirst.

And while Aditsingh went to fetch a drink,

Within that time, Laichi was already in the netherworld.

And that's how she saved the honor of three generations.

Laichi sister, preserved the honor of three generations.

MEENA DEVI, MISRAULIA, CHHAPRA

In the verbal sparring that occurs before Laichi is abducted, Laichi 's higher caste and class status is clearly established. Her suicide, whereby she resolves the threat the abduction poses to the honor of the clan, is presented as the most praiseworthy outcome, the most acceptable exercise of female questioning. In the narrative, the abduction of the woman threatens the honor of the entire clan, caste, and village community, and this honor must be restored at all costs. The last two lines of the narrative deliver an approving judgment, thus presenting the episode as a pedagogical tool for showing how any threat to women's chastity is a threat to the honor of her caste and clan, and it is this honor rather than the woman's per se that must be appropriately restored.

The concerns the narrative takes up reflect the prevailing upper-caste anxieties that upwardly mobile groups adopt when seeking to alter the public's perception of their status. Thus the narrative operates as discourse defining gender behavior for the upwardly mobile groups as well. Perhaps no other narrative matches the content and serves so well the function of a morality tale. While, for the purposes of the story, the means of Laichi's death remain obscure, the tale points to suicide in general as the only option available to good girls caught in bad circumstances.

With reference to songs in this section, Prem Chowdhury argues that in Haryana the implicit duality of women's voices is apparent in the figuration of lower-caste men as the lovers of upper-caste women. In these songs, women covet the marginalized and outcaste lovers, generally specialists in their crafts—ascetics, tailors, and artisans—that upper-caste women are likely to meet (Chowdhury 2001, 35–46). North Indian folklore is replete with appeal of the ascetic orders, particularly given that holy men were known to cure women's barrenness. Indeed, as Chowdhury argues, "this in a way acknowledges the impotence of the husband or his class/caste men and underlines the virility and potency of men occupying the margins" (36).

11

DOM LOVER

Jan tuhūn Domvā hamke lobhāniyu ho Ram, Domvā Baba joge hathiyā besārau
  ho Ram
Hasī hasī Domva hathiyā besārai ho Ram, are Rama royī royī carhe le Baba ho Ram
Bhaiyā uthū ke karā datuaniyā ho Ram, bahini kaisan karī datuaniyā ho Ram
Bahini Domva moharā chenkaike baithal ho Ram
Jo tuhūn Domva hamke lobhānieu ho Ram, Domva Bhaiyā joge ghorvā besārau
  ho Ram
Hasī hasī Domva ghorvā besārae ho Ram, Rama royī royī bīran bhaiyā cārhai
  ho Ram
Hame joge dariyā phanāvau ho Ram, are Rama carhein gayin Kusuma betī ho Ram
Bhaiyā nahin dehin piyarī moharavā ho Ram
Eik ban gailin, dūsar ban gailen, tīsar ban Bhaiyā ke sagarvā ho Ram
Kaharā dekhleitin Bhaiyā ke sagarvā ho Ram
Cup rahān biyahiti dhaniyā ho Ram, Dhanā āngane me sagarvā khodiahen ho Ram
Domva bhaiyā ke sagarvā barī dūrvā ho Ram
Kusumā nikali parī bīce sagarvā ho Ram
Eik būri būrain, dūsar būri.
Are Rama tīsare me būri gailī patahuvan ho Ram
Royī royī Domva

If you've fallen in love with me, then for my father please get an elephant, Dom.
Dom happily gets the elephant for father; weeping, father mounts the elephant.
"Brother, rise, perform morning ablutions." "Sister, how can I? Dom blocks the
  entrance."
If you've fallen in love with me, Dom, then for brother, do get a horse.
Dom happily gets the horse for brother; weeping, brother mounts the horse.

Now the carriage is ready and Kusuma daughter mounts it.
Brother did not give her the auspicious saree at the entrance.
She went to the first, the second, and the third forest.
"Kahar carriers stop! Do let me see my brother's lake."
"Hush! Wife, I shall get a lake built in our own courtyard."
"Dom, but brother's lake stretches out far."
Kusuma stepped out in the middle of the lake.
The first dip, the second, and on the third, the bride drowned.
The Dom wept bitterly.

MUNRAJI, BARSARA VILLAGE

This excerpt comes from an inordinately long ballad about a lower-caste Dom lover, who cheerfully supplies horses and elephants for the woman's male kin and articles of clothing for her female relatives. The marriage is solemnized and the bride mounts the carriage and sets off for her marital home. On the way they pass through her brother's lake. The bride requests that the palanquin bearers stop, and she drowns herself in the lake. Note the extended negotiations that the heroine enters into with the lower-caste man to appease her family members, as if purchasing their consent for the union. It is interesting that the Dom blocks the doorway of each of the relatives, until he is able to elicit their reluctant and weeping consent, albeit after presenting his bribe. Even more surprising is that the rich Dom complies with and fulfills every demand.

In my conversations with the singers after making these recordings, it always appeared to me that they were in agreement with the song's underlying messages. For instance, Munraji informed me that by committing suicide "the woman had saved the honor of her family." Munraji pointed out that by drowning herself in her brother's lake, "the heroine chooses to return to her brother" and thus to "keep his honor." Munraji pointed to the significance of the line in the song wherein, as an expression of his displeasure, the bride's brother refuses to give her the ritual gift of the yellow sari (*piyarī*). The women present during the recording suggested that the brother, through this action, made clear his intention to sever relations with the bride. These lower-caste singers, intently listening to the song and joining in the chorus, endorsed the upper-caste heroine's refusal to transgress her caste norms. Surprisingly, they commended her choice to drown herself rather than live out her life with the Dom.[13]

The song reinforces Chowdhury's argument that "articulations in women's songs indirectly attack the self-image of the upper-caste male as strong, virile, and sexually potent, shattered not by his kinsmen or caste-men but by an inferior, who is denigrated and ridiculed by them" (39). Through such songs women indeed appear to provoke and challenge male authority within their own castes. These songs also appear to challenge "the reality of sexual exploitation and liaisons with lower-caste women by men from dominant groups" (43). Thus men may see these songs as representations of the sexuality of women they seek to control: "Women do not see themselves as transgressors nor condemn their sexual activity/desires/lustfulness. Men are brought in as sexual players in a total reversal of sexual roles and in a clear subversion of the dominant fixation and idol-ization of female chastity, and the very concept of the ideal woman" (45).

WOMEN'S COMMUNITIES

The texts of these grinding songs provide unique perspectives from which to understand the restrictions nineteenth-century caste reformers placed on women of intermediate occupational caste groups such as Yadavas (dairy and cattle keepers), Koeris (market gardeners), Kurmis (cultiva-tors), and Kalvars (distillers). These restrictions ranged from prohibitions against women's public singing and their attendance at marriage proces-sions (barāts) and fairs and festivals to controls on women's interactions with bangle sellers and other itinerant peddlers. In the early decades of the twentieth century, the even stricter controls against women of up-wardly mobile groups such as Yadavas, Ahirs, and Kurmis, going as far as banning women from visiting fairs where interactions with such caste specialists would have been inevitable leveled, articulated this anxiety. Many pamphlets advocating the upward mobility of castes actually rec-ommended that women's contact with tattooers and bangle-sellers be monitored. As these pamphlets' concerns echo those of the grinding songs, we can assume that they likely based their arguments on the folk understandings embedded within these traditional narratives by and about women.

While it is not possible to date these women's ballads, it is possible that social reformers received their cues about the purported dangers for women in public spaces from women's own narrative traditions, which, in the reformer's hands, were ironically turned against them. More to the point, the songs' purported obscenity, as indicated by the reformers, did not stem merely from hints at sexual transgression, but, as we have seen, from "the transgression of caste/gender boundaries. Also, such transgressions crucially attacked upper-caste masculinity. Since notions of masculinity were themselves undergoing considerable change, with the growth of a so-called martial Hindu identity, masculinity acquired more aggressive and physical overtones" (Gupta 1998, 727–36). It was these changes that appear to have encouraged the dominant castes to mount protests against women's songs in which "their" masculinity could have been ridiculed (ibid). As a corollary to the evolving masculine aggressivity, emphasis was now placed on feminine chastity and purity. The popular literature, including women's manuals and tracts of the period, emphasized the *patīvratā* models of women's behavior.

In addition to the unease in the nineteenth century generated by the explosive content of many women's song genres, another concern related to the customs of women's singing lay at the heart of the severe strictures against the practice. Women's power as enacted in community singing was threatening to the patriarchal order. As has been noted in other contexts, women's collectivities invariably arouse patriarchal anxieties. For instance, Abu-Lughod cites similar evidence from the Middle East, where women were called upon to be good wives and companions to the "new men." She contends the process was "linked to a denunciation of women's homosocial networks that encouraged certain kinds of subversions of men's authority" (1998, 12). It seems clear that the restrictions imposed on women's singing indeed ensured the dispersal and fragmentation of women's communities, especially where these communities were also inclusive, cutting across caste and class divides. In the interest of forging strong caste identities, the breakup of the more inclusive women's collectivities could well have been a significant strategic move on the part of caste patriarchies.

We have no way of assessing the long-term impact of such fragmentation, nor is there documentary evidence to suggest how successful these measures were or how they were implemented. Yet, we may conclude that the proposed reform sought to drive a wedge within even the most informal and spontaneous of singing communities. Signifying social protest as well as social control, a variety of women's songs, including jatsārs, while anathema to social reformers, articulated the dominant patriarchal values even as they critiqued them.

Several related themes emerging from these narratives would benefit from some discussion in terms of the pedagogical functions the genre served. One might argue that the narratives succeed in preparing women to confront misfortune and face adversity. With so much going against them, women can find in these narratives encouragement to cultivate their reserves of inner strength. From brothers who may never offer the necessary assistance, to husbands who may one day bring home a Bengalin, to mothers-in-law who, happy to poison their daughters-in-law, are tantamount to one's worst enemy, the songs hint at the need to cultivate nerves of steel, like Sita's. In fact, Sita's trial by fire is never far from the reality the women of these tales face. Knowing the nature of the adversity that could strike from many quarters is one step toward being prepared for it, even armed against it.

It would be useful, for instance, to know how to deal with an unwanted pregnancy, how to handle an elder brother-in-law's advances, and even how to handle the consequences of elopement. The narratives imagine in detail the many solutions these fictional women adopt to solve their problems, the nature of the risks they take, and where they end up. Thus, the songs are not only about what happens to women and the many possible ways in which the system oppresses them but also the miseries women might inadvertently end up wreaking on themselves. In this sense, jatsārs weave together cautionary tales and dark, disturbing stories.

Songs that take up the theme of elopement, for instance, suggest that even when women decide to elope, they must still confront the problems inherent in working within caste-based occupational structures, this time within structures unfamiliar to them. And since the heroines of these tales never elope with a noble, for instance, they must also contend with a drop in status. Just as the urahari was, upon her arrival, handed torn clothes or the swineherd's hook for grazing pigs, the narratives force both listeners and singers to reflect on what will befall the elopers next, for women, lacking a caste themselves, adopt the caste of their men. Despite such dire warnings, the songs nevertheless highlight the considerable attractions, indeed the very irresistibility, of lower-caste men, including bangle-sellers, tattooers, soldiers, and even the low-caste Dom. These songs therefore are not simply about sexual transgression per se, but the transgression of caste and gender boundaries in ways that target upper-caste masculinity. While the stories' warnings and morals are quite clear, their genius lies in their capacity to open the imagination to alternative scenarios in which women's sexuality does, sometimes, transcend the confines of class and caste.

These refreshingly candid and nonjudgmental songs in fact celebrate women's ingenuity at many levels, including seeking solutions for unwanted pregnancies. In a culture where the clash of interests between women within the conjugal household is a given, reinventions of the sister-in-law figure provide alternative scenarios and create ambivalence, belying norms and stereotypes.

Finally, looming large in these narratives is the threat of incest, a reality that aids our comprehension of cultural codes regarding women's avoidance of their elder brothers-in-law and fathers-in-law. The songs play out the possible repercussions of a woman's refusal to observe veiling in the company of these relatives. That the logic of these avoidance relationships is worked out so effectively in sung tales serves as another significant illustration of the genre's pedagogic function.

I have suggested throughout this chapter that songs sung in the village courtyard about tensions within kin relationships are not just a method of enforcing gender and caste norms on women, but have implications for the agrarian labor these women perform. It is important to recognize, therefore, that a discourse delivered by women to women about intrakin relations (i.e., fidelity, caste endogamy) may also contain as an ideological subtext a discourse licensing female subordination to patriarchal authority in other nondomestic situations. In short, the discourse about the desirability of female obedience in the domestic domain can also be translated into the desirability of women-worker obedience in the sphere of agricultural production, whether this sphere involves female laborers working on land owned or operated by the male head of their household or working on his behalf on holdings owned or operated by nonkin. This economic dimension, which disempowers women not just within the domestic sphere but also beyond its confines, is frequently overlooked. Collective acts of singing remain ubiquitous, particularly in the sphere of agricultural production. The next chapter examines some implications of a genre sung while women work in the fields, the lighthearted, and pithier, *kajlī*.

CHAPTER TWO

→ Singing Bargains

Shakti's violence to Brahma and Vishnu persuades Shiva to try bargaining instead of refusal, and Shakti is quite willing to bargain. The
assaulting decapitating goddess quite readily relinquishes some power
(her masculine power, her third eye) in order to achieve her goal of
creation. Cooperation, not murder is the way to get things done, but it
is negotiated only after a violent display.

ANN GRODZINS GOLD, "GENDER, VIOLENCE AND POWER," 26

All over north India, agricultural operations carried
out by women are accompanied by rich and varied
song genres, so much so that these songs are inseparable
from women's work cultures. Since songs lighten repetitive tasks, agricultural production and cultural creativity
proceed hand in hand. With the exception of ploughing,
women participate in varying measure in every agricultural task, including tilling, sowing, spreading manure,
irrigating, weeding, cutting and reaping, carrying and
transporting the harvest, threshing, winnowing, and the
processing and storing of food (Jassal 2001, 70; Bhargava
1996). Nevertheless, until as late as the 1980s, women's
work in agriculture remained invisible and their enormous contributions were largely subsumed under the labor of the male peasant. That women's songs accompany

agricultural tasks provides at least one, albeit unexpected, source of proof that women labor as agricultural producers and further established the need to link cultural and economic analysis. This chapter investigates the usefulness of work songs as source material for unearthing the labor conditions of women on lower rungs of caste and agrarian hierarchies. The song genre explored here is the *kajlī*, a generic term in the north Indian countryside for songs performed largely by female agricultural laborers on the lowest rungs of caste hierarchies and, occasionally, by women of intermediate castes. Arjun Das Kesari, the folklorist and renowned compiler of the kajlī genre who based his collections on those of the villages of Mirzapur and Sonebhadra, argues that the genre originated as a musical offering to the goddess of the region, Kajjala Devi (1996). What might we learn from these songs about the conditions of these women's labor? Alternatively, what might we learn about the relations of production from the songs sung during this production?

In 1975, the Report on the Committee on the Status of Women (CSWI) exposed the degree to which official statistics highlighting unpaid family labor underestimated women's contributions. In 1988, a Commission of Enquiry on Self-employed Women and Women in the Informal Sector submitted its report on the nonrecognition of women's work (Shramshakti 1988). Yet women's contributions, so crucial to the livelihood and security of agrarian households, remained peripheral to the way "work" was defined, and numerous inadequacies in its documentation persisted. During the 1980s, the concept of work and the invisibility of women's work—two major areas of scholarly research—emerged from feminist concerns and the recognition of gender as an analytic category (Kalpagam 1986; Deitrich 1983). This focus on women's roles in agriculture, in turn, yielded the new understanding of the peasantry as a vastly differentiated, rather than homogenous, group. The taken for granted character of women's agricultural activity, which was subsumed within the labor performed by peasant households, and its hidden and uncompensated nature has attracted the attention of feminist scholarship over the past decades (Boserup 1970; Tinker 1990; Agarwal 1995; Jassal 2003).

Just as the labor of women in the countryside was obscured by the assumption that women's work in the fields was an extension of their household duties, a predisposition not to hear women who labor has likewise muffled their voices so that, even today, little is known about their lives. This predisposition does not mean that women have been silent, but rather that women on the lowest rungs of caste and class hierarchies have not been heard, especially within the privileged enclaves of the academy.[1] Paradoxically, songs about women's intimate worlds are best heard in the relative anonymity of open spaces. Such anonymity is also relevant to discussions of the fluidity of folksongs and, as Wendy Doniger has argued in relation to folk traditions in general, "the anonymity of the text makes it appear to be part of communal experience, like a ritual, like the whole sky; the author is as fluid as the text" (Doniger 1995, 31).

Paul Stoller's suggestion that we "learn how to hear" is pertinent to this inquiry, as is his plea that we "consider in a new light the dynamic nature of sound, an open door to the comprehension of cultural sentiment" (Stoller 1984, 561). Quite apart from the information song texts impart as "maps of shared experience," therefore, the chapter focuses on the melodic structure of work songs, and treats the transformative aspects inherent in music and those qualities that promote women's sense of community as equally worthy of attention (Feld 1987, 200). Indeed, the sensation that the sounds and feelings of the songs engender lingers powerfully, long after the songs' performance.

Against the backdrop of women's invaluable, though uncompensated, contributions, the work songs examined in this chapter suggest how women might try to make their work conditions less onerous. Yet, the strategies that women adopt to advance their own interests, their "bargains with patriarchy," often end up reproducing prevailing gender ideologies and structures (Kandiyoti 1988). As gender orders involve mutually binding constraints, Deniz Kandiyoti argues that women must strategize within a set of concrete constraints. Since the inner workings of gender arrangements vary across societal contexts, contestation is "always circumscribed by the limits of the culturally conceivable" (147). Moreover, as the household is the locus of competing interests, rights, obligations, and resources, where members are often involved in negotiation and conflict (Moore 1994, 87), patriarchal bargains influence how women's gendered subjectivities are shaped. This chapter investigates how songs might offer clues about how this gender asymmetry is created and reproduced and, sometimes, contested. In addition, this chapter moves beyond the household to explore the economic, social, and political milieu in which households are embedded.

A significant question this chapter takes up is how the "voice" of song might be different from that of speech. Beginning in the 1990s, ethnographers, particularly Ann Grodzins Gold and Gloria Goodwin Raheja, who, in their pathbreaking study of Rajasthan, sought to overturn prevailing assumptions about the purported subordination and passivity of rural women, have provided us with important new understandings of women's voice. Through women's expressive traditions and through the "hidden transcripts" within speech and song, we learn about women's own self-imaginings, quite often contrary to the construction of women in much of the prescriptive literature on gender, sexuality, and kinship. Capturing the fun, ribaldry, and irony of the songs, Raheja and Gold argue that Rajasthani women's genres were highly effective at momentarily subverting patriarchal ideology, even if what constituted this subversion or resistance remained undertheorized. This chapter goes beyond Raheja and Gold's theorization of the management of women's kinship bonds and the negotiations between conjugal and kinship networks to index, instead, the diversity and multivocality of women's voices and to highlight the multiple viewpoints and layers of interpretations possible in each musical rendering, which in turn prompt us to refine and complicate the so-called limitedness, in these contexts, of notions such as resistance. Moreover, as work songs are intrinsic to women's agrarian production, I seek, as I indicated above, to illuminate the processes of production within which these songs emerged.

The chapter also examines the extent to which work songs allow us to move beyond the conceptualization of women's agency, per the contributions of Laura Ahearn (2000; 2001) and Saba Mahmood (2005), as the sociocultural capacity to act within the existing power relations that in turn impact structures of subordination. I depart from the purported antinomy between subversion, on the one hand, and the reproduction of power structures, on the other, and in so doing follow Kirin Narayan's recommendation to stop seeing songs merely as texts to mine for so-called folk points of view and to focus instead on contexts within which each performer might creatively assign new meanings to the songs (Narayan 1995).

A characteristic feature of the songs in this chapter is their spirit of abandon; carefree in mood, they also express an unrestrained sexuality, especially when at a safe distance from the controlling patriarchal gaze. Prem Chowdhry's following observation about women's songs in Haryana is relevant to the kajlī genre: "Occupying an almost autonomous space outside the male presence, most of them are not to be heard or viewed by men. Yet often they are sung addressing the men and in close proximity to them. The lurking presence of men in the periphery is not obvious or acknowledged by either of them. This ambiguity in relationship to the male presence, or rather private-public space allows a full and frank expression of women's desires and I would venture to suggest perhaps affords them greater pleasure" (Chowdhry 2005, 113).

Despite its association with agricultural tasks, kajlī possesses as its outstanding feature a light-hearted quality that likens the genre to play. It is perhaps an overarching contempt for manual labor that causes the genre's connections with the labor processes representing the collective voice of laboring women today to be effaced and lead to its sanitized understanding as a genre of songs representative merely of the spirit of a particular season. Do laughter, play, jokes, and humor—themes associated with the kajlī genre in particular—help us to arrive at a more nuanced understanding of women's agency? Again, as Raheja and Gold have pointed out, jokes and laughter disrupt the stereotypes of female subjectivity based in an unrelieved victimhood. On the other hand, if women must negotiate cultural restrictions to gain the opportunity to play, a state presumably free of such restrictions, how is play to be theorized? Here, it is worth revisiting J. Huizinga's characterization of play as an activity outside of ordinary life that is not serious despite the player's intense involvement, that takes place in a delimited area or space where nonplayers are kept at a distance, that has its own time and duration, and that serves as a mechanism for forging social groupings (Huizinga 1955, 13). This conceptualization of play emphasizes the temporary suspension of ordinary life, which is also a feature of the women's songs examined in the last chapter.

I heard most of the songs in this chapter while conducting fieldwork on women's labor conditions in agriculture in the villages of Atara, Barsara, Pilkicha, and Sauraiyan in the heart of Jaunpur district. As I pointed out in the introduction, Atara and Barsara are large multicaste villages, while in Sauraiyan more than half of the population is Dalit and the rest is multicaste. The nongovernmental organization (NGO) Bharatiya Jan Sewa Ashram has been active in Sauraiyan, and as a result the Dalit population has been steadily educated about its rights. Much of the research on laboring women in Jaunpur that I reference in this chapter was facilitated through my contact with this NGO and through my participation in the activities of the Abhiyān Samitī for Land Reforms and Labor Rights in the late 90s. I recorded the songs in Sadiapur, on the other hand, in 2003, as part of a separate inquiry on marginalization processes along the Ganga. Here the focus of my fieldwork was entirely on the challenges faced by communities that derive their livelihoods from the Ganges, particularly the river-faring caste of Mallah.

This chapter is divided into five sections. The first section addresses songs that reveal the nature of the peasant household, the site of women's productivity. The second shifts its focus to the context within which I made my recordings and to the kinds of issues that surfaced. The third section takes up women's involvement in agricultural production and examines problems such as unequal wages. In section four, I examine the importance in this region of songs of migration. Finally, in the fifth section I discuss songs in which negotiation and bargaining predominate, including the implications of women's negotiation to play.

THE PEASANT HOUSEHOLD

The task of safeguarding food, averting danger, and, in a broad sense, attending to the grammatical rules which govern the relational idiom of food, falls upon women.

DUBE, *ANTHROPOLOGICAL EXPLORATIONS IN GENDER*, 159

In this section, I focus on the functioning of the household as an economic unit, exposing, where that unit is the extended household, many kinds of tensions, both social and cultural. As women of upper-caste households are not involved in laboring in the fields, the household remains their center of existence, so it seems entirely appropriate to begin here. While it is often impossible to separate songs by caste and class, as most of them constitute the common heritage of the people, I nevertheless found it something of a surprise that the women of the relatively prosperous households of upper castes in Atara village sang so many songs about scarcity and the management of scarce resources. These recordings, then, force us to reflect on the issue of persistent gender inequalities in nutritional allocations and on the overall unequal distribution of resources even in relatively prosperous households. Such discrepancies must include basic necessities such as health care, education, access to property, resources, earnings, and so on across caste and class divides. Development studies over the past decades have dealt with the implications of these assumptions for women at length, especially where the household was seen as an undifferentiated unit (Agarwal 1995; Jassal 2001). The songs then serve to flesh out in concrete terms what the sharing of scare resources might entail. Such songs are indicative of the rich qualitative data that could be collected to supplement dry statistics on agrarian class structure.

I

Pahile pahile gavanvā āinī, apane sasurvā āinī ho
Saiyān samjhāvain lāge, Dhan māi ke jinke au
Ki māi mor garvā se jor bāti ho,
Eik cammac bhar cāvar dihin, cammac bhar ke dāl dihin,
Cammac bhar ke ātā dihin, sutuhī bhar ke namak dihin, eik the gohariyā
  dihleen ho
Bahuvā itanai rasanvā hamre bātai, banāi ke khiyāi dihu ho
Sorah the manseru bāte, satrah the mehrāru bāten
Bīs the larikvā bāten, Kukur, bilariyā bāten
Gaunvā caravahā bāten ho, Bahuvā, itnā pariniyā hamre bāten
Banāi ke khavāi dihu ho

When I just came to my marital home, to my marital home,
My love began advising me that Mother is very powerful and proud.
She measured out just a spoonful of rice, just a spoonful of lentils she measured
  out.
A spoonful of flour, just a pinch of salt, she handed me and one shout she gave,
"Daughter-in-law, this is the ration we have, prepare and feed them all."
Sixteen men, there are here, seventeen women
Twenty children there are, and dogs and cats,
There are the village ploughmen. "Daughter-in-law, so many people are there.
Prepare, and feed them all!"

SHANTI TEWARI AND FRIENDS, ATARA JAUNPUR

Shanti, a Brahmin woman from Atara village and one of the singers, drew my attention to the contrast between the powerless inmarrying bride and her controlling, though stingy, mother-in-law. She marveled at women's skills in food preparation and distribution, given the scarce resources available. Shanti explained that while upper-caste households in this area are generally well off, the distribution of household resources is a concern for all households in the countryside. Inmarrying wives, therefore, must be socialized into preserving and maintaining the family's food traditions, especially those regarding prescriptions and proscriptions about various foods. The song presents a scenario in which both the senior and junior woman of the household are involved in an exchange with each other, allowing us to imagine the gradual progression from the extreme disempowerment of the youngest brides to their increasing responsibilities, which over time lead to their transformation into powerful matriarchs who have significant clout in household decisions. The next song continues the motif of scarcity, but introduces other elements relating to the distribution of both resources and power within the household.

2

Ser bhar gehuān e Ram sāsu jove dihilī nu re ki
Kuch pisanvā e Ram kuch herāil nu re ki
Pīsī a pīsī e Ram rotiā pakval nu re ki
Sāsu mānge rotiā e Ram nanadiyā garaivali nu re ki
Urakh purukhvāiye e Ram, din khoje bāsī nu re ki
Sāsu dukh sahab e Ram nanadiyā gāri sahab nu re ki
Sāmī ke irkhve e Ram, jamunavā dhansi jāib nu re ki

Just a handful of wheat, mother-in-law gave to grind.
Some was ground into flour, the rest was lost.
First I ground and then I baked the bread.
Mother-in-law demanded bread and sister-in-law just abused.
All day long I search for some leftover crumbs.
I'll bear mother-in-law's oppression and sister-in-law's abuse.
But for husband's wrath, into the Yamuna I'll throw myself.

Where female members of the groom's family, such as unmarried sisters, mothers-in-law, and other inmarrying brides, are also present in the household, new brides are kept under constant surveillance, their actions carefully scrutinized and reported. Inadequate nutrition, abuse by their female relatives, and, worse, a husband's indifference combine to produce the explosive mix described here, themes I explore more fully in the next chapter. The depiction of scarce food resources also highlights how the interests of the female relatives are in conflict with those of the new bride, leaving her chances of integration to hinge on her careful cultivation of a persona above reproach. In spite of this, such integration is never easy and meets with much resistance, and it could take several years and many children before a woman is integrated into the environment that is her marital home.

The process of integration may be described in terms of working one's way up the social ladder. The song makes sense against a cultural back-drop wherein repetitive tasks are assigned to the in-coming bride, until either a sufficient number of years have elapsed or there is another new entrant in the form of a young bride of a husband's younger brother. In other words, the recognition of seniority by age confers benefits and rewards upon senior inmarrying brides, including the easing of their work burdens or their gradual movement into positions of greater respon-sibility within the household. One such gain might be the taking over of the task of food distribution rather than its preparation, since this task offers greater control over household resources and decisions about who gets to eat what. Time-consuming tasks such as grinding, cutting—the preparation of ingredients—might be relegated to the lower-status junior bride, while the actual cooking, a more prestigious task, is performed by the senior one. The following song elaborates on these concerns to reflect on how a new bride is likely to adjust to her marital home.

3
Apane ghar me kaisan, kaisan bahinī dīdī
Tu rahiu bahinī dīdī
Apane ghar me aisan ham rahe bahinī dīdī, ham rahe bahinī dīdī
Sasuru morā aisan ki taisan bahinī dīdī
Nau hasiyā khet me kāti bahinī dīdī
Tabahun kahen ham ghar me baithī bahinī dīdī
Ham baithī bahinī dīdī
Jeth morā aisan kī taisan bahinī dīdī
Sorha hāth ke lehangā lāye, nau hāth ke ghunghat kārhe

Tabahun kahen ham bahu dekhin, dekhin bahinī dīdī
Devar morā aisan ki taisan bahinī dīdī
Solah roti gin ke khāyen tabahun kahen eik phulki, eik phulki bahinī dīdī
Apane ghar mein aisan ki taisan bahinī dīdī

In your home how do you fare, how do you, sister?
How do you fare, sister?
In my home I fare this way and that, sister, just fare, sister.
My father-in-law is like this, so like that, sister.
Nine sheaves I cut in the fields, sister.
Still says I sat at home, sister.
Just sat, sister.
Elder brother-in-law is like this, so like that, sister.
Wore a sixteen width skirt, nine lengths of face covering.
Yet, he says saw me, saw the bride, sister.
Younger brother-in-law is like this, so like that, sister.
Eats sixteen loaves to the count, still says a single loaf, just a loaf, sister.
In my home, I fare just this way and that, sister.

SHANTI'S COURTYARD, ATARA, JAUNPUR

This ironic song supports Shanti's observation that it was "common-place for the new bride to be subject to intense scrutiny and criticism" by her in-laws. The song evokes the mood of galīs, abusive wedding songs, which I take up in chapter 3, in which the new relatives in the conjugal home are paid back for their critical appraisal of the bride. The song spells out just how hurtful and difficult this scrutiny can be. The complaints voiced in the song suggest the practice of heavy veiling before elder male in-laws, a largely upper-caste norm, as well as the labor of reaping in the fields, a lower-caste one. While this suggests that upper-caste practices are adopted by all castes, especially the upwardly mobile, its universal message of complaint enhances its appeal for all castes. In a surprisingly reflective and self-critical way, Shanti added, "the criticism of the new relatives often serves to break the bride's morale so that she ends up being even more submissive and subservient."

For the purposes of this chapter it is useful to remember that the equitable sharing of resources among genders within households, a key assumption of the development paradigms dating to the 1950s, was overturned by later research. Studies conducted in the 1970s and 80s

16   Wives of prosperous Brahmin (center) and Rajput (left) landlords in Barsara, Jaunpur.

17   Near the granary of Brahmin landlords in Atara, home of Shanti Tewari.

demonstrated that far from the egalitarian sharing of resources within households, the division of resources, especially of scarce food resources, was differentiated by gender, with women being the most deprived. Women in the field affirmed that males receive the best and most wholesome diets. Many conceded that this was often to the detriment of women and girls, though they noted that this inequality was changing rapidly. Sarah Lamb's observations from Bengal hold true for other parts of north India: "Women are expected first to serve others in the households as young wives and daughters-in-law and then to be served as older mothers and mothers-in-law" (2000, 74).

In these villages, in contrast to the house-bound upper-caste women whose songs are cited above, women of the intermediate peasant castes, such as Yadavas (dairy producers), Telis (oil-pressers), Kumhars (potters), and Kahars (water-carriers), were usually circumscribed by duties that included work both in the fields and in the home. In peak agricultural seasons such as harvest time, the responsibilities of women of these castes included such a range of tasks that younger women rarely had time to rest. During the fieldwork I conducted in the villages of Jaunpur district, I found that women of peasant households rise two hours before the men and go to bed at least one or even two hours after the men have retired. Tasks such as washing up, watering the cattle, and putting the children to bed continued well after the men had called it a day. Peasant culture in the region appeared to endorse these discrepancies, with the care of cattle and children, the fetching of firewood, and the collection, cooking, and processing of food—rendered even more exhausting where women must walk miles to procure food, water, or fodder—all falling to women.

In Barsara village, I found that newly married brides were the earliest to rise. Amraoti of the Teli (oil-pressers) caste, my young-bride informant, explained: "To be caught asleep after daybreak as a new bride invites hostility, social sanction and gossip from extended kin and even neighbors. This can be very hard to combat. I couldn't bear the loss of face, especially since the values and training received from the natal home are called into question. Mothers of brides are always careful to impart this training."

Amraoti's explanation supports the well-known fact that a bride's work culture, productivity, sense of responsibility, duty, and industrious nature would be judged through her work as well as her sleeping and waking practices. The song below provides insight into the hierarchies within the household, once again subverting received wisdom about the household as a site of equitable sharing.

4

Nimiyā lehar lehar kare pāti, māre bhavachāri ho nanadī
Rangmahal bīc sasurū sovain, māre bhavachāri ho nanadī
Jevanā uthā chalā ho jewain sasurū, māre bhavachāri re . . .
Rangmahal bīc jethvā sovain, māre. . . .
Rangmahal bīc devarū sovain. . . . .
Rangmahal bīc sajanā sovain, māre . . .
Jevanā uthā chalā ho jevain saiyān

The neem branches sway, sprays of rain drench me, sister-in-law.
In the center of the palace, father-in-law sleeps, rain lashes, sister-in-law.
Rise, father-in-law, the meal is ready, lashes of drenching rain.
In the center of the palace, elder brother-in-law sleeps, rain lashes, sister-in-law.
Rise, brother-in-law, the meal is served, lashes of rain.
In the center of the palace, husband sleeps.
Rise, dear husband, for the meal is served, lashes the rain.
MUNRAJI, BARSARA, JAUNPUR

When Munraji, a woman of the Mallah (river-faring and fishing) caste sang the above song, she described it as "prescriptive," showing women of all castes how they need to live in their marital homes, serving the elder males first in order of seniority: "See, how she (the song's protagonist) cooked the meal and then one by one, woke up everyone and served them all, keeping in mind, proper respect for age and seniority. Going back and forth she is surely drenched in the rain. Then at last, she finally serves her husband too" (Munraji, Barsara, Jaunpur).

A number of women's songs spell out the order of male relatives by age within the extended patriarchal household, thus reinforcing hierarchies and the appropriate deference owed to each member. The song is addressed to the sister-in-law, here the husband's sister, and therefore the relative who could be both an ally, as seen in the grinding songs, as well as a potential enemy, owing to her prior claims on the affections of the husband. In this case, the song suggests camaraderie between these two women. Just as it was surprising to learn from the songs cited earlier in

18   View from Munraji's hut in Barsara village, Jaunpur.

this section that upper-caste women face food shortages, the lower-caste Munraji's reference to palatial living conditions appear equally to challenge the stereotypes and expectations we have about the subject matter of lower-caste women's songs. However, it must be stressed that the song is entirely in keeping with folk conventions of remarkable exaggeration, wherein humble peasant dwellings are invariably referred to as palaces endowed with the world's riches, including horses and elephants, gold and silver, and other trappings of wealth. The next section highlights the significance of the context in which the songs are performed.

THE PERFORMANCE CONTEXT

While many of the songs I heard in the field appeared to serve the purpose of keeping time during the execution of labor, other songs illuminated specific issues or opened the way for wide-ranging discussions. This section is based on my fieldwork in Sadiapur village on the outskirts of Allahabad, a district adjoining Jaunpur. It describes my participation in an evening session, when laboring women and Mallah caste women assemble after a day of hard work. The following recording illustrates forcefully the significance of the performance context. Some of the women had returned after working as day laborers in neighboring fields, while others had spent the day hawking fish. A fairly routine exchange about the day's events, earnings, and familial preoccupations gave way to relaxed banter and jokes. The song below was a spontaneous and uproarious conclusion to the mutual recounting of everyday woes. While exchanging stories about their men's infidelities, the women collapsed with mirth as they sang out this song about a two-timing husband in which the wronged wife gets to enact her revenge on the other woman.

5

'Khāvo na more sāmī dāl bhāt rotiyā, kajarī khelan ham jābai re duirāngi'
Kajarī khelat hoi gayi ādhi ratiyā, are ādhī ratiyā
Payi kaune bahāne ghar jāūn re dūirāngi
Hathavā me leu dhanī sāndi goithiyā aur kāndi goithiyā
Payi adhiyā bahāne ghar jāva re dūirāngi
'Kholau na more sāmī chananā kevariyā aur bajrā kevariyā
Payi hamai dhānā thāri akelā re dūirāngi'
'Kaise ke kholā dhānā canānā kevariyā, bajrā kevariyā
Payi more godī savatī taharā re dūirāngi'
'Kholau na more sāmī canānā kevariyā, bajrā kevariyā
Payi dekhatiun savatiyā ke rūpā re dūirāngi'
'Tumhare ke dekhai dhāni savatī ke rupvā aur savatī ke rupvā
Payi candā sūrujvā ke jotā re dūirāngi'
'Tore lekai havai sāmī candā sūrujvā
More lekai mātiyā ke dhūla re dūirāngi'
'Tore lekai dhaniyā taravā ke dhurvā aur paiyā ke dhulvā
Payi more lekai mahakai kapūr re dūirāngi'
'Tore lekai sāmi mehakai kapūrva, mehakai kapūrva
Payi more lekai naliyā ke kīca re dūirāngi
Are dharaun silavā, ūparū dharaun lorhavā
Payi kūncatiun savatiyā ke gāl re dūirāngi.'

Eat, husband, the meal of lentils, rice and loaves, I'm off to play in the rains.
The games went on until past midnight.
With what excuse shall I go home, dear one?
Take some fuel and firewood in your hand.
Return home with the excuse of fetching fuel.
"Open, husband, the sandalwood door, the strong door.

Your wife stands alone outside."
"But how can I open the sandalwood door, the strong door.
In my lap sits another woman, your other."
"Do open the sandalwood door, the strong door.
Let me see how she looks, the other woman."
"How can I show you, wife, her looks, how she looks.
She is the very light of the sun and moon."
"Maybe for you, husband, she's the moon and sun,
But for me she is just the dust of the earth."
"Maybe for you, wife, she's the dust of the feet.
For me she is as fragrant as camphor."
"For you she may be camphor,
But for me, she's the waste of drains.
On the grinding mortar, with the pestle above,
Her cheeks between, I'll bash them in, you two-timer."

SITARA MALLAH AND OTHERS, SADIAPUR, ALLAHABAD

Here, the opening lines about playing in the rains capture the spirit of the season in which it is sung. The loosening of restrictions and controls on women reveals the significance of the rainy season within the annual agricultural cycle. The song's poetic imagination offers insights into the rainy season's life-giving potential, providing release and relief from the scorching heat. Even the most secluded of women appear to have been encouraged to drench and frolic in the season's first showers. The inner courtyards of upper-caste homes facilitate the conduction of women's revelries uninterrupted and unseen by outsiders, but drenching in the rain is openly encouraged across caste and class divides. The medicinal properties of the first showers are widely perceived as an antidote for a host of heat-related skin disorders such as boils and prickly heat, to which even the most sheltered are subject. This remedial nature of the first rains accounts for women's encouragement to play in the showers. However, like the warnings issued in grinding songs, a note of caution is sounded: too much sport and play may lead one to neglect husband and home. One may end up being locked outside and, what's worse, having to deal with the other woman ensconced within! The repeated refrain of *duirāngi* (colorful one, also two-timer) adds to its ironic appeal.

The song generated considerable merriment, but the collective singing

19a Sitara Devi (center) with her singing companions in Sadiapur, Allahabad.

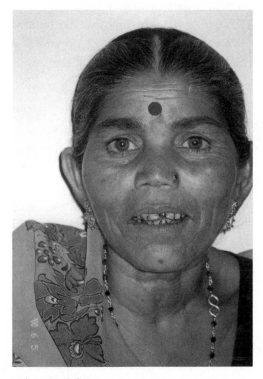

19b Mala Devi in Sadiapur.

also brought up issues related to women's financial anxieties, their everyday struggles, and their lack of support from their husbands. The women spontaneously recounted their personal stories. When Mala Devi said that her husband had died young, Sehdei ruefully interjected, "I, on the other hand, have a husband, but he has deserted me." Sitara spoke about not expecting financial support from men since opportunities for employment had been steadily decreasing for several years and men often traveled outside the village in search of work. Lower-caste women have always worked alongside their men, so it was clear that the women who sang the song above were by no means passive victims. The Sadiapur women expressed both sympathy and admiration for each other, and the session was marked by abundant goodwill and bonhomie. Between fits of explosive laughter, Sitara remarked, "In search of livelihoods we are forgetting to sing." Old Dhaniya replied, to shrieks of laughter, "Come, let's sing such a song so that if someone's youthfulness is on the wane, it can be revived," adding mischievously, "You wouldn't believe the excesses of my youth! It was simply explosive, like lighting a match."

In keeping with the buoyant mood, and as if in response to Dhaniya's challenge to revive their youth, the women zestfully concluded the session with the following song.

6

Hamrā bālam eik diliyā ke naukar, diliyā ke cākar
Diliyā se ākar cale jāye re sakhī re, Āye, cale jāye re sakhī re
Jab calā āve, pahariyā mai dakālun
Dāntava se kātalun janjīr mor sakhī re
Ab bal hatt kar dagariyā nāhin dūbe, Dagariyā nāhin dūbe
Thar thar kāpat hai sarīr mor sakhī re
Mai bahiniyā ke cithiyā jab bhejat, caupatiyā jab bhejat
Raniyā ke bhejat-a birog mor sakhī re
Dhaniyā ke bhejat a birog mor sakhī re
Māi bahiniyā ke cunarī jab bhejat
Raniyā ke bhejat hai darpaniyā mor sakhī re,
Dhaniyā ke bhejat hai darpaniyā mor sakhī re
Māi bahiniyā ke pīyarī jab bhejat
Dhaniyā ke bhejat dūi rumāl mor sakhī re
Dūi rumāl mor sakhī re

Are, rovelā ponchaike dui rumāl mor sakhī re
Māi bahiniyā ke cunarī jab bhejat
Raniyā ke bhejat hai virog, mor sakhī re

My lover is the servant of his will, heart's slave, he comes, then goes back,
  my friend.
Comes and goes but when he does come,
I could jump across the highest mountains.
With my teeth, bite off the chains, my friend.
Now, hope his return path will not be blocked, his path does not disintegrate.
Oh! my body trembles and quivers, my friend.
To his mother-sister when he sends letters and missives,
For his queen just separation, my friend.
For his wife he wishes separation and sorrow, my friend.
To his mother and sister, when he sends festive sarees,
To his queen he sends words of separation, my friend.
To his mother and sister when he sends auspicious sarees,
To his wife two little handkerchiefs, my friend.
Oh, just to wipe away all those tears, my friend.

SITARA NISHAD AND MALLAH WOMEN, SADIAPUR, ALLAHABAD

The masculinity described in this song fully conforms with patriarchal norms, which prioritize mothers and sisters over wives. The husband of the song readily accepts the condition of separation and is equally non-chalant about the strains these periods of prolonged absence induce in the conjugal bond. This song also hints at work cultures wherein men are likely to be away for long spells and women, perforce, must be strong and assertive. When I asked the singers to explain the meaning the song held for them, Mala Devi underlined the plight of women who receive words of anger from their absent husbands instead of precious gifts, which men reserve for their sisters and mothers. These words appeared to describe Mala Devi's own reality, and, without a hint of self-pity, she added:

"See, our men don't provide anything for us."

"We have no support from men," underlined another woman in the group, matter-of-factly.

"Why two handkerchiefs?" I persisted.

Sitara laughed. "So that when the first one gets completely drenched with tears, the other one can be used."

At this, everyone was in splits again.

"Just keep crying and wiping away the tears, crying and wiping," added Sehdei.

Collapsing with mirth, Mala Devi added, "Now you see, how necessary the second one is?"

This sparkling sense of women's community appeared to be strengthened and reinforced by the singing session. Perhaps as noteworthy as the song texts themselves were the nature and quality of the women's interaction. Such fragments of women's everyday conversation are valuable for the insights they offer into group interactions and, thereby, the construction of gender. Through the predominant note of playfulness and making light of some of their harsher experiences, the women also effectively underlined their strength as a collective. Further, by reacting, responding to, engaging with, and creatively building upon the texts of the songs, they demonstrated how they carry forward and further develop the discourses these songs present. In this sense, resistance and subversion scarcely capture the range of possibilities inherent in the songs, in women's singing practices, and in the ensuing interactions. Nevertheless, one could argue that it was the amusing personas and playful and rather irreverent stance that the Sadiapur women adopted that allowed them to critique the male world represented by their husbands and employers or landlords. Since playfulness and spontaneity are two components of the creative process with the potential to transform and redefine work or to imbue it with positive energy, women, by making time for song and discussion, were at once fulfilling their emotional, aesthetic, and psychic needs. As we will see in the third section, the spirit of this session is in stark contrast to the grimness of the everyday reality within which these women labor. In what ways, then, are women's songs and singing practices shaped by this grim reality?

WOMEN'S "UNFREEDOM"

The songs above, as well as my exchanges with Sitara and her friends in Sadiapur that I have recounted, contextualize the mood I encountered in the countryside, namely, a stoic acceptance of the fact that laboring women must continue to labor because their families and households are dependent on them for the security of their livelihood. This work ethic is typified in a song from another Jaunpur village that serves as a classic example of the genre's bittersweet, though largely upbeat, mood.

8

Rimi jhimi barase la paniyā, āvā cali dhān ropai dhaniyā
Sonavā ki thaliyā me jevanā banaulī, āvā cali dhān ropai dhaniyā
Jevanā na jevai mor balamuā, āvā cali dhān ropai dhaniyā
Gage geruvā me gangājal paniyā, āvā cali dhān ropai dhaniyā
Geruvā na ghotai mor balamuā, āvā cali dhān ropai dhaniyā
Lavang-ilaicī ke birvā sajaulī, āva cali dhān ropai dhaniyā
Birvā na kunce mor balamuā, āvā cali
Phulvā mai cuni cuni sejiyā banaulī, sejiyā na sovai mor balamuā

It's raining, let's go transplant paddy.
In a golden plate I served the meal, he refuses to eat, my beloved.
In a glowing pot, I offered the purest water but he refused a sip.
Arranged a fine betel leaf with cardamom and cloves but he refused a bite.
With handpicked flowers, arranged the bed but he refused to lie on it.
Let's go transplant paddy.

BHAGIRATHI DEVI AND URMILA MAURYA, CHACHAKPUR, JAUNPUR

It was very common to come across songs like this one in the villages in which I conducted my fieldwork. Strikingly, the song's deceptively simple, gritty message provides no indication of women's ongoing struggles. While such songs might lead one to speculate about women's disappointments in love, the struggles they faced were often of an altogether different kind. Issues related to wages and the gender division of labor in the countryside came up for discussion several times during my fieldwork in the Jaunpur villages. People from Barsara explained, for instance, that women and children form a relatively high proportion of the labor force, because their labor is economical for the employer and also because men from these areas seek employment outside of agriculture. They complained that now that the harvester is fast replacing the agricultural laborer in areas of mechanized cultivation, it is the women laborers who are being left with almost no alternative sources of income. They lamented the low wages paid to agricultural laborers and bemoaned the fact that, on average, no more than forty days of continuous wage work per season is available within agriculture. They spoke of migrant labor from Bihar that served to keep their wages low.

Through women's song and discussion sessions, I learned that while men seek employment in industry and the service sector, women remain dependent on agriculture for their livelihood. In the villages where I conducted fieldwork, the shrinking agrarian labor market had closed a significant avenue of wage earnings for both men and women in the village economy, but its impact was particularly devastating for women of landless families who were unable to travel outside the village to seek wages as laborers in brick kilns and so on. The decreasing bargaining power of labor and the related decline in job security made it impossible for many men to earn a family wage. On the other hand, deep-rooted cultural beliefs continue to associate masculinity with the role of provider and femininity with reproduction and nurturing.

The women of Barsara observed that their wages were at least 20 percent below those of men. On average, where men receive Rs.50 for a day's work, women get little more than Rs.30 for the same work. The women explained that in many villages the custom of *lehanā*, whereby the laborer is allowed to take home the amount of harvested grain they are able to carry with both hands, was still in operation. This custom was often simply a verbal agreement made between landlords and their agricultural labor. Thus, an able-bodied wage laborer could carry home 10–20 kilograms or one headload of grain at the end of the day. Naturally, women felt shortchanged when they were unable to pick up as much grain from the threshing floor as the men.

During my years of fieldwork in Jaunpur, landless laborers resisted low wages for ploughing and irrigation tasks, as well as the "beck and call" arrangements that had traditionally existed between upper-caste landlords and their lower-caste, landless laborers (see also Lerche 1997, 14). In the Jaunpur villages, despite occasional threats from village landlords, women found themselves unable to give up working for them altogether.

20 Women labor
in Barsara village,
Jaunpur.

21 Intermediate-caste
women in Atara
village, Jaunpur.

22 Intermediate-caste
women in Atara
who have leased land
from landlords for
cultivation.

It was clear that the brunt of laborers' resistance was invariably borne by the women of the laboring households who chose to stay behind in the village rather than accompany their husbands in their search for work.

The songs make more sense when heard in the context of the gendered division of labor within the laboring household. The weeding of land-lords' fields and the carrying out of other tasks for landlords during the slack seasons, sometimes without any direct payment, fell to the women while allowing men to migrate in search of more remunerative employ-ment. Thus, women's maintenance of goodwill relations with their land-lords ensured employment in the peak seasons for both men and women of the laboring household, besides access to fodder for cattle, grass, and credit, in times of need. Clearly, women ended up paying the price for their men's freedom to seek better work opportunities (Lerche 1997, 19). In Barsara, Mallah women also relied on cordial relations with landlords to obtain at cheap rates on the *sarpat* grass used for rope making, an important source of alternate livelihood security for this caste. The lands bordering the Gomti River, though rich in sarpat grass, are owned by Brahmin landlords, and Mallah women could therefore not afford to incur the displeasure of their landlords, even when their wages were abysmally low (Jassal 2005, 269).

During my fieldwork in Barsara, I witnessed on many occasions the clout the Brahmin village landlords had. One of the wealthiest landlords, members of whose extended family own several acres of land in the village, observed a practice that provides a telling commentary on the nature of landlord-labor relations. From early morning until sunset, this landlord would sit on a chair at the far edge of the field under a makeshift umbrella to keep an eye on his hired labor. At the end of the day, by means of the *jarīb*, a long wooden measuring scale, he and his staff would measure the distance each of the hired laborers had covered for weed-ing, planting, or other specific tasks. Men and women hired for the day worked in teams in separate parts of the fields. While the women occa-sionally sang or conversed among themselves as they worked in their respective rows, any interruption in the work itself would have adversely affected their daily wages. Hence, the prudence of our collective decision to record their work songs only after the day's work was done.

Despite the fact that the structure of landholding in this district has changed substantially since Independence and that large landholdings

23　Jarib in Barsara.

24　Powerful Brahmin landlord in Barsara. A Mallah leader stands behind
him with B. D. Upadhyaya, a fieldwork assistant, seated.

have given way to smaller ones, most comprising no more than five bighas, where a bigha is approximately one third of an acre, pockets of traditional privilege nevertheless remain. In such pockets laboring women still experience a range of vulnerabilities. As late as 1998, an incident from the neighboring village Dehiyan served to revive a collective memory about the feudal past and to create a furor in surrounding villages as well as within the Jaunpur administration. An upper-caste landholder's attempt to sexually violate a Dalit woman laborer was met with severe outrage and concerted resistance with the support of the local NGO, the Bharatiya Jan Sewa Ashram at Badlapur. The village Dalits moved the courts, the offending member of the former Brahmin village elite remained in police custody for several days, and the entire neighborhood of Dalits boycotted work on the Brahmins' fields, forcing the Brahmins to hire laborers from neighboring villages at higher wages. Thus, a struggle that had begun as an effort to restore the Dalits' *izzat* (dignity) ended as a powerful movement for Dalit and laboring class solidarity. Protest against this incident of sexual violence in fact served to increase wages in the region, and, since it was the women who had organized in opposition to landlords, it also served to collapse wage differentials between men and women for the same kinds of work (fieldnotes, Sauraiyan village, 1998). Once a minimum wage had been enforced and gender discrimination in wages had ended, women initiated another protest against the persistent issue of forced labor.

In my years of fieldwork, I heard many versions of this episode from villagers in Dehiyan and Sauraiyan. For them, it appeared to constitute a watershed in the changing agrarian scene. In recent years, under the Mayawati-led Bharatiya Samajwadi Party (BSP) government, many villages have been declared by the state as "Ambedkar" villages, making them eligible to state-sponsored development schemes targeted specifically at improving the conditions of Dalits. Since male migration was a major preoccupation of the women of rural Jaunpur and since it remains a recurring motif in their oral traditions, I turn next to the migration motif in women's work songs.

PROTESTING MALE MIGRATION

The scale and histories of migrations from the subcontinent since the mid-nineteenth century leave no doubt about the profound impact upon the "more intimate relationships within households" and ways in which gender relations are destabilized through migration, a theme that has received only marginal attention in the social sciences. F. OSELLA AND K. GARDNER, *MIGRATION, MODERNITY, AND SOCIAL TRANSFORMATION IN SOUTH ASIA*, XVI

The singers I introduced in the previous section that hinted at migration from this region to neighboring towns, as well as to the service and transport sectors in Delhi, the industrial centers in Mumbai, and the rural belt in the Punjab, make the phenomenon an immediate reality rather than one consigned to a distant past when men migrated largely to the port city of Calcutta and, thence, to the sugar colonies of the Caribbean. Since the region has experienced male migration since the nineteenth century, it comes as no surprise that the migration motif suffuses its song culture. Kajlī is an important source for reconstructing that history, though other genres, such as the songs I explore in chapter 6, also feature the theme of migration. The repertoires of both men and women[2] feature the migration theme, the history of which is kept alive in the collective consciousness through this song culture. The continuing phenomenon of migration in contemporary times makes the theme even more relevant. Women's experiences during industrialization in colonial India show that the industrial working class was reproduced through the intensification of women's and children's labor in the rural economy, as urban employers depended on a steady supply of male workers from the countryside (Sen 1999, 3). Samita Sen's research points to the importance of examining the continued linkages between the shifting gender equations in the countryside and the emergence of the urban working class. The laborers in the jute mills of Bengal, for instance—almost exclusively single, male, and temporary—were migrants hailing first from Orissa and Bihar and later from the United Provinces and Andhra Pradesh, which not only changed the contours of Calcutta's labor market but also revived the casual nature of the labor force (26, 48).

It was the earnings and labor of women in the rural economy that enabled male workers to return home periodically, largely in accordance with the mill's requirements. Thus, mills passed on the entire cost of migration, as well as the costs of maintaining and reproducing the rural household, to the workers, whose wages were already insufficient and sometimes even subsidized by the rural household (Sen 1999, 51). For small and marginal peasant households, however, it was remittances from the city that provided the essential source of cash for servicing their debts (69). The redefinition of gender roles arising from the new expectations of the women left behind, and the intensification of women's direct involvement in agrarian production, were necessary outcomes of male migration. However, women's involvement in agricultural production remains largely undocumented and unacknowledged as it is presumed to be either marginal or merely supplemental to the male income (76).

9

Are haraiyā ban jariga
Hamre bālam pardesvā nikariga
Are hamke naiharvā mein tajga
Are sejiyā na sove haraiyā ban jariga
Are pānc rupaiyā sāmi tohrī naukariyā
Das hamhin gharhi me debai na
Rakhbain ankhiyā ke sāmanvā
Piyā ke jāye debe na
Cithiyā na bhejai caupatiyā na bhejai
Apane jiyarā ka bavalvā sāmī likhi bhejai na
Cithiyā pe cithiyā likhai mehraniyā
Apani chori ke naukariyā ghar calā na autā na
Cithiyā pe cithiyā likhai mahrajvā
Ghar kabahu na aubā na, apani chori ke naukariyā
Ghar kabahun na aubā na

Oh the green woods are scorched.
My love left for foreign lands.
Oh, abandoned me in my natal home.
The bed holds no charm, the green woods, burnt up.
O beloved, your service worth just five rupees.
Ten, I could give you in my own home.
And keep you before my eyes
Not let you go, beloved.

No letters, not a four-liner did he send,
About the state of his heart, he didn't write.
Letter upon letter sends the Meherin,[3]
"Return home!
Leave service and return home."
Letter upon letter sends the Maharaj,
"I shall not return home,
Giving up my job,
I shall never return home."

TENGRA KAHARIN, ATARA, JAUNPUR

In this song a woman proclaims that she will raise the paltry sum her husband earns abroad, provided that he remains at home. The song effectively captures the angst of abandoned women, who sometimes spent their entire lives waiting for news from their migrant husbands. The *Maharaj*, or lord and master of the song, categorically refuses to give up his job and return home. While the reasons for male migration may have changed over time, the conditions of existence for the women left behind continue much the same. Thus while the songs shed light on the economic factors that prompted the migration, they are also good sources for understanding the current economic imperatives that burden peasant households today (Kumar 2001; Sen 1999).

The mood of protest and defiance in these songs is such that the threats could be taken as ironic, funny, or serious. In one powerful song of protest against gender inequalities, a wife threatens to get rid of the signs of her matrimony. She announces that she will wash the vermilion from her hair part in the river, smash her glass bangles, and rip off her velvet sarī (*lorhvā uthaike curiyā phor naibe ho; gorvā uthaike sariyā phār naibe ho, piyā jaibe bidesvā*) if her husband migrates in search of work. What stands out in these songs is the desperation of the women, since male migration usually consigned women to lives filled with loneliness and long periods of separation from their husbands. The song below plays on the myriad anxieties of women abandoned by migrating men.

10

Sakhiyā so Rama Madhuban, ke kaise ham jiyabe ho Ram
Are are kāli badariyā tī, hai mori bahinī ho,
Bahinī rimik jhimkī, Deva barisau rainī,

Rama barse ho Ram, Rama jab carhlen naiyā par
Âdhe Gangā gailen ho Ram, are ohi pār se kewatā pukāre
Navariyā tohrī dūbal ho Ram
Sanjhavahi badrī ghamāsal, masi rāti barsahī ho
Rama chhatvā lagai ke harī gailen rainī, nāhi bāsain ho
Ohi pār se kewat pukāre, sunahun Raja Dasrath ho
Apane biyahī k dhara manāvahu, navariyā tohri dūbai ho Ram
Kāu ham dhara manāvahu, sunhu bhaiyā Kevat ho
Apane biyahī k kiyahu apmān, navariyā hamarī dūbai ho

Friend, my love goes to Madhuban but how am I to live, O Ram!
O dark cloud, my sister, just rain, sister.
It rained and rained, Rama, it rained, Rama when he stepped onto the boat
Half way across the Ganga, that's when the boatman called out,
"The boat sinks, O Ram."
Since the evening clouds gathered, into the night it rained and rained.
But holding an umbrella he had left, and did not stay back.
That's when the boatman called, "Hey Raja Dashrath!
Call upon your wife's good fortune to save you, your boat sinks!"
"How shall I invoke her fortune to save me? Listen, boatman.
I heeded her not, but insulted her, alas, now my boat sinks!"

SHANTI'S COURTYARD ATARA, JAUNPUR

When Shanti and her friends sang this song, I thought of the so-called karmic connection it draws between the husband's misfortune and his arousal of his wife's displeasure. About the motif in this song Shanti says, "Women are auspicious and bringers of good fortune, so the spurned woman of the song reminds listeners about the importance of women's roles for the continued good fortune in the life of a married couple."

The song is a powerful articulation of the way in which women might perceive their contribution to the harmony of the universe. It also evokes the qualities of female power (*sat*) described in the previous chapter, whereby chaste wives are able to accumulate and exercise spiritual power for the benefit of their families. Like the grinding songs, this song evokes the potency of the superhuman feminine strength to be derived from women's purity, a strength that usually remains latent but continues to bestow good fortune. However, if tampered with, this latent strength also has the potential to wreak havoc.

While the song might be interpreted as providing a glimpse of men's fear of feminine power and the need to appease their women for their own wellbeing, ordinary women, making no claims to any of the inflated ideals of chastity, use the song to assert and underline the need for men to recognize the importance of their perspectives. The song makes a powerful argument that men ignore women's needs and desires at their own peril. Here, when a husband, in defiance of his wife's entreaties, sets off in the rain armed only with his umbrella, leaving his wife disconsolate, misfortune strikes and his boat capsizes. At this point, the boatman's words suggest that it is only a wife's accumulated merit, righteous power and good fortune that can save her husband and prevent her from becoming a widow. It is in this line that we learn that the errant husband is none other than the mythical and just King Dashrath of Ayodhya, a man of his word and the father of Rama (see chapter 4).

The striking parallels between this song and one that Narayan cites from the Sumba genre, especially their motifs of a punishing rainfall that brings an arrogant husband to his senses, suggest the extraordinary thematic commonalities that exist across regions (Narayan 1995, 248). Narayan's suggestions for using dialogue to elicit oral literary criticism about particular texts provided additional parallels between women's interpretations and their acknowledgment that such songs provide commentary on contemporary social relations (251). The songs below reinforce the notion that while agrarian production depends on the men and women of peasant households working as a team, the men remain the decision-makers and heads of these households.

NEGOTIATIONS FOR PLAY

Where the men and women of a household work together as a team, their labor and industry is evident in a mere glance at the fields. All over the Jaunpur countryside, it is easy to identify the fields that belong to the hereditary cultivating or peasant castes of Kurmis, Koeris, Yadavas, and Kahars; their fields are neat, manicured, weeded, and watered, largely because these castes enlist the labor of the women of their households. Where, on the other hand, the households are prosperous or upwardly mobile, as is the case with a large percentage of the Yadavas in the region, women are withdrawn from laboring in the fields in the interest of raising their household's status, although senior women may still contribute in a supervisory capacity.[4] The advantages peasant women's uncompensated labor offers peasant households, and the perceptions these women have about their own contributions as extensions of their duties as members of peasant households, are reflected in the bargaining tone of songs wherein women negotiate time off for leave, play, or recreation.

The fact that women negotiate to visit their natal homes precisely in the slack season hints at the importance of their labor and suggests the appropriateness of expressing this need at the juncture in the agricultural cycle when there are fewer demands on women's labor. While the need to negotiate and seek permission to visit one's natal home is romanticized and appealingly celebrated in this genre of song, the reality it disguises is troubling and one that I encountered repeatedly during my fieldwork. The songs endorse the findings of research conducted in the 1970s, namely, that women regarded much of their agricultural labor as an extension of their household duties and that this labor therefore remained unrecorded. It is the bargaining tone of these songs that allows us to see the extent to which women have internalized the ideology of women's agricultural tasks as an extension of their duties as wives. Against the understandings of patriarchal bargains, the songs below offer rich evidence of both accommodation and negotiation. The songs further reinforce the notion of women's work as essential, albeit subservient, to male productive activity.

In the agricultural cycle, the rainy season is when agricultural activity is at its slowest, making it the ideal time for wives to spend a couple of months with their natal families. Women's lack of autonomy emerges as key since this leave, more likely to be understood as "time for play," must be effectively and strategically negotiated, as demonstrated by the mood of coaxing and cajoling in these songs. In this section, I highlight two melodious and lively songs, both of which I heard while conducting fieldwork at the onset of the monsoon season, that capture the mood of such bargaining. As the women sung these songs while laboring, the question that came to my mind was how women are socialized into their roles as compliant laborers. The songs are light-hearted and deceptively simple but provide an unexpected window on the contexts within which women must negotiate their time away from work. They reveal hitherto lesser-known aspects of women's work cultures. Paradoxically, then, it is in songs about women's negotiations for leisure time that we encounter rich perspectives on women's work cultures.

11

Àī re jijiyā kajariyā more sāmī, kajariyā more sāmī
Kajariyā khelei jāvai re naīharavā, kajariyā khelei jāvai re
Jab tum raniyā kajariyā khelei jāyau, tikuliyā dhare jaye re sejariyā
Nathuniyā dhare jaye re
Nathunī ke raiya chamākai ādhi ratiyā, gamakai ādhi ratiyā
janavale dhanā sovāi re sejariyā, janavle dhanā sovāi re
Aī re beriyā kajariyā more sāmī, kajariyā khelei jāvai re naiharavā
Jab tum raniyā kajariyā khelei jāyau, kajariyā khelei jāyau
Pāyaliyā dhare jāyo re sejariyā, bīchuiyā dhare jāyau re sejariyā
Pāyal ke ghunghrū bājai re ādhi ratiyā, janavle dhanā sovāi re more lagavā
Kajariā khelei jāva re naiharavā
Jab tum raniyā kajariyā khelei jāyau, kardhaniyā dhare jāwau re sejariyā
Kardhaniyā dhare jāyo re sejariyā.

"It's the rainy season, love, the season of kajlī
To frolic in the rains I go to my natal home, to play kajrī I go."
"When you go, my queen to play kajrī, be sure to leave your forehead
   ornament on the bed,
Your nose ring on the bed.
When the nose ring glistens at midnight, it will seem as if wife sleeps on the
   bed."
"The season of rain is here, to frolic in the rain I go to my natal home."
"My queen, when you go, be sure to leave your anklets on the bed, toe-rings on
   the bed.
When the anklets tinkle at midnight, it will seem as if my wife sleeps
   alongside."
"I go to play kajrī at my natal home."
"When you go to play, leave your waist-belt on the bed."

SITARA NISHAD AND OTHERS, SADIAPUR, ALLAHABAD

Note how the song draws attention to items of jewelry, the significant markers of matrimony, as well as to items that represent women's submission to their husbands. As Gold has rightly pointed out, female coyness is often a pose, masking a superior power: "Female adornment is an explicitly acknowledged form of restriction, signifying women's submission to men (although women also celebrate their beauty as a form of power)" (Gold 1994, 36).

In listening to the many layers in the song, one might argue that apart from reminding wives of their marital duties, the casting off of women's jewelry may also express a brief liberation from women's primary roles, which are characterized by subservience and duty. Or, as, Mala Devi suggested, "the husband of the song is simply expressing his protest and displeasure since she will not be with him in the days to come." Sitara pointed to the song's feel-good element, suggesting that the husband's requests "make women realize that their absence will be strongly felt."

In addition to the women's explanations, this ambivalently coded text could be interpreted as a classic of patriarchal bargaining. There are many possible ways to interpret the song, wherein the woman's jewelry is so intimately linked with her body that the former becomes metonymic of the latter. On first hearing, one might observe how the husband's authority is romanticized, and since the women sang the song with a touch of irony as well as with aplomb, the likeliness that the woman will consent to the husband's demands in the song becomes immediately apparent. One might even conclude that the husband, in his requests for his wife to remove her ornamentation before her departure, is demanding that the wife be desexualized when she travels beyond the physical confines of the home. Where women's entry into public spaces requires monitoring, especially over long journeys, it is possible that this may be achieved in as nonthreatening a way as possible through the erasure of women's sexuality. The construction of the "queen," even "goddess," within the household seems to erase woman's sexuality outside it. That no concessions are made, even if the movement is for the purpose of visiting the natal home, further underscores the stringency of the conditions. The coupling of the song's loaded upper-caste symbolism, with its references to strict controls and its use of jewelry as a marker of social status, with the fact that it is sung by poor laboring women adds to its irony. In spite of these possible readings, Sitara's interpretation struck me as the most convincing and appealing, especially given the harsh separations many married couples endure when husbands are compelled to migrate in search of work. Since women in the region dwell so intensely on the pain of separation, their desire to be desperately missed by their lovers and husbands is poignantly captured here. In the next song, the ironic elements are further enhanced.

12

Kajarī bād aube soc mat man kar sāvan me bhajan kar na

Sab sasure se sakhiyān aihen e jirva jhālariyā

Ho tani bhent akvār hoi jaihen he jirva jhālariyā

Eik sarī liyāya, jhamphar barhiyā khūb sīyāya

Mor cijiyau ko chorāvai ka jatan kar sāvan me bhajan kar na

Kajari bād aube soc mat

Sab sakhiyā t karihen singaravā ho jirvā jhālariyā

Jaihen bābā mor ho, jaihne bābā mor hamare sagarvā

He jirvā jhālariyā

Jhulbe jhulvā ka dār gaihen kajrī malhār

Cār din saiyān culhā bartan kar sāvan me bhajan kar na

Apane bahineu ke ho, apane bahineu ke le tū bulwāi

Unahūn sasure me hoihen ūbiyāi, he jirvā jhālariyā

Dekhihen ghare ka sab kām tohen ho jāye ārām, hamai jāyai de

Jina khan gan kar sāvan me bhajan kar na

Eike samahje na tū maskhariyā, je jirvā jhālariyā

Bhaiyā ānai āvat ba ātvariyā

Pandit tū catur hayā kāhe soch me bhayā

Tani subah shām pūja kīrtan kar na, he bhajan kar na

Kajari bād aube soch mat man kar sāvan me bhajan kar na

When the rains end, I'll return, in the rains do not think, just sing songs of devotion.

The girlfriends will come from their marital homes, dear one.

Reunions and warm embraces there are going to be, for sure, dear.

Just get a sari and a top stitched for me to wear.

Get detached from my things, just try to sing devotional songs.

When the rains end I'll return, don't think in the rains, instead, sing songs of devotion.

My girlfriends will dress up of course, dear.

To visit their fathers, our own worlds, dear one.

Swinging on the swings how we'll sing, melodies of the rains to sing.

Just for four days, dear, take care of those kitchen chores for me.

Send for your sister, call her over here.
By now she too must be bored at her in-laws, for sure.
The housework she'll manage, then it's easy for you and I may leave.
Just don't go grumbling, sing those devotional songs.
This isn't a joke, don't scoff, dear, please.
My brother will arrive to fetch me this very Sunday.
Like a pandit, you're clever, but why silent like this?
Morn and night say some prayers, sing some devotional songs.
When the rains end, I'll return, remember not to think.
It's the devotional songs you must sing, you must sing.

While, as Sitara illustrated, the first song in this section describes the ways in which permission is elicited, the second establishes and articulates the conditions under which it is grudgingly granted. Note the arrangements that must be made before the wife's departure. In such songs the request for permission to take leave is made on the flimsiest of pretexts. In a kajlī that I heard during a brief interlude of fieldwork in the neighboring district of Mirzapur, which, according to sources, is the birthplace of the kajlī genre, a woman asks that she be allowed to visit her natal home because a parrot flew off with her handkerchief and she needs to fetch a new one:

Rajkā rumāl ho suganvā leke urī gainā
Ihe hamare bābā ka bhariba dukān ho
Kahā t bālam calī jāīn.

Such a little hand towel and the parrot flew off with it.
But my father has a well-stocked shop.
If you say, beloved, I could visit, if you say I could go.

These themes, all staples of kajlī, illustrate how women negotiate the fulfillment of their desires and seek permission from their real masters, their husbands. The songs endorse Sarkar's observation that "visits to the parental home were a rare pleasure, dependent upon the whim of the new authorities and mostly withheld, since the bride soon became the source of the hardest domestic labor within the household" (1997, 59).

Since natal visits involved the marital household's loss of the inmarrying women's labor, male resistance to such visits would appear to have structural roots. Hence, as Sarkar found in Bengal, "control over labor is a concept that needs to be masked and mystified, whether in political or domestic economy. Control over the wife's sexuality, the other argument against long absences from the new home, on the other hand, was a more familiar one, securely grounded in sacred prescription, and therefore, possible to articulate more openly" (59).

In the context of the production of a labor force, the songs suggest that husbands are entitled to unconditional rights over the labor of their wives. Elsewhere, I have shown that in colonial times it was understood among the cultivating castes that the labor of the women of peasant households would be readily available in the fields (Jassal 2001, 65–86). During my fieldwork on the subject of concealed tenancy in the late 1990s, villagers who leased out their lands for cultivation revealed to me that occasionally what proved decisive in granting a tenant an oral lease was the knowledge that both the husband and the wife would be cultivating the land (fieldnotes, 1999–2000).

On the other hand, not all women were interested in securing time away to visit their natal homes. Nevertheless, these women would still need to negotiate so-called playtime, and on this level they too relate to the words and spirit of the songs, which articulate deeply felt structural tensions that require both assertion and resolution. These songs reveal a space open to women's negotiations and the context in which their requests might be legitimated and endorsed. It is the gendered nature of the distribution of power within households that emerges here. Women sweet-talk their need for a break from family and household responsibilities, without disturbing existing arrangements. These sung narratives appear to establish the parameters within which women's negotiations would not only be acceptable but also serve to impart the sense that the women have negotiated a deal for themselves. One could argue that by allowing women to take credit for such short-term negotiations, their husband's secure their wives conformity in the long run and keep real autonomy out of reach.

The songs in this section evoke Gopal Guru's important observation that Dalits had been systematically deprived of the right to their own space and time (Guru 2000). In the late 1990s, it was clear that the marginalized women who attended the Abhiyān Samitī meetings, held by a loose coalition of NGOs working on labor and land rights, had received permission to attend from their husbands or mothers-in-law, who were

25 Mallah women cultivators mind their crops near the Ganges, Allahabad.

26 Young Mallah sisters take a break from cultivation on their plot near Allahabad.

27 Islands of fertile cultivable land on the Ganges near Allahabad.

convinced that the interests of the family or society at large would be served. Had the sole purpose of the meetings been for play or entertainment, the women would likely have found it much harder to get away. On the whole, younger wives, who were still in the process of establishing themselves in their marital homes, were rarely present at meetings and workshops unless accompanied by a senior woman of the family, usually the mother-in-law, who was also participating. In these matters, the spadework the NGOs carried out was important in breaking down the resistance of the village patriarchal communities to the new ideas and initiatives the NGOs offered.

While the reputation of a particular organization for sustained and systematic grass-roots work counted toward whether a husband or mother-in-law would grant a woman permission to attend the NGO's meetings, the fact that women had to secure this permission before they could attend meant that women's bargaining skills were always being tested. For this reason, I usually preferred to meet individual women in their homes in the late afternoon. When, on the other hand, I initiated focus-group meetings, I invariably had to base our initial discussions around how the women would elicit permission to attend or how they would arrange for dinner preparations or the efficient conclusion of a range of household tasks ahead of time in order to elicit this permission.

For instance, on one occasion during my fieldwork in Sauraiyan village, Meena Devi, a Dalit agricultural laborer, arrived panting and puffing well after the meeting had begun. Impeccably turned out in her best sari, she summed up her late arrival thus: "My mother-in-law was initially reluctant for me to go and until this morning she was adamant that I should not join the meeting. But I completed all the cooking and washing up before dawn and served everyone at home. Then, seeing that all the work had been done, my mother-in-law relented. She said, 'why not go and see what that lady from Delhi has to say. After all, she's also come all the way from Delhi.'"

Another woman, Susheela, proudly recounted her own boldly defiant stance: "When I was coming, my father-in-law said, 'where are you going? There is no need to attend those meetings-pheetings. Go and work.' But I said, 'work goes on, today I shall not work, tomorrow I'll do it.' Earlier, it was my mother-in-law I used to have conflicts with." Like Meena Devi and Susheela, women were constantly negotiating and making small adjustments in order to earn certain small freedoms for themselves. The opportunity to attend meetings and workshops proved to be one such gain. However, during my fieldwork I encountered numerous instances of women looking over their shoulders for fear of disapproval from their family members. Many such instances also underlined women's lack of autonomy in decision-making and the strong patriarchal controls under which they operated.

Elsewhere, I have described my experience of conducting fieldwork among Mallah women in Madhubani district, who had formed a women's collective to manage fishponds to raise and harvest fish for sale (Jassal 2003). Resistance to the formation of women's cooperatives came first from the men of the Mallah community, as fishing is seen as typically male work. The women remember being subjected to varying degrees of hostility, suspicion, and jeers in those early days in the mid-1980s when the cooperatives were being formed. Women's attendance at meetings was a new phenomenon, and during my fieldwork, the women of village Usrar in Andhrathari recalled that so threatening was the prospect of a women's fishing cooperative that male relatives sneered at them, remarking that the women were "off to drink cups of tea and lounge around on

28 Members of a fishing cooperative in Madhubani, Bihar.

chairs." While the remarks were often harmless, that they were remembered fifteen years later seems particularly poignant.

Some women conceded that initial hostility of male family and village members did eventually give way to support, and then to grudging admiration when, at last, the ponds were secured in the names of the women's cooperatives and over time proved to be the pillar of economic prosperity that the women had promised they would be. The intervening stages of this unique experiment, however, were replete with hurdles and conflicts at every step: concerted struggles involving litigation, protests, and collective action; visits to the government offices for discussions with functionaries; hard labor to clean out and make the ponds functional; mastery of new technologies of fish production; the purchase of fish eggs and then round-the-clock vigils to guard the fish crop against theft and poisoning by disgruntled elements; the keeping of accounts and disbursal of profits; and so on (Jassal 2003).

In Pilkicha village of Jaunpur, Malti, a Mallah woman, who was otherwise very articulate and opinionated, once made it very clear to me that she would have to conclude our conversation because her husband had seen her conversing with me at length and was making angry eyes at her (*ānkh tarerat hain*). Just before, she had forcefully expressed her opinion about the functioning of the Dalit *pradhān* (headman) with these words: "What does the headman do? Nothing. He struts about like a navāb. If he were to grant us a small patch of land from the uncultivated area in the village, we could also grow some greens, herbs, and garlic for sale in the market to improve our livelihood security."

While Malti's statement struck me as poignant for the very meagerness of her request for a small cultivable patch to keep herself financially afloat, even more surprising was the fact that her husband was keeping an eye on her from a distance. Compounding this irony was the fact that Malti was not only an extremely outspoken woman who vended fish but also a woman who was also otherwise economically independent and exuded confidence in her dealings with the outside world. However, her visibly increasing discomfort under the vigilant and disapproving gaze of her husband so close to her homestead spoke volumes about the nature of the restrictions under which she lived and the gender inequality within her household. Her husband's reaction, on the other hand, was typical of the men who perceived the efforts of local NGOs striving to achieve greater gender parity in the countryside as a threat to male authority in the household as well.

This chapter examined how a culture may be heard and how we may listen to women who are rarely heard. It argued that laboring women's musical practices and songs are an important source of information about women's conditions of labor and about agrarian production as a whole. While women's own perspectives on their songs were significant, the chapter also focused on the work songs' value as sources for unearthing women's labor conditions. For instance, songs about women's negotiations to obtain leave from work offer insights into the nature of their involvement in labor processes, both as wives and as producers. In this sense, the chapter also rethinks the relationship between music and production, poetry and power.

The chapter emphasized the texts of the songs, women's ideas about what they sing, and how and when they articulated these ideas. Particularly illuminating are the meanings women attach to these articulations and the ways in which they can be claimed and applied to specific situations. The songs show how women respond to structural constraints by creating systems of meaning that reconstitute the social structure (Holland and Eisenhart 1990). My fieldwork suggested that what is important to bringing to light the nature of emotions in women's collectivities is not only the texts of songs but also their rhythms. Women's experience of working together under common conditions appeared to spill over into their discussions, allowing me a glimpse of the sparkling sense of community. My experience is in fact consonant with the Indian experience of music, wherein melodic structures are quite explicitly linked by convention to particular emotional contexts. The convergence of bodies in music and rhythms in shared work, creating the sense of shared space outlined by scholars of embodiment and music (Feld 1987; Stoller 1984), spilled over into women's camaraderie during their hours of relaxation. Facilitated precisely through such shared space, my fieldwork unearthed a range of viewpoints that might not otherwise receive an airing. Thus, women's solidarities arising from shared work experiences appeared to forge the emotional and public spaces within which women could constitute, express and affirm their sense of belonging.

Thus, it was possible to see in section two that as women came to terms with the strains and disappointments of their daily existence, they tended to use the songs as points of reference for further elaboration on their own conditions. The camaraderie they shared through work appeared to induce a relaxed and upbeat mood, rendering immediate difficulties somewhat bearable. This section drew attention to the commonalities of women's experiences, the fact that such experiences are rarely isolated but rather are shared by others, and, furthermore, that it is possible for women to delve into their oral traditions to find endorsement and affirmation for ongoing struggles.

The leads the songs provided opened a range of questions about women's changing roles within the agrarian economy. While some songs, especially those about the peasant household and migration, provided direct clues as to the conditions of labor, others, often ambivalently coded, were not quite as direct. Thus, many of the songs appeared to simultaneously uphold and challenge patriarchal ideologies. However, taken together, laboring women's songs provided a fruitful and unusual point of entry into learning about the processes of production. For instance, the changing division of labor, especially the fact that men's victories in labor organization are leaving women even more tied to their unattractive work conditions, was an important insight prompted, in part, by the song material. Equally striking was my finding that in work settings involving one form of patriarchal arrangement under employer-landlords, women chose to sing about another kind of the patriarchal control—that wielded by their husbands.

As specific forms of women's bargaining, the song texts have wider implications for women's consciousness, struggles, and politicization, even as they caution against seeing all women's folklore as resistance (Narayan 1993, 181; Gold and Raheja 1994; Abu-Lughod 1990, 41–55). In this sense, the songs in this chapter also challenge us to rethink conventional understandings of the relationship between patriarchy and complicity. The songs and women's responses suggest that we must introduce greater diversity, even ambiguity, into our conceptualizations of agency, especially since, as we have seen, not only are women deeply involved in negotiations for both minor and major gains, but multilayered and competing interpretations about agency also appear to be equally valid and plausible. In their interpretations of the songs they sang and in the various contexts I have described, women affirmed their ability to transcend the limits of their particular conditions and hence demonstrated agency.

The direct association of the kajlī genre, the subject of this chapter, with women's monsoon frolic and the immense opportunities it provides women to laugh, joke, and engage in humorous banter point to contexts where one might search for multilayered and complex evidence of agency. Those who have worked with rural laboring women in India will be familiar with the infectious nature of their jokes and laughter. In this chapter's concluding section, we saw how even the most pedagogical of NGO-sponsored projects and workshops offered women opportunities to have some fun, or, at the very least, to momentarily escape the tedium of their daily work schedules. The empirical evidence therefore points to the rich potential of theorizing the role of fun and laughter in constructions of rural women's subjectivities, a subject I could only peripherally address here. In the next chapter, I turn to the celebration of marriage and the genre of songs associated with this critical rite of passage in the lives of women.

CHAPTER THREE

→ Biyah/Biraha

EMOTIONS IN A RITE OF PASSAGE

Feelings are not substances to be discovered in our blood but social
practices organized by stories that we both enact and tell.
MICHELLE ROSALDO, "TOWARD AN ANTHROPOLOGY
OF SELF AND FEELING," 143

Anthropological evidence from many parts of the
Indian subcontinent points to structural reasons
such as village exogamy as the chief causative factors in
women's feelings of vulnerability and dependence in their
marital homes. However, the emotions associated with
marriage and generated at this rite of passage deserve
greater attention than the anthropological literature has
hitherto accorded them (Macwan et al. 2000; Trawick
1990, 1991; Raheja 1994; 2003; Narayan 1986; Gold 1992;
Ramanujan 1986). The principle of village exogamy ensures that while daughters are permanently transferred to
other households at marriage, sons remain in their natal
homes to carry on the patriline. This arrangement gives
rise to a logical question: does the relative residential ad-
vantage sons enjoy induce a corresponding emotion in
daughters? As the ideology of son preference permeates
all castes and classes in north India, the question is a
significant one for learning about the emotions of those

implicated in these structural arrangements; nevertheless, the tendency to impute emotions to others is common in ethnographic writing, and researchers may sometimes project their unstated assumptions onto the fieldwork situation (Leavitt 1996, 514–17). Since the disciplinary emphasis on structure has, at least until recently, kept the realm of emotions hidden, this chapter explores folksongs as potential forms of cultural production that will allow us to unearth these emotions. The chapter investigates what songs associated with marriage celebrations in particular might teach us about emotions.

Lila Abu-Lughod and Catherine Lutz have emphasized the discursive, performative, and social character of emotions. Since people deploy emotional talk for various purposes, the analysis of discourse reveals much about social life in different societal contexts. Hence, Abu-Lughod and Lutz emphasize the need to "examine discourses on emotions and emotional discourses as social practices within diverse ethnographic contexts" (1990, 14). Highlighting how emotions are manipulated in power hierarchies, the authors show that emotional discourses establish, assert, challenge, or reinforce power or differences in status (14). This chapter treats songs as discourses of emotion in hopes of gaining insights into the purposes they serve. By adopting this approach in her analysis of Bedouin love poetry, for instance, Abu-Lughod and Lutz find that this poetry serves as a discourse of defiance. Thus, since "emotion can be said to be created in, rather than shaped by, speech" (12), this approach also supports the examination of how appropriate emotions are generated through singing that is specific to certain ritual or seasonal contexts. As emotions are socially and culturally produced, it is possible to translate meaning through feeling and thereby to suggest alternative ways of feeling. I therefore proceed by searching folksongs for affective associations in order to track the shades of feeling and emotional nuances these songs produce (Leavitt 1996, 529).

Since several genres of song relate to marriage, this subject allows for the widest possible range of emotions, both at the level of the collective and of the individual. In Van Gennep's theory of life-cycle rituals, *samskāras* serve to mark the passage from one stage or status to another, that is, the culturally defined transitions that first separate the individual from their previous status, next put them through a symbolic transition or passage, and finally, incorporate them into their new status (Van Gennep

1960, 3–11). However, as saṃskāras affect every aspect, and not just the spiritual life, of the individual undergoing the transition, they have an impact on the individual's physical as well as mental states, altering and affecting the outer and the inner, the visible and the invisible (Inden and Nicholas 1977, 35). Within the sequence of saṃskāras, this chapter is concerned with *biyāh-vivāha* (marriage),[1] and the impending rupture village exogamy causes—a parent's separation anxiety at losing a daughter to strangers.

DAUGHTERS DEPART

When, during my field visits, I attended weddings or participated in wedding preparations, I observed that a range of moods characterized the emotional disposition of the bride-givers. Fathers usually looked careworn and weighed down with worry, and not only because of the expense of the wedding. In upper-caste households and among the upwardly mobile who have adopted the practice of *kanyadān*,[2] fathers are also physically weak by the time their daughter's weddings are performed as this ceremony must be carried out in the ritually pure state achieved by fasting. In this context of these heightened apprehensions, the wedding as "eclipse" offers an unexpected, though culturally apt, metaphor through which to frame a daughter's marriage ceremony, as seen in the song below. It underlines the extremely destabilizing effect of the marriage both on the daughter and on her immediate kin.

I

Dhiyavā garhanvā bābā mandvani lāgelā
Kabbdoni ugrah hoī e?
Hamrā he bābā ka sone thāriyavā ho
Chūvat jhanjhanī hoī e
Ūhe thariyā bābā damāde ke dīhito ho
Tab rauvā ugrah hoī e

The daughter's eclipse begins in the wedding space.
When does that eclipse pass?
My own father had a golden plate
That resounded at just a touch.

That very plate father gifted to his son-in-law.
That's when the eclipse passed.

UPADHYAYA 1990B, 43

In this song, the metaphor of an eclipse, which is a threat to the cosmic order that requires the giving of alms in exchange for the return of peace in the heavens and purity on earth, serves to naturalize and make acceptable the fact that the rite of a daughter's marriage involves gift giving (Guha 1985, 16). Those who must be appeased are the bride-takers, who depart not only with the daughter, the most precious and purest of gifts, but also with large dowries and any additional material goods they may demand. In one eclipse myth, when the malevolent planet Rahu blocks out the sun, only by giving alms to outcastes is the cosmic order restored. Here, the lower castes serve as the mediators who have the power to induce the demons to release the moon (16), allowing them to ask for their due, while the upper castes are equally obliged to share their resources and match the lowest castes' requests for alms with generous gifts.[3] Hence, gift giving on the part of the bride-givers is likened to the giving of alms at the time of an eclipse.

The eclipse metaphor is effective at other levels, too. For the parents of a daughter, while the wedding is a cause for celebration, it is also fraught with complex and contradictory emotions, since it signifies the permanent departure of their daughter from the home of her birth. Bittersweet and paradoxical, the joyous celebrations are accompanied by sadness since the daughter is departing on an unknown journey and will henceforth return to the natal home only as a guest. The combination of village exogamy with virilocality (i.e., the relocation of a bride at marriage to reside with her husband and his family in patrilineal societies) mandates that the daughter be ritually severed from her natal home, and, in most cases, subject to greater restrictions and controls in her new one. Even on the lowest rungs of the hierarchies of caste and class, where spatial distance between natal and marital households may not be vast, an internalization of loss of the natal home dominates, for "a woman belongs to the caste of her father at birth and then that of her husband" (Oldenburg 2002, 37). The notion of biyāh-vivāha, or separation from the natal home and its nurturing environment, underscores this rite of passage in north India, making it not only irreversible but also the universal experience of women across social divides. Typical of the financial anxieties associated with the daughter's wedding is the following song.

2

Bhaile bīyāh parelā sir senūr
Nau lakh mānge re dahej re
Ghar me ke ba bhārā āngan dei patkelī
Saturū ke dhiyā janī hoī re

The wedding over, *sindur* (vermilion) ceremony completed,
They asked for a 9 lakh dowry.
In despair Mother threw out the cooking pots into the courtyard.
One should not wish the birth of daughters even to enemies.
SRIVASTAV 1991, 112

As the song articulates, a critical source of this anxiety is the gifts the bride-givers must make to their daughter and her in-laws, and here its articulation appears to prepare mothers for another related, though traumatic, eventuality. The song evokes last minute demands for dowry and the embarrassment a daughter's parents could face were the groom's wedding party to stage a walkout, either without solemnizing the marriage or just after the nuptials and before the formal send-off. The song suggests anxieties a family may have about their daughter being thus left stranded and eventually abandoned by the bride-takers.

Despite the unsettling imagery of the eclipse song, both historical and contemporary evidence from rural settings suggest that efforts are made to promote the participation of the bride-givers' entire village in the wedding. The notion of shared responsibility can still be observed in villages in eastern Uttar Pradesh where each household, particularly those within the same caste and often, class, offers a quantity of grain or rice to the celebrating household to build up adequate food resources for the forthcoming ritual banquets. While this practice ensures that debt incurred by the already overburdened bridal household remains within manageable limits, in Jaunpur I found that women from the village also volunteer their time in the grinding of grain and spices. Their contribution toward the processing and preparation of food required to feed the *barāt* (the groom's party) are a necessary component of the festivities. Such institutionalized arrangements appear to have evolved over time, precisely to ease the kinds of uncertainties associated with the daughter's departure that the song about the eclipse alludes to.

Dube cites an example from central India where mothers of departing daughters wail that had their daughters been sons, they could have ploughed the fields, instead of being sent off like a corpse (Dube 2001).[4] Similarly, among Yadavas in Bihar, a mother's ritual lament includes the placement of a stone on her heart as her daughter departs (A. Kumar, personal communication). Indeed wedding rituals appear to enact the logic of the separation, while also making the separation both bearable and unbearable for the departing daughter.

3

Bāsavā ke jariyā sunrī eik re jamlī, sagare Ayodhyā ke anjor re
Sunrī dhiyavā caukvā carhī re baithe, Ama kamaravā dhaile thār re
Chati cūhuvāile betī nayan dher loravā, ab sunrī bhailū parāi re
Jāhu ham janatī dhiyavā kokho re janamihen, pihintī mai miricī jharāi
Miricī ke jhāke jhuke dhiyavā mari re jaihen, chūti jaiti garuvā santāp re
Dāslī sejīyā urasi bālu re dihitī, sāmīji ke rahrī chapāi re
Bāral diyarā bujhāi bālu re dihitī, harījī se rahitī chapāi re.
Būkali sonthiyā dhūrā ho phānki lihatin, sāmī jī se rahitī chapāi re

Near the bamboo, a beauty took birth, the light of all Ayodhya.
The beauty mounts the wedding space as her mother looks on.
Breasts overflowing, eyes tearful, now my beauty belongs to another.
Were a daughter's birth foretold, a concoction of chilies I'd have consumed.
Or smoked chilies to abort and escape the unbearable sadness.
Given up the decorated bedchamber, hidden from the husband in the *arhar* field.
I could have extinguished the flame, concealed from my husband.
Dried ginger powder I could have gulped, behind his back.

UPADHYAYA 1990B, 130

The above song, like the metaphor of the eclipse, introduces dark and disconcerting notes. It lists some of the strategies women adopt to both avoid and abort pregnancies, such as the consumption of dried ginger and chilies. In this case, however, it is the daughter's departure that induces the mother's agonized cry, which contradicts the popular contemporary understanding of daughters as economic burdens; rather, the song seems to suggest that it is the daughter's transfer to her marital home that evokes the deepest despair. In folk consciousness the dense and long branches of the arhar lentil crops are understood to provide the ideal hideout for lovers and the perfect cover for extramarital sex (see Kumar 2001; field interviews 2000). In a surprising reversal, the very arhar field that should have served as the ideal hideout for a love tryst here figures as the perfect place to hide from a husband.

I heard a version of this song on the occasion of the ritual of *cumāvan*, a performance context that served to highlight the altogether paradoxical and contradictory nature of the daughter's wedding. One of several meaningful ceremonies associated with minimizing the pain of the daughter's transition, the cumāvan (offering of kisses) is by far the most moving. In an intermediate-caste household in Atara village in 2002, I witnessed the performance of the ceremony, which involved the bride's ritual massage with a concoction of turmeric and oils by her mother and female kin, the day before the wedding. Ronald Inden and Ralph Nicholas's account of this samskārā in exceptionally dry, mechanical terms captures none of the rite's emotional charge (Inden and Nicholas 1977, 41). From the songs, and from my own experience of the ceremony in Atara, I would suggest that something more than a massage transpires, something at the emotive level. Here, I transcribe from fieldnotes recorded in 2002 my response to what I observed.

One by one, pairs of married women from the bride's extended family anointed the bride's joints and limbs with sprigs of *dūb* grass, sprouted just for this purpose. Crossing their hands and dipping the grass into the turmeric and milk, they brought it first to the feet, knees and shoulders and forehead of the bride and then to their own lips, while the surrounding women sang out their blessings. One married woman after another thus bestowed blessings on the bride. At the completion of the blessings, close female kin continued with the bride's herbal oil massage, foregrounding the abundantly tactile nature of the ceremony and its nurturing aspects. The ritual appears to underline the care and adoration showered on the bride in her natal household and, perhaps, to contain the grief of her departure. (fieldnotes, Atara, May 2002)

4
Apane man k dhīr dharāvai ke calī
Jahān māi bāp sag bhaiyā nahī
Huvān naihar ke tej dikhāvai ke calī

Apne man k na dhīr dharāvai ke calī
Jahān hāt bajār dukān nahī
Huvān niti bhojan banāvai ke cāhī
âpan man ke na dhīr dharāvai ke calī
Jahān Ganga Jamun Tirbeni bahī
Huvān niti tirth karāi ke cahī.

With a stoic heart she goes
Where there's no father no mother, no real brother.
There, to show the glory of the natal home she goes.
With a stoic heart she goes.
Where there isn't a shop, a market or bazaar,
There too, the daily meal must be prepared.
With a stoic heart she goes,
Where Ganga, Jamuna, and the Triveni flow.
There, everyday is a pilgrimage to be made.

SHANTI TEWARI, ATARA, JAUNPUR

In carefully listening to the song, we hear that its predominant notes are ones of trepidation, rendered even more so because at stake is the good name of the bride's natal home, which will be judged by her behavior, under even the most trying of circumstances. Subjected to intense scrutiny and yet deprived of emotional support, a bride finds her fears of criticism heightened. The song effectively captures the uncertainty of the next stage the young bride is entering. From the bride's point of view, then, the predominant emotion associated with this rite of passage is fear of the unknown. The songs in the following section, which address women's shares in their natal property, are more reflective in mood, as women contemplate all that they are leaving behind. These songs also suggest a highly evolved interrogative consciousness on the part of the bride.

DAUGHTERS VOICE THEIR LOSS

As women give voice to their vision of gifts and of their ties to brothers and to husbands, their words undermine the north Indian ideology of the *pativratā*, the ideal wife who moves silently and submissively from natal to conjugal kin and makes no claims of her own. GLORIA GOODWIN RAHEJA, "'CRYING WHEN SHE'S BORN, AND CRYING WHEN SHE GOES AWAY,'" 38

Since the 1970s, rising dowry-related violence has given rise to an anti-dowry discourse that has effectively sidelined the primary functions of a dowry as a bride's safety-net and personal insurance voluntarily put together by her natal family in accordance with the means at its disposal and as an index of a bride's emotional bonds with her natal village. Oldenburg's analysis of historical data from Punjab links the emphasis on dowry with the growth of private property in land under colonialism.[5] The songs below serve as the proverbial "nail in the coffin" as they articulate the anxiety of the daughter, the very individual whose life is to be transformed. In the final analysis, the wedding is about a fundamental change in the status of the daughter, and it is her anxiety that is likely to be most pronounced and that rituals occasionally strive to resolve. The songs focus on what precisely women might lose through the virilocal residential arrangements. While many marriage songs grapple primarily with the emotive issue of women's sense of displacement at being severed from their natal homes, they also regularly include, if only peripherally, brides' concomitant anxieties about being deprived of a gamut of rights. While the songs reference a bride's demand for her share of the natal home, in practice brides "have little control over the way in which dowry is given and received" (Sharma 1993, 342).

The following song articulates a bride's demand for a share in her father's property, if not in his ancestral property, then at least in all that he has acquired and earned during his lifetime. Through these songs it is possible to find links between the demands of contemporary feminists and the women's movement, on the one hand, and what peasant women have been demanding in their songs through the ages, on the other.

5

Uttarī caitvā ho bābā, carhī baisākh
Des paisī khojahaun bābā, nanuā damād
Ban paisī kañihun ho bābā, khamhavā pacās
Cār khamavā garihaun ho bābā, cāru je kon
Mānik khamavā gārhihū ho bābā bediyā ke bīc
Dhūrat dhūrat ho betī baithe bābā jāngh
Je kuch arajihau ho bābā, se kuch adhiā hamār
Adhiyā kārn ho betī, sarabe tohār
Citukī ke senurvā ho betī, bhailū parāi.

The month of caīt over, Father, then spring comes along.
All over the land, Father's search for a little groom is on.
In the forest father cut fifty logs of wood.
Four poles for the home, Father, for the corners four.
In the canopy's center, Father erects the jeweled ritual pole.
Tumbling along comes daughter, sits on father's knee.
"Of whatever you earned, Father, half belongs to me."
"Why just ask for half daughter, all of it is yours.
A pinch of vermilion, daughter, to another you belong."
TEWARI AND SHARMA 2000, 308

Here, a daughter's request for her share in her father's property triggers an ambivalent response. One hears in the father's response a note of relief that his daughter will be gone before he actually has to give her her share. Hence, it is possible for the father of the song to make the grand gesture of offering her his entire property. Here is the articulation of a structural conundrum whereby the social order can flourish only by denying daughters their share in the landed property. That a marriage song posed the puzzle so effectively was startling, given that in north India the denial of land rights to women is axiomatic. Where this denial is so taken for granted, even daring to raise the question could be perceived as potentially threatening. Hence, the request must come from the mouth of a mere child, presumably innocent and utterly unaware of the implications of posing it. While such songs hint at the systemic logic at the heart of the denial of land rights to women, they also reflect on the question of the balance of power. As I have shown elsewhere, rural women's access to and control over land is arguably the single most empowering strategy they have at their disposal in their fight to achieve gender parity and redress existing power imbalances (Jassal 2001).

The song below continues our exploration of the relief fathers experience when their daughters are to wed. The song seems to suggest that the marriage rite also marks a girl's passage into womanhood, with its accompanying responsibilities.

6

Bābā ham pahirab līle rang cunariyā
Līle rang cunariyā re betī gorī tor badaniyā
Larhi jaihen na, betī chailan se najariyā

Chailan se najariyā dūi cāri dinavā
Larhi jaihen na
Cali jaibe betī apane sasurvān
Chailan se najariyā dūi cāri dinavā
Calī jaihen na

"Father, I would like a blue stole to wear."
"Blue stole, daughter, your body so fair
Will attract the gaze of the lads out there.
The gaze of lads, for just two to four days,
The meeting of glances and stares.
Then off you go, daughter, to your marital home.
Glances exchanged for just two to four days.
Then you'll be off and away."

FIELD RECORDING, ROBERTSGANJ, MIRZAPUR

Here, a daughter's request for appealing clothes raises anxieties in the father about the unwanted male attention the clothing would trigger. Yet the song also expresses the father's relief that such a period would be brief and would end with the daughter's final departure to her conjugal home. Here, while the father's relief arises from not having to manage the sexuality of a growing daughter, the mood is very similar to that of the previous song where the father is relieved at not having to actually partition the property. In both songs, therefore, we encounter fathers relieved at being absolved of their responsibilities toward their daughters—and the earlier the better!

Songs that, like the one above, present the bride's point of view were relatively rare, yet the few that do so flesh out a critical dimension, namely, that of the bride's state of mind. The song below is a classic within the genre. It questions the culture of gifting material goods to daughters, goods that in any case can never make up for the loss of the daughters' real rights or power.

7
Har har basavā katāyo more Bābā, āngan tamuā tanāyo re
Aaj ki rāyin rakh le re Bābul mai to pahunī terī re
Sonvā tū diha Bābā, rūpavā tū dīha
Aur diha ratnā jarāyo re

Ghorvā tū diha Bābā, hathiyā tū dīha
Eik nāhin diha Bābā sar kī kangahiyā
Sās nanad bolī bolein re.

"The young bamboo[6] felled Father, you got the canopy erected in the
   courtyard.
For this night let me stay, Father, I am at your beck and call.
You gave me gold, Father, you gave me silver.
You gave me precious stones crafted and set.
You gave me horses, elephants you gave.
One thing you didn't give, Father, is the head ornament.[7]
Mother-in-law and sister-in-law jeer and mock."

KHATUN, JAUNPUR CITY

Hovering over the excitement and preparations for the daughter's wedding and the father's proud installation of the wedding canopy are a
daughter's disconcerting and unanswered questions. Foretold are the
bride's loss of status and eroding self-confidence that no amount of gifts
can restore. Here women rightly perceive that the gifts they receive are
more "display of status rather than a parallel fund of wealth" (Basu 1999,
225) and while a bride's dowry may bring her self-respect and prestige
in the household (and indeed in the community) if her parents have
been particularly generous, it will not of itself bring her economic power
(Sharma 1993, 347).

The head ornament may be read as a euphemism for the ability to hold
one's head high, an ability the departing daughter, so much at the mercy
of others, experiences as singularly missing. The daughter naturally wor-
ries that despite the transfer of moveable wealth, without any real rights,
she may nevertheless be the subject of ridicule, even contempt, in her
conjugal home.

Indeed such songs also appear to protest the fact that while gifts to the
bride, such as cash, jewelry, and even horses and elephants, constitute
strīdhan (woman's property), they also reflect women's "concomitant exclusion from a formal share in the patrimony, especially land" (Tambiah
and Goody 1973, 93). The songs also appear to endorse the argument that
"contrary to the dominant ideology and the terminology of traditional
Hindu law, dowry property is not women's wealth, but wealth that *goes*

with women. Women are the vehicles by which it is transmitted rather than its owners" (Sharma 1993, 352; italics mine).

Finally, while the daughters in each of the three songs of this section address their fathers directly, the strategies they deploy vary, from the pointed and confrontational to the more common pliant and cajoling. These daughters are not interested in seriously challenging or unsettling the patriarchal order as much as asserting their awareness of its inherent injustices. Through the songs, then, departing daughters come to terms with their exclusion. In the following section, we see how daughters perceive the advantages their brothers enjoy relative to their own exclusion.

QUESTIONING THE PRIVILEGES OF BROTHERS

Wedding songs serve both to explain the action taking place during the ceremony and, more significantly, to induce the appropriate emotional responses to this action. As "harmonized multivocality" in situations charged with tension, the songs offer "verbalized expressions of misunderstandings and debates, conflicts and confusions" since, by and large, these sung conversations would be unlikely to take place in real life (Gold and Raheja 1994, 42). Thus, "songs imagine rather than replicate human interactions, making speakers forthright in unlikely contexts, and at times, making women articulate and assertive where they would probably be tongue-tied and acquiescing" (42).

The songs highlight the temporary nature of the daughter's position relative to the son's and reveal the remarkably explicit privileges brothers enjoy vis-à-vis their sisters. Leela Dube and Prem Chowdhry (1994) have argued that the "contrasting fortunes of daughters and sons is a common theme in the wailings at the send off of a bride from her natal home and also in subsequent visits and departures of a married daughter" (Dube 2001, 93). A bride's ritual act of throwing grains of rice over the threshold as she departs her natal home can signify differently; while for brides in Punjab, the act signifies their wish that their natal homes prosper, in Orissa the same act signifies the return of all the rice the bride has consumed to absolve herself of her debt to her natal home. Such logic might also explain why the wedding ritual in our region, Uttar Pradesh, is termed *lāvā parachhnā* (the scattering of parched rice) or, simply, *lāvā* (parched rice). Gloria Goodwin Raheja's graphic account of a postwedding ceremony among the landed Gujars of Saharanpur, in which the groom, before his ritual departure with the bride, plants rice seedlings on his wife's natal homestead, enacts the same logic (Raheja 1988). Yet, despite the songs' seeming acceptance of these structural inequalities, the songs also provide a legitimate space to question them, and in this capacity they deserve a closer look.

8

Gamkai bājā bājai naihar ke nagariyā, ho gujariā
Sāsurariyā ko calī
Are bhaiyā pāpī bhaiyā pāpī, chorain sunvā
Kai ohariyā ho gujariyā
Sasurariya kai calī
Are bhaujī pāpinī hamke dehlīn ankvariā, ho gujariā

The music of sorrow plays in the streets of the natal home, beloved.
She leaves for her conjugal home.
O Brother sinner, she leaves, listen.
To the other side, O beloved.
For the conjugal home.
O brother's wife, the sinner, gave a warm embrace, beloved.

BHAGIRATHI DEVI, CHACHAKPUR, JAUNPUR

Here, the bride's departure for her marital home is likened to the soul's final journey to meet with the divine. Bhagirathi Devi explained that the song also evokes the "urs" (wedding) of the souls of Muslim saints with god. In the Jaunpur region, where Sufi shrines dot the landscape, the Islamic influence is pervasive enough for the physical death of saints to be understood as a moment of joyous union with the Beloved (Ernst and Lawrence 2002, 91). The song is a stunning example of the spiritual and mystical dimensions of subaltern consciousness that I encountered repeatedly throughout my fieldwork. A deep understanding of the inherent divinity of humanity emerges through such songs (see Urban 2001; Dube 1998; Hardiman 1995).

When I asked Bhagirathi Devi why the brother is referred to as "sinner" in this song, she offered this simple explanation: "Bhaiyā pāpi hain jo āpan bahin k pare hānth saunpat hain" (We often refer to a brother as a sinner because he is someone who willingly gives away his own sister) (Bhagirathi Devi, Chachakpur, Jaunpur). Prof. Rakesh Pandey,who guided me to some important sources in Benaras adds: "*Bhaiyā* (brother) is often referred to as a *pāpī,* 'sinner,' because he parts with a sister and for the same reason, the brother's wife (*bhaujī*) is also a sinner since she ousts the daughter from her own home and even replaces the sister in the brother's affections" (Rakesh Pandey, Benaras, October 2008).

Bhagirathi Devi's and Pandey's reasoning endorses similar approaches in north India, where the terms *sar, sālā, sarau* for a wife's brother are known terms of abuse. In Punjab, a brother, by giving his sister in marriage to another man, "not only makes a gift of that which he most jealously guarded but also exposes himself to the possibility of personal dishonor." Here, too, sālā is a taunting abuse, carrying the emotive power of one who gives his sister to another to violate (Hershman 1981, 191).[8] Yet another song about daughters' disadvantages further emphasizes the relative privileges their brothers enjoy.

9
Hamahi bhaiyā ho eko kokī janmīlen
Dudhvā piyālā daphdor
Bhaiyā ke likhal bābā caupariyā ho
Hamke likhal dur deus

Brother and I born from the same womb,
Raised on the same mother's milk.
Brother's destiny is father's inheritance,
While mine, exile far away.

ATARA, JAUNPUR: SRIVASTAV 1991, 30

The song expresses women's envy at the fate of their brothers in patriliny, contradicting Kakar's assertion that in spite of the preference for sons, there is little evidence in the psychology of Indian women of male envy (Kakar 1988, 48). In these songs, however, women voice and confront deep-seated feelings of envy, which underlines the enormous value of such songs. They emphasize the poignancy of women's lack of rights in their natal homes, accepting the system even as they harbor strong undercurrents of protest. These articulations and the ritual injunctions about singing them only at appropriate moments during the wedding ritual are significant. Indeed, if these rituals were not in place, such songs would have long been expunged from marriage repertoires.

10

Kekar hain bāri phulvariyā
Kekar hans cunai phulvari Rama
Bābā ke hai bāri phulvariyā ho
Bhaiyā ke hans cune phulvāri Rama
Phūl gaye phūl, kachnār bhain pāti
Birnā ke hans cunai ho phulvarī
Phalan gaye phulvā, jhurāi gayin pāti
Biran ke hans cale ho sasurārī Rama.

Whose is the lovely garden?
Whose swans play in the garden?
Father's is the lovely garden.
Brother's swans play in the garden.
Flowers bloom, the kacnār tree is green.
Brother's swans in the garden.
The flowers droop, leaves shrivel up.
Brother's swans leave for their marital home.

SHANTI TEWARI AND FRIENDS, ATARA, JAUNPUR

The numerous approaches to this theme these songs adopt signal a bride's need to understand the paradoxes she must nevertheless accept. Shanti, one of the singers of the above song, explained that the swans in the brother's garden signify the sister who must eventually leave the garden, here, the natal home, causing the leaves and flowers to shrivel and droop. The imagery of loss contrasts with the bounty and prosperity of the natal home. The pathos of the sister's departure seemingly impacts the entire universe, which mourns in sympathy for the brother's garden bereft of its swans. In this song, brides are made to realize that indeed they will be missed in their natal homes. The songs serve to contain the emotions associated with women's structural exclusion from their natal homes, a fact perceived so starkly at marriages when women begin to imagine what it will be like to return merely as guests, as well as provide relief and psychological succor. However, women have strong reasons besides emotional ones for maintaining contact with their brothers.

As Shanti explained, while brides do experience sorrow at leaving their natal homes, which will henceforth belong only to their brothers, other songs emphasize the comings and goings and periodic gift giving that make the bride's exclusion bearable, at least in the early years. To illustrate, Shanti sang out her version of the first grinding song of chapter 1, "Brother Don't Tell Them," which narrates the ritual visit of a brother to his married sister, who hopes to count on her brother's support in the natal home when conditions in the conjugal one are hostile. Citing the song, Shanti drew my attention to another important dimension—that of the *keluwa,* the symbolic ritual gift that brothers bring to sisters.

Jevan baithen hain sār bahnoiyā
Sarvā ke cuvein hain ānsuiyā ho Ram
Kiyā mor bhaiyā tiriyā sudhiya āin
Kiyā samjhayā maiyā ke kaleuvā ho Ram?

Seated for a meal, a brother and brother-in-law.
The wife's brother dripping tears O Ram!
What bothers you brother, is it your wife you miss,
Or is it about the ritual gift mother was to send?

Shanti explained that the ritual gifts brothers brought to their sisters were a source of great comfort and that "women looked forward to receiving them as symbols of love and appreciation from their natal homes." Indeed since women experience leaving their natal homes as traumatic, it is easy to appreciate the extent to which brothers' ritual visits were loaded with emotional and symbolic significance.

Further, were the marital household to discourage these visits, isolating the bride even more, as we see play out in the same grinding song, then we might read a bride's efforts to maintain a close connection with her brother against all odds as a form of minor resistance on her part. In fact, through continued ties to natal kin, especially brothers, women often try to resist the authority of the husband's kin (Jeffrey et al. 1989, 34–36). As Veena Talwar Oldenburg notes, such visits from the natal home are routinely discouraged: "Virilocality, this common feature of north Indian Hindu society, created for women and men vastly different destinies and vastly different experiences . . . isolat[ing] married women even further, robbing them of the company of siblings, friends, confidantes, and partisans" (2002, 187).

The circumstances under which women's contact with their natal homes was policed are poignantly invoked in the ballad of Gobind and Maina, well-known in rural homes across eastern Uttar Pradesh and Bihar. This grinding song stresses the isolation of brides but also prepares them for it. I heard numerous versions of the ballad about the young Maina, who is betrothed and sent off to her conjugal home, leaving her childhood sweetheart disconsolate.

11

Cah re mahinā Maina sasurā me rahelī ho
Bansiyā bajāvat Gobinā gailan re ki
Nāhi morā āve sāsū, bhāi re bhatijvā ho
Nāhi more jorī ke milanvā hūve re ki
Hamrā bābājī ke rahelī dhenū gaiyā ho
Ham Gobina bachrū carāvale bāni ki
Kholi d na āve re Bahuvā, lahangā patorvā ho
Calī jā na Gobina ke sāthūn re ki.

For six months Maina lived in her conjugal home.
Then playing the flute, Gobina landed up.
"It is not, mother-in-law, my brother or nephew
Nor is it simply a companion.
My father had a herd of cows
Gobina and I used to graze them together."
"Then, daughter-in-law, undo your fancy skirt and top
And leave with your Gobina."

MEENA DEVI AND MOTHER-IN-LAW, MISRAULIA, CHHAPRA

In this upper-caste version of the ballad, which I heard in a Brahmin household, Maina's meeting with her childhood sweetheart is thwarted and Maina remains concerned with preserving her natal family's honor; in other versions, however, she pays for the meeting with her life.[9] Nevertheless, the song underlines the isolation new brides experienced, given that visits from members of their natal villages were as equally discouraged as visits from their brothers. As the system is concerned with ensuring that a bride assimilates into her conjugal home, minimizing her reliance on her brothers and severing her relations with her natal home serves to solidify the authority and influence of the husband's kin. In many folksongs, a "fortunate" girl is understood to be the sister of as many as seven brothers, as seen in the grinding song of Satmal.[10] Yet, in keeping with folksongs' often contradictory messages, the following fragment questions the very reliability of brothers.

12

Ek din gailīn naihar
Koī kare na kadar
Bhaujī naihare me tāne carpāi piyā
Âvelā rovāi piyā
Bābā rahelin hamār
Âne āve bār bār
Bhaiyā kabahūn na sudhi mori leyī piyā
Âvelā rovāi piyā
Māi jo hotin, daurī sāj jāti
Bhaujī dihi gatharī banvarī ho
Māi jo hotin cauparat pahuncavatīn
Bhaujī devaiyā duāre ñīhārīn banvārī ho
Māi jo hotin, karejā nikār bheñtīn
Bhaujī dihin akvārī ho

Once, on a visit to my natal home,
Not a soul cared.
In the natal home, brother's wife stayed in bed.
Overcome with tears am I.
When father was there,
I was invited again and again.
Brother never once inquired about my welfare.
Overcome with tears am I.
Were it mother, she would have decorated a gift basket.
Brother's wife just gave a bundle, my dear.
Had mother been around, she would have seen me off at least until the village
    center.

Brother's wife left me at the door.

Had mother been around, she would have done anything, given her heart.

Brother's wife just gave a formal embrace.

SHANTI TEWARI, ATARA, JAUNPUR

The song bemoans the gradual distancing of a bride from her natal home that comes with the passing of her parents. We learn about the indifference of the brother's wife and the bride's growing disappointment at her sister-in-law's inability to replicate the warmth and hospitality of past visits when her parents were alive. The song references the appropriate gestures and rituals (or codes) for leave-taking, so that the desired emotions related to parting are adequately expressed. These codes allow the sister to effectively read the intensity of her sister-in-law's emotions, or the lack thereof. In a diachronic way, the song succeeds in explaining the gradual weakening of the brother-sister bond, allowing women to imagine the waning intensity of their emotional ties with their natal homes.

The song reminds us that since a brother's wife must, eventually and in time, as the senior female of the household, fulfill her duties as wife of the householder, including the maintenance of relations with her husband's kin, women might be forced by circumstance to reevaluate their expectations of their natal homes. However, as the song indicates, tensions between women and their brothers' wives loom large in this reevaluation.

The weakening of the brother-sister bond has crucial implications for the question of women's rights to land. A key finding of recent research on this subject is that even among castes and classes where there is immovable property to be shared and where daughters' legal entitlements to equal shares in that property are clear, women are uniformly reluctant to claim their shares for fear of antagonizing their brothers. Ursula Sharma found, for instance, "that a sister who claimed her share of the land would seem greedy and might risk forfeiting her brother's goodwill. Had she not already received her share of the family property at marriage?" (Sharma 1993, 351). Srimati Basu further explains that "while most women were unable to alter extant property relations, they strongly contested dominant notions that marriage ended their ties with the natal family, both by helping and taking help from the families in some cases, and more prevalently, by claiming to forego property shares in order to keep the natal connection alive" (1999, 226).

As the songs reveal, the environment of the marital home is often a hostile one, and the maintenance of cordial relations with brothers, the sublimation and sacrifice of claims to equal shares in the natal home, and even the acceptance of gender inequality as a given in the natal home are all necessary to buttress a bride's badly needed sense of security. Over the last decade, research on women's land rights has shown that daughters hardly ever use ideas about gender equality to seek their rightful inheritance shares in their natal homes, despite being aware of recent enabling legislation.[11] It seems clear that the reason women forego their claims is the potentially high cost of doing so, including the loss of their brothers' support.

Anthropological literature on the importance of the ritual role of brothers (Agarwal 1995; Vatuk 1975; Wadley 1976) has underlined the considerations that prevent women from taking such a bold step. A number of studies support Basu's findings that many women actually gave up their shares in the natal property to avoid "angering their brothers and sisters-in-law and to preserve the natal home as a space of emotional wealth contrasting with the quotidian realm of work, duty and abnegation in married life" (Basu 1999, 227). My fieldwork suggests that while women would prefer the equitable distribution of property between sisters and brothers, for the reasons the songs articulate, they are reluctant to initiate legal action against their brothers. On the other hand, men in north India rarely have to tell their sisters that they would break off all contact should they demand their ancestral shares; indeed, the men can do so at low economic and social cost to themselves (Agarwal 1997, 7). It is against the layered emotional and cultural backdrop I have described above that the brother emerges as the symbolic link between the natal and marital household, as Bina Agarwal concludes: "What we therefore see in the sister-brother relationship is an idealized and complex construction of roles and expectations—ceremonially ritualized, culturally elaborated, economically necessitated, and ideologically reinforced" (1995, 266).

GALI: ABUSIVE WEDDING SONGS

Folksongs have declined in popularity in some areas and are undergoing transformations in others, yet many genres, such as the *gālīs* or songs of abuse integral to wedding celebrations, not only survive but also continue to be sung and performed at appropriate occasions. Anthropological explanations for the survival of abusive songs point to their symbolic function in restoring the power balance between groups linked together by marriage, namely, the "wife-givers" and the "wife-takers." According to the north Indian marriage rule of hypergamy, a daughter must only be given in marriage to a group higher in status than her own, making the occasion of a daughter's marriage one marked by a momentary loss in status that must be restored. The ritual abuses directed at the wife-taking group effectively accomplish this restoration at the symbolic level by containing potential rivalries and animosities.

Underlining the natal family's affection and love for its departing daughter and emphasizing its reluctance to part with her, gālīs provide much-needed assurance to brides. But since the daughter is also severed from her natal home, the tensions associated with being uprooted demand immediate resolution. When songs address these tensions humorously, they also serve to defuse a potentially explosive situation. Abusive songs sung at the bride's departure, then, address the bride's two main anxieties—the loss of her natal home and the uncertainty of establishing a home among relative strangers, features that testify to the structural logic of the customary singing and hence to the continued relevance of these songs.

13

Are mai to thāri duariyā ke oat, hamen to nanadoiyā bulāvain na re
Sasurū hamāre caudhari re, sās mughal harjāi
Hamen to sāri duniyā lajāvai na re
Jethvā hamāre moulvī re, hamen to pānc vaktā parhāven na re
Mai to thāri duariyā ke oat, hamen to nanadoiyā bulāvain na re
Devarā hamrā hijrā re, hijr nikal ta ta thaiyā nacavāi na re
Hamen to sāri duniyā lajāvai na re
Thāri pakariyā ke oat, hamen to nanadoiyā bolāvain na re
Nanadī hamārī bijūlī re, giren kauno chailā ke ūpar na re
Thārī dūariyā ke oat, hamen to nanadoiyā bulāvain na re

Behind the door I hide, do not call me brother-in-law.
My father-in-law a Chief, mother-in-law a Mughal Tax Collector.
The whole world is embarassing me.
Elder brother-in-law, a priest, makes sure I pray five times.

Behind the door I hide, just do not call me brother-in-law.
Younger brother-in-law, a eunuch, breaks into dance at the sight of the full moon.
The whole world is embarrassing me.
I stand at the corner of the door, do not call.
My husband's sister a streak of lightning, what if she were to fall upon a
    young man!
Behind the door I hide . . .

KHATUN, JAUNPUR CITY

The song above, sung by Khatun, a Muslim singer from the city of Jaunpur with a wide-ranging repertoire, illustrates other subtle goals gālīs fulfill, most importantly, the immense psychological support they offer the young bride. The shy young bride of the song acutely observes each of her husband's relatives from her hiding place, relatives to whom she has probably only been introduced at her wedding. The situation of the song is significant as it is likely to be sung by her natal relatives in earshot of the bārāt, members of the wedding party who will, in due course, depart with her for her marital home. For the bride, these last moments as a daughter in her natal home are likely to be full of mixed emotions, and the funny but acute observations the song makes about her new relatives help to make her transition into the new household less overwhelming. The lighthearted mood of the songs serves to lessen the blow for the bride, who in all likelihood feels that she is being handed over to rank strangers. The above song, while it evokes a Muslim social universe, parallels similar gālīs sung at Hindu weddings. In fact, Khatun is a popular singer at weddings in Jaunpur city's Hindu households, owing to her rich voice and repertoire.

When the loss of a beloved daughter is imminent, the more humorous and hard-hitting the lyrics, the better they serve as an emotional outlet. Hence, while the emotional state of the bride-givers may be somber and tearful, the songs we hear, at once absurd and funny, belie this fact. They cause a shift in perspective and mitigate the mood of despair and separation that has no doubt been building up. It is possible to imagine this mood reaching a crescendo on the morning of the bride's departure. The belting out of jocular songs, then, serves to defuse the tension, effectively containing and releasing it. The songs the bride's relatives sing reassuringly propose improbable and unlikely scenarios that may never actually transpire. In helping the powerless bride to imagine and enact a script of power over her new relatives, such songs have the potential to be profoundly morale-boosting. Not only does the bride's community of close relatives express its emotional bonds with the bride who will soon depart, but by humorously identifying, for her benefit, each of her new kin, they render them familiar and less threatening. Many gālīs force the bride to reflect on potential sources of conflict with her new kin, thus both preparing and cautioning her.

While gālīs are sung at marriages, other songs that likewise explore interkin tensions and conflicts are sung throughout women's lives. A typical example of relations that need management through women's life cycles are those between a woman and her husband's sister. In the song below, the brother's wife reveals her grudging attitude. The gālī is also a form of anticipatory socialization, through which young girls are able to imagine themselves as adult women.

14

Darjī bulāu Patane se
Kasak Coliyā nanadī ke siehen
Dono dehein lagāi, morhavā
Apane nanadiyā ka karbai gavanvā
Duno daehein dahej, morhavā
Jab nanadoiyā kothariyā me jaihen
Morhavā, duno hasen khakhāi, morhavā
Jab nanadoiyā coliband kholihen
Duno karain guhār, morhavā
Kahiyā ke bairī, rāji ho nanadī
Morhavā, duno delā dahej, morhavā.

Call the tailor from Patna
To sew a tight blouse for husband's sister.
With peacocks designed on both breasts,
Sister-in-law to her marital home, I'll send,
And two peacocks will be her dowry.
When the groom entered the nuptial chamber,
The peacocks burst into laughter.
When the groom undid the blouse-ties,
The peacocks set up wails and cries.

For the longest time, this enemy of mine,
Two peacocks for her dowry are just fine.

DALIT SINGERS, ROBERTSGANJ, MIRZAPUR

In this funny and ironic song, the simmering and often unstated conflict between the two sisters-in-law is made explicit as the brother's wife
succeeds in playing a dirty trick on the husband's sister on the occasion of
her marriage. When heard alongside song 11 of the previous section, an
ongoing war between these rivals is evoked in which this trick is possibly
the sister-in-law's retaliation for similar provocations in the past. In any
case, the enmity stems from the emotional demands of the two women
linked to each other by marriage, demands so engrained that the tension
between them remains unresolved. It is worth recalling, however, that
sometimes these kinswomen do act as allies as in the grinding song entitled "Pregnant Solutions: Disguise," of chapter 1. The songs in the next
section describe the conjugal ties that develop as the bride finally moves
to her marital home.

GLIMPSES OF CONJUGALITY

15

BRIDES' TEARS
Jab ham rahlei ho bālī kunvārī ho na
Are Rama tabhei bābā kailen morā biyahavā ho na
Jab ham bhailī das barisivā ho na
Are Rama tabhai mai kailī mora bidaiyā ho na
Kailīn bidaiyā bhāi bābā ke gharavā ho na
Are Rama ham to khelalī sapulī mahuniyā ho na
Jab ham rahelien bāri kunvāri ho na
Are Rama tabain sāsū paniyā bharvāvai ho na
Paniyā ham bharī bharī dhailī kararvā ho na
Are Rama tabhai sāsū māren hamai hucvā ho na
Paniyā ham bharī bharī ailīn jab gharavā ho na
Are Rama gore mūre tānali cadariyā ho na
Haravā jotai āilen, kudariyā gorai āilen
'Māi nāhī dekhalin tirīyavā ho na.'
'Tohrī tirīyavā bhaiyā garvā gumānin ho na

Bhaiyā, jāike kothāriyā me sūtai ho na
Itanā bacan bhaiyā sune to na pāvalenī ho na
Bhaiyā basavā paithī sutukunī kātilinī ho na
Eik sutukun mārlin, dūsar sutukun mārlinī ho na
Bhāi mārilī tiriyā marāvavlieu ho na.

When I was a little maiden,
O Rama, that's when Father had me married off.
When I was 12 years old,
O Rama, that's when mother bid me farewell.
Sent me off from my father's home.
O Rama, I played Sipuli Mahuniya
When I lived in Baba's home
I used to play Mahuniya.
When I was just a little girl,
O Rama, mother-in-law made me fetch loads of water.
And just as I had some respite from that,
Mother-in-law dealt me a punch.
When I had fetched the water,
O Rama, I lay down covered from head to toe.
With the plough and sickle he came home.
"Mother, I don't see my wife anywhere?"
"Your wife, son, swollen with pride
Is in the room asleep."
He barely heard the words, wouldn't hear more.
He cut the bamboo and fashioned a stick.
One stick he dealt and then another,
That beaten down wife, he then just killed her.

BHAGIRATHI DEVI, CHACHAKPUR, JAUNPUR

When Bhagirathi Devi, a woman in her late 70s of the caste of vegetable growers and market gardeners, sang this song in Jaunpur's Chachakpur village in 2002, a hushed silence fell in the courtyard. Those who had
gathered to remember and record songs and discuss the nature of wom-
en's lives and struggles slipped into a reflective mood. Since we had already heard many songs of pathos, such as the grinding songs, this song
was by no means the first to grapple with the troubling emotions that
attend domestic violence within the home. While the audience was visi-

bly moved, Bhagirathi Devi's own emotional state as she sang the song was not immediately apparent.

This song highlights the vulnerabilities of brides sent off to the homes of virtual strangers owing to the principle of village exogamy. The vulnerabilities are likely compounded when daughters are married at a very young age or when the spatial distance separating the natal from marital kin is great. The following songs were recorded in a single sitting over an afternoon in April 2002 and serve to examine the frequency with which the motifs of violence and women's vulnerabilities in the conjugal home occur. They were heard interspersed with a number of other songs addressing a variety of subjects and concerns. The singers who had assembled for the recording were from upper and intermediate castes such as Brahmin, Baniya, Kayasth, Yadava, and Thakur, highlighting Atara's multicaste composition. In contrast to Bhagirathi Devi's song, these songs were heard in the relatively prosperous neighborhood and inner courtyard of the household that Shanti, an upper-caste Brahmin woman, belongs to. As the songs unfold, we see why the departure to one's marital home might require the cultivation of a stoic heart, as song 4 (121–22) describes.

16

Sāsū marlī mahenvā kaise saparī
Jab dekhlin sāsū hamrā ta kahin hamse ki choti ho
Caukā belenā na sambhrai, to povai hānth se rotī
Gīlā sān ke pisanvā kaise saparī
Ham kahlīn apanī sāsū se dher dharā mahranī ho
Ganga ji mein dūbi ke marbain abkī barhai d pāni
āpan taj debai paranvā, kaise saparī
Atana sun ke sāsū hamrī kailīn khūb badhaiyā ho
Jauno din tu mar jaibū, apane betvā ke karab dūsar sagaiyā
Mārlin tān ke belanvā, kaise saparī
'Ham cat pat kailin apane betvā ke dūsar sādī ho'
Būrhā kahain kalakh ke sabse, bhail mor barbādī
Aguvā milal baimanvā, kaise saparī

Mother-in-law's taunts, how are they to be endured?
When she saw me, she said I'm too little.
"If you cannot manage the rolling pin, use your hands."

But how to manage when the dough is sticky?
"Mother-in-law," I said, "Be patient, queen!
This time when the waters rise, wait and see, I'll drown myself in the Ganges."
Give up my life, how else to endure all this?
Mother-in-law heaped her congratulations.
"The day you die, I'll have my son betrothed again."
How are beatings with the rolling pin, to be endured?
"I'll soon get my son remarried!"
The old woman tells everyone she's been destroyed,
That the matchmaker deceived her, oh how to endure!

SHANTI'S COURTYARD, ATARA, JAUNPUR

This song identifies the nature of the young bride's anxieties. We learn that the apprehensions of young women as they depart for their marital homes, articulated in the songs of earlier sections, are not unfounded. While the song evokes a bygone era, the persistent violence it describes resonates with the singers. The reality of the marital home turns out to be more grim and unnerving than expected. The repeated taunts of the mother-in-law, punctuated by her threats and acts of physical violence, are not merely intolerable but also induce alarming suicidal thoughts in this young bride. Here, it seems that the threat of a husband's remarriage served to control women. The song hints at the reserves of inner strength a bride would need not only to endure but also to survive repeated abuse.

As young women grow up hearing at least some such songs, their socialization likely conditions them to be prepared for the worst, as outlined in the grinding songs. The singers, especially the older women who connected with the note of despair in the song, affirmed the relevance of the song's simple message for women today. For feminists who continue to struggle with questions of ongoing violence against women in the domestic sphere, the song is a reminder of the persistent, ubiquitous, and hidden nature of domestic violence. Despite its prevalence across caste and class divides, the problem of domestic violence was not collectively confronted until the 1980s.

17

Likhen angurī se khunvā nikār citthiyā
Māi siyahiu ke tarase tohār bitiyā
Sāsū kahen beci āyi tohain hatiyā

Kahen kulbornī, pukārain din ratiyā
Aisan garībin se kāhe bhai sadiyā
Dubiyā ke charī na chuāyo morī dehiyā
Tohre anganvā atab kahiyā
Hamri jinigī me nāhī sukh nindiyā
Māngiyā ke sindūrā aur mathvā ke bindiyā
Khāi soyī jaharvā ke tikiyā
Tab to kahat rahī sunā morī dheiyā
Tohke mangāibe lagate joriyā
Cithiyā na bheje bitī gayī tithiyā
Beci dārā abkī tū sagaro phasaliyā
De dārā inkā tū motorcykiliyā
Nahin phir paibū hamār lasiyā
Māi siyahiu ke tarase . . .

She writes a letter dipped in blood from her finger.
Mother, your daughter yearns for ink.
Father-in-law says we'll sell you in the market.
They say it's their clan I destroyed,
Rue the marriage with a girl so impoverished.
All day long just one thought,
Not a blade of *dūb* grass has touched my skin.
Now mother, your daughter yearns for ink.
When will I enter that courtyard of yours?
In this life there's no sleep of peace for me,
The sindūr of parting or the forehead bindī
I could consume a poisoned pellet.
Then you had said, "Listen my daughter,
we shall send for you at the auspicious hour."
You did not write, the date has now passed.
This time, you must sell your harvest
To purchase for him a motorcycle
Or else, this corpse of mine is all you may find.

SHANTI'S COURTYARD, ATARA, JAUNPUR

This song communicates the searing emotion of a young woman's abandonment within her marital home. The nature of the violence appears to be compounded by structural conditions regarding the transference of brides. Without a single ally in the marital home and alienated from virtually all of its members including her husband, the bride in the song finds herself in an alarming scenario, and the suicidal thoughts she entertains signal a collective cry.

Referring to signs of matrimony such as the *bindī*, the young bride bemoans the fact that not only are her femininity and sexuality ignored but also that she is deprived of participation in rituals and ceremonies, as confirmed by the reference of the dub grass, an essential ingredient of ritual. As we have seen above, the customary maintenance of social distance between a daughter's natal and conjugal households precluded frequent visits from her parents. This fact prevented natal families from closely monitoring their daughter's welfare in her conjugal home, at least in the initial years of integration, which could have precluded such occurrences. The last straw in the song is the reference to a dowry demand (the motorcycle) and the language of threat in which this demand is couched, a feature of the north Indian social milieu since the 1980s, when dowry-related violence became the subject of heated public discourse and outcry. As potential sources of evidence, however, these songs likely remained hidden from mainstream discourses until the easing of conditions permitted such taboo subjects to be openly discussed. The importance of unearthing and documenting such songs can scarcely be overstressed.

18

Mathavā pe hathvā ke jhokelī tiriyavā
Piyā beci khāi ho gailen na
Hamre naihar ke gahanvā piyā beci khāi gailen ho na
Karā chharā, painje challā imirti dār
Gūngī nindiyā sūtale me more dhīre se nitāle nissār
Ki jiyarā derai ho gaile na
Ham to cor cor goharaulīn
Ki jiyarā derai ho gailen na
Jāgi gayin morī sāsū nanadiyā
Ghar bakharū ke log
Bac gailen nahin to bahutai pitaiten, achā rahā sanjog
Ki jiyarā lajai ho gailen na
Dekhalin cor rahā ghar hi ke, ki jiyarā lajāi gailen na
Kamar kardhani dhīre se more le gailen uthāi

Na jāne kaun saut ke dihalen na janī kā kihlen
Ki isko pachāi ho gailen na

A wife holds her head in despair.
The husband has sold off, consumed her wealth.
"The jewels of my natal home, husband consumed them all,
Bracelets and necklaces, anklets and amulets.
During my silent half sleep he crept up stealthily,
Scaring me like that.
I cried out 'thief thief.'
So scared was I then.
My mother- and sister-in-law awoke,
And the household too.
He was saved a thrashing, that's lucky for him.
So ashamed I felt.
A thief within the family, how embarrassing!
Gingerly, he picked up my waist belt.
Who knows to which 'other' woman he gave them
Or finished off with them."

SHANTI'S COURTYARD, ATARA, JAUNPUR

In this song we learn of the theft of the woman's strīdhan, the jewelry and valuables that constitute a woman's personal wealth. Unlike the previous song's reference to dowry, this one introduces the notion of women's rights to their strīdhan, the "wealth given with the daughter at her marriage to use as the nucleus of the conjugal estate" (Tambiah and Goody 1973, 63), as well as women's rights to property and to receive gifts from their natal households. Since husbands and relatives-in-law acquire no interest in this wealth, the song voices a woman's justifiable grievance where this prohibition is violated. Such violations could not have been uncommon, and the song suggests the unlikelihood of women receiving justice in situations where the "thief" is none other than their husband or member of their close kin. Here, the husband takes his claims on his wife's jewels for granted, but the woman's sense of outrage is compounded by her speculation about their whereabouts.

The inconstant husband is a recurring theme in songs of the region. These songs flesh out husbands' wayward tendencies, as well as the tendency for various pieces of their wives' jewelry to be distributed to other lovers. They capture the anxieties of wives bound by the sacred bond of matrimony, a bond that is, however, repeatedly violated by their husbands. Many such songs also idolize the wandering hero, and the folklore is replete with the charms and attractions of yogis and ascetics of all kinds—men whose appeal is enhanced because, as wanderers and travelers, they remain free of worldly ties.

Songs by women of various castes, therefore, affirm the presence of domestic violence expressed in Bhagirathi Devi's song. These songs provide windows on the ongoing violence in conjugal homes. However, the songs stress the fact that dowry is by no means the only cause of the domestic violence. This material evokes the 1980s, when the middle-class women's movement mounted antidowry agitations, highlighting atrocities against women and disturbing the glamorized notion of the Indian family as the bedrock of Indian society (Agnihotri and Mazumdar 1995). It became clear that, far from being a deep-rooted Indian tradition, dowry had attended the spread of caste hierarchies and consumerism. Recent research has highlighted the many atrocities perpetrated against women, some of which were only tangentially linked to dowry but have tended to get lumped under the term. However, it is dowry-related violence that has received special attention, with the term *dowry murder* papering over a range of sins (Oldenburg 1998, 220). Either way, the songs confirm the finding that while dowry may be associated with upwardly mobile groups seeking to emulate the practices of upper castes, all castes and classes of women are subject to forms of violence that exploit their extreme vulnerability as a result of village exogamy.

AN ALTERNATIVE SCENARIO

Are you coming from your *naihar* (natal home) or your *pīhar* (marital home)? QUESTION ADDRESSED TO A FIELDWORKER

Lest these disturbing songs suggest that only tragedy, trauma, and violence characterize conjugality, women's repertoires also feature playful songs that convey joyful messages about conjugal life. To put the above songs into perspective, therefore, I present the following two alternative scenarios. These songs were sung in groups amid relaxed laughter and teasing. However, since every recording session had its share of tragic and buoyant songs, a realistic assessment of the variety of women's emotions must draw on both. These songs highlight how joy and suffering are inextricably intertwined, with one emotion giving way to another and with experience existing in the shades of grey, within the interstices.

19

Dhīre dhīre āvā naiharavā me bātī
Sone ki thālī me jevanā banavalī
Dhīre dhīre āva kitchenvā me bātī
Jhajhare gervā, gangajal pānī
Dhīre dhīre āvā mashinave pe bātī
Lavanga elaichī ke bīra banaulen
Dhīre dhīre āvā ham birvā lihe bātī
Cuni cuni kaliyā mai sej lagāiyon
Dhire dhire āvā ham duarvā pe bātī
Dhīre dhīre āvā naiharve me bātī

Come gently, I am in my natal home.
In a golden plate I served the meal.
Come gently, I am in the kitchen.
Cooling Ganga water in the mud pot.
Come gently, I am at the refrigerator.
Made a paan with cloves and cardamom.
Come gently, I have the pān ready.
Picked the buds to make the bed.
Come gently, I am just at the door.
Come gently, I am in my natal home.

SHANTI'S COURTYARD, ATARA, JAUNPUR

The flirtatious playfulness of this song is characteristic of the kajlī genre, which I discussed in chapter 2. Unlike the grim messages of the preceding songs, the playful hide-and-seek motif here conveys both the joys and strengths of the marital bond. In songs with amorous motifs, "swinging" signifies sexual play, and women recount their sexual frustration when their overtures are deliberately thwarted. In hundreds of such women's songs, water and delicious food elegantly served are invariably followed by an offering of fragrant *pān* and an enticing conjugal bed brushed with petals, a recurring motif. Alas, the lovers in such songs refuse each of their women's offerings, and the successive denial of each delectable offering builds the mood of rejection and abandonment, underscoring women's sexual disappointments. Each motif follows the next in a formulaic way, perhaps underscoring both the sensual pleasures as well as the rejection and denial of them.

Like the reference to the motorcycle in the song above, the reference to the refrigerator as a symbol of consumerism serves to illustrate how contemporary motifs and concerns creep into songs. In the song below, women search for a standard against which to measure the qualities of a good husband.

20

Galiyā khari car sakhiyā batāvā sakhī kiske patī hain
Pahilī bolī more Rama patī hain
Sitin ke rachavaiyā, batavā sakhi hamrā patī hai
Galiyan khari caron sakhiyan batāvā sakhi kiske pati hain
Dūsrī bolī morā Lachman patī hai
Sajīvan būtī ke leivayān batāvā sakhī hamrā patī hai
Tīsrī bolī morā Bholā patī hai
Damarū ke bajavaiyā sakhī jī mere patī hain
Galiyān kharī cāron sakhiyā bbatāvā sakhī kiske patī hain
Cauthi bolī morā Kānhā patī hai
Bansīyā ke bajavaiyā, batāvā sakhī merā patī hai

Four friends in the lane take a guess about their husbands.
"Mine is Rama," the first said.
"He who wed Sita, friend, he's my husband."
"My husband is Laxman," the second said.
"He who brought the life-giving herb Sanjeevini, that's my husband."
"My husband is Bholenath [Shiva]," the third said.
"The one who plays on the damaru drum."
"My husband is Krishna," the fourth said.
"The one who plays the flute, my friend, that's my husband."

MUNRAJI AND SUBHAVATI, BARSARA, JAUNPUR

In this lighthearted song, women playfully declare the standards against which husbands will be judged. One of the ways in which the marital bond might be imagined as sacred is elaborated here. The song puts into perspective the contrast between ideal, even god-like, husbands and the traumatic reality of the marital home, as witnessed in the preceding songs. The gulf between women's imaginations and the realities they face could hardly be starker. The opposing moods and emotions in the two sets of songs allow us to see just how contradictory the experience of marriage is for women. The following section explores other strains in the conjugal bond and the incompatibilities arising from various causes.

STRAINS IN THE CONJUGAL BOND

Misalliance in marriage was thought to be disruptive of "the ideal continuity of the sequence of matrimonial conjunctions" in a manner not unlike the way an eclipse disturbed the order of planetary movement. GUHA, "THE CAREER OF AN ANTI-GOD IN HEAVEN AND ON EARTH," 3

In the section below, the young maiden departing for her marital home has finally transitioned to the next phase. The difficulties inherent in this transition, however, are rendered even more complex when the couple is mismatched or incompatible. Early marriages and alliances with substantially older men or with those much younger, and the resulting sexual incompatibilities, are hinted at. Despite the fact that misalliances and inappropriate matches are universally frowned upon, the songs of the region testify to their not infrequent occurrence. As such, the songs provide insights into what women perceive as constituting an inappropriate match.

Songs enumerating mismatches are particularly poignant given that in north India there is clearly an economic imperative for families to arrange good matches for their daughters (Papanek 1989, 103–4). Derne points out, "A father knows that arranging a proper marriage for a daughter supports a family's prosperity by protecting its honor and expanding its network of social ties" (Derne 1994, 83). The three songs below provide a glimpse of the incompatibility arising from a marriage between a woman and a significantly younger male. The recurrence of this image in the folklore is noteworthy for highlighting not only this particular lack of marital fulfillment but also, perhaps, its functioning as a metaphor for women's perceptions of other, harder to voice, incompatibilities.

21

Jhuruke pavan puruvaiyā
Balam mor sanjhvai se soye gaye ho
Apanan mein phane batlaiyā balam mor
Sanjhvai se soi gaye ho
Sāsū jethāni karein bolā-cālī
Na jānin ratiyai ki pavatihi khālī

Gusts of easterly winds blow.
My love asleep since early evening.
My love converses with himself alone.
Asleep since the early evening.
Mother-in-law and elder sister-in-law talk on.
They know not my nights are empty.

SHANTI TEWARI, ATRA, JAUNPUR

In this song about a woman's disappointment, long nights stretch out interminably as the husband retires to bed early. On the other hand, household members who stay awake are perhaps able to guess at the woman's dilemma. They are undoubtedly aware of the woman's frustration, which further fuels her embarrassment. Since the husband is also disinclined to engage his wife in conversation, the song suggests that the incompatibility exists on several levels. The fact that newlyweds are surrounded by household members that seek to hinder the emergence of close ties between them is the theme of many songs.

Another recurring theme in these songs is of women lying in wait for truant husbands who sometimes return in the wee hours of the morning just when their wives are about to rise and begin their household responsibilities. Hence, frustrations and unfulfilled longings remain unresolved and are simply carried forward into the next day. Since the bond between husband and wife must be kept from developing in a way that would threaten the interests of other family members in the marital home, the new bride also personifies the risk that the groom might transfer his loyalty and affection to her. Thus, signs of developing attachment between the newlyweds are jealously monitored, and "attempts are made to curb a too rapidly developing conjugal intimacy, in the interests of maintaining the solidarity of the husband's patrilineal kin" (Raheja 1994, 28).

A whole genre of songs captures the brevity, furtiveness, even clandestine nature of the meetings between the new bride and groom. Kakar cites Gore's study of men from the Agarwal community where "these constraints, masterminded by the older women, usually succeed in their aims" (Kakar 1988, 64).

Shanti Tewari and her friends sang this song with irony and good humor. When I asked Shanti about the meaning of the song for her, she explained, "women's songs are precisely about such disappointments as well as pleasures, both big and small." Shanti's song reminded me of the following song, which I heard often in the countryside, a version of which is presented below.

22

Banvāri ho, hamrā larikā bhatār
Larikā bhatār leke sutalī osaravā
Banvāri ho, rahrī me bolelā sīyār
Khole ke t coli-bandā, kholele kewār
Banvāri ho jari gaile airī se kapār
Rahrī me suni ke siyariyā ke boliyā
Banvāri ho, rove lagale larikā bhatār
Anganā se māi ailīn, duarā se bahinā
Banvāri ho, ke māral babuā hamār?

Dear god, my husband is just a little boy.
With my boy-husband on the roof I slept.
Lord, the jackal calls in the field of *arhar*.
Instead of my blouse ties, he opens the door.
God, that burnt me up from heel to head.
From the field, when the jackal calls he heard.
Lord, the husband-boy just started to cry.
From the courtyard came mother and sister next door.
God, who's been beating our little one so?

UPADHYAYA 1990B, 122

The incompatibility arises from the immaturity of the husband. The song is a lighthearted commentary on incongruous situations that might arise from age disparities, such as when older brides marry younger grooms. The singers agreed that such songs served as warnings against unnatural marriage alliances. Here, the reference to the "jackal in the field of *arhar*" hints at the likelihood of extramarital affairs developing in the face of such incompatibility. Since the fields of the long arhar plants are known to serve as the ideal hiding place for lovers, the reference to the arhar fields evokes clandestine meetings and infidelity, the lover being like the jackal, a treacherous animal that creeps into the fields in the dark. Songs that cast an ironic glance at social mores usually promoted great mirth and relaxed banter during our recording sessions.

23

Bārah baris sāsū naihare mein bītāvale
Tab le āye u gavanvā na
Bārah kisim ka sāsū jevanā banāveli
Pūt taharā na āiye bhavanvā na
Abahi t bahuver pūt larikā nadanvā
Mālin sange khele phūlgenvā na

Twelve years, mother-in-law, I spent in my natal home.
Then he brought me to my marital one.
Mother-in-law, I cooked twelve different dishes.
But your son does not visit me in the boudoir.
"Daughter-in-law, my son is yet a child immature
Plays flower balls with the gardener's daughter."
MUNRAJI, BARSARA, JAUNPUR

Elaborating on this theme of marital incompatibility, this fragment from a longer ballad voices the complaints of a young bride who has just joined her groom's household. However, the groom, who, owing to a reference to a "palace," is clearly upper caste, remains oblivious of her while sporting with the gardener's daughter. The fragment is interesting for its pun on "play" or "sport," which suggests that the upper-caste groom will engage in sexual play with the lower-caste gardener's daughter once he has matured. These meditations on the nature of incompatibilities enrich our understanding of the complexity of the marital bond. However, it is not just the obvious age factor that contributes to sexual inadequacies and women's perceptions of incompatibility. Women's songs document other sources of conjugal dissatisfaction and afford women a space within which to voice their anxieties and frustrations with their conjugal lives.

This chapter, though a focus on songs associated with marriage, aimed to analyze those emotions that cannot be apprehended by observing the ritual structure of the wedding ceremony alone. My concern with emotions also highlighted the structural ambivalences and contradictions that attend momentous phases in a woman's life cycle. For instance, the songs might reveal the presence of mixed emotions: anxiety with joy; affection with anger; feelings associated with the loss of rights with feelings of excitement. The tendency of prior research to refer exclusively to structural patterns while ignoring the rich emotional life that forms the backdrop to these patterns has left us with an understanding of marriage as a rite of passage that is at best partial and empty of its powerful emotive content. One could also argue that since the ritual action serves to disguise and contain the attendant emotional states, the songs alone hold the key to these emotions.

Moreover, since emotions cannot be rigidly controlled, they tend to spill over into successive phases of the life cycle. While the rites of passage seek to formalize and facilitate the transition from one phase to the next, the emotions associated with these transitions are not so easily contained. Thus, for women, unity symbolized by the biyāh also spells sorrow, separation (*birahā*), and uncertainty. Thus, throughout women's lives, the continuously mounting pressures may sometimes be alleviated and released through song or through other rituals in which singing plays a critical role. In this sense, I also sought in this chapter to advance Max Gluckman's (1965) theoretical insights into rites of passage that disguise, but ultimately cannot completely control, the uncertainty inherent in such transitions.

If one were to take seriously, as Gluckman and others do, the idea that rituals of rebellion function like valves that let off steam, then these songs allow us to imagine the process as a diachronic, sequential movement. However, these songs could just as well be seen as "letting in steam," especially given the affective quality of many of them. It is precisely the multidimensional, multilayered nature of such expressions that allows for complex, sometimes radically divergent and counter-intuitive, readings.

The songs not only reflect the social reality but also pose alternate worlds for women who do not yet participate in them. They allow women to imagine their lives by creating the worlds they desire, thus giving meaning to their aspirations. These images, embedded deep within the collective consciousness, serve then to justify the anxiety produced in the bride and her kin at her departure. Moreover, despite the integrative impulse that seeks to incorporate the bride into her marital home, the immediate effect of separating her from her natal home is one of isolation. In fact, it is rare that such integration is achieved at all, and if it is, then only incompletely, gradually, and after considerable struggle.

A key insight that emerged from my conversations in the field was the paradoxical nature of weddings for brides. Indeed, in their specific ritual contexts, the songs serve to underline these contradictions: the heightened sense of tragedy combined with relief; repeated feasting followed by wrenching, prolonged farewells and leave-taking. It is the lack of resolution, the incomplete nature of the process that comes through in the songs. It is the loose, jagged edges of reality that are effectively captured therein. By presenting the context within which these songs are typically heard, I aimed in this chapter to highlight the power of the astonishingly candid articulation of women's lives as they apprehend them. The anxieties reflected in the songs are likely to ease with women marrying when they are older in years and with decreasing emphasis on village exogamy and virilocality, the alarming isolation of women is also bound to reduce.

Women's increasing familiarity with the Hindu Code bill promulgated in 1986 whereby women have a right to the self-acquired property of fathers and their increasing ability to sustain ties with their mothers, siblings, aunts, and other natal kin point to changes. Moreover, today sisters and brothers enjoy an equal share in their families' urban property, usually houses etc. rather than cultivable land (Basu 1999). Meanwhile, dowries have grown, as the value of agricultural land and urban property has increased exponentially and as the line between dowry and property has faded (Oldenburg 2002, 224). The songs alert us to the need for interventions at the policy level and for consciousness-raising to encourage women to think of their natal homes not as temporary shelters but as their anchors and birthrights (224). Finally, as women rebel and assert their rights, violence against women is expected to grow; therefore women must create their own institutions and organize not only for reform but also for social justice and rights (225).

CHAPTER FOUR

—✐ Sita's Trials

Sita's almost absolute stillness counterbalances Rama's extreme activity. Wherever he journeys, she is "home," the place where he stops or returns to. His actions are completed by her stillness; his moves to the periphery are answered by her presence at the center. Where she is, he must go to. . . . She is a model of the orthodox Hindu construction of "wife."
RICHARD SCHECHNER, "STRIDING THROUGH THE COSMOS," 174

A good starting point for an inquiry into the meaning of Sita for peasant women living in Uttar Pradesh is the Ramlīla of Ramnagar, an annual ritual reenactment of Tulsidas' Ramcaritmānas performed over the course of a month. Located on the outskirts of Benaras, the theatrical action of this Ramlīla takes place on separate sites and makeshift stages erected in a vast field.[1] Peasant women, at once spectators and pilgrims, often choose to keep the stage Sita company, rarely leaving her side as she sits in captivity for days in the Ashoka garden of the demon king, Ravana. While the audience moves with the actors to the site where the battle scenes are staged, it is the way women express solidarity with Sita and identify with her plight that lingers in all its poignancy and pathos, inviting questions about the place Sita occupies in peasant women's consciousness.

Sita's significance for women and her continued hold on the popular imagination is a phenomenon many scholars have investigated (Kishwar 1999). Whereas Sita, and her reputedly passive personality, has been a controversial figure among (mainly upper-class) feminists in India, in this chapter I focus on the relationship that members of the intermediate and lower castes have with Sita. If feminists have largely identified Sita as the model for *patīvratādharma*,[2] that is, the social ideal of female chastity, what accounts for the large number of Sita songs in the repertoires of peasant and lower-caste women? Since Sita's persona is also claimed and "domesticated" by women from a range of castes, this chapter, in addition to seeking insight into peasant women's attitudes about feminine power, investigates how this domestication is achieved and what purpose it serves.

Specifically, this chapter seeks to learn about the lives of women through the alternative narratives women's songs offer beyond those of the mainstream Rāmāyanā myth. I single out a range of Sita songs known as Sita Mangal, sung on ritual occasions such as weddings, for the insights they offer about peasant women's experiences of conjugality; these songs form the core of this chapter's analysis. As Usha Nilsson asserts, "in an unbounded, fluid, and flexible discourse, women have reconstructed alternate tellings of the Rāmāyanā. Neither harshly nor stringently, they have refashioned them into statements from women's points of view" (2001, 158). Similarly, Velcheru Narayana Rao's findings from his fieldwork in Andhra Pradesh suggest that women "have long used this language to say what they wish to say, as women" (Rao 1991, 114).

Reenactments of the Rāmāyanā myth conclude with the victorious battle and the return of the divine couple to Ayodhya, but several genres of women's songs, from the jatsār to wedding, childbirth, and ritual ceremonies, evoke, often metaphorically, Sita's suffering from the often unreenacted Uttara Kanda portion of the Rāmāyanā. Interestingly, it is these later episodes of Sita's ordeal and her eventual banishment that are supposed to represent the fate of Sita in *kaliyuga*.[3] Consequently, these epsiodes are not recited, but left out of the propitious yearly ritual reenactments of the epic, spread over nightlong sessions. Thus, "the Uttara Kanda of the Rāmāyanā, which is the shortest segment in the canonical versions, constitutes the longest fragments in the women's songs"

(Chakravarti 2006, 242). Since women's songs about Sita draw liberally from these episodes, we can consider these episodes unique in their resonance with women's perspectives.

SITA SONGS AND THE RAMĀYANĀ TRADITION

Ramāyanā scholarship has unearthed the existence of diverse Ramāyanā texts in different regions of India, as well as in Southeast Asia, each perspective reflecting different social locations, aspirations, and ideological concerns (Richman 1991, 4). Significant variations in the myth's plot in turn create new conceptualizations of its characters and meanings (Thapar 1989, 4). The women's narratives explored here exemplify the vitality and diversity of these plural traditions. Class, gender, and ethnic variations in Ramāyanā narratives are the subject of ongoing research (Richman 1991). Feminist concerns have led to renewed interest in contemporary women's performative and dance repertoires that grapple with Sita's so-called passive persona and often, as in Bina Agarwal's poem, a silenced Sita is entreated to finally claim her voice and speak out (Hess 1999, 17).

The first of the three episodes upon which women's songs focus deals with Sita's ordeal by fire, or test of chastity, after Ram's victory in the Great War and before they return to the kingdom of Ayodhya. The second pertains to Sita's subsequent abandonment in the forest when she is pregnant. The last episode in the sequence relates to Rama's request that Sita return to Ayodhya after she has spent several years of exile in the forest and her twin sons are grown, but not before she undergoes another trial by fire. In this final and conclusive episode, Sita's refuses to return and the Earth responds by granting her wish and opening to receive her. Next, I explore how these three episodes are expressed, reworked, and engaged with in women's songs.

EARTH, FIRE, AND SACRIFICE

First is the *agni-parīkshā* in which Sita, at the end of the great war between Rama and the demons, must undergo a test of chastity that requires her to throw herself into a blazing fire. LINDA HESS, "REJECTING SITA," 3

The ethos of pativratadharma places much of the power and responsibility for the husband and his social context in the hands of his wife. . . . In the wife's ideal moral universe, the husband functions as the point of orientation for her actions, as the king does for the warrior, the teachers for the student, the deity for the priest, and so forth . . . in addition to being empowered and responsible for the husband's well-being, the wife is also understood to be his "half-body" merged ontologically through the ritual of marriage. COURTRIGHT, "SATI, SACRIFICE, AND MARRIAGE," 187–88

In Rajasthan, Ann Grodzins Gold found that the appeal of female goddesses was attributed to their inner strength in the face of adversity. She notes that when talking to informants in Ghatiyali about goddesses, they seemed to mix "familiarity and intimacy with respect for their potency and violent capacity, a capacity not necessarily embodied in weapons" (Gold 1994, 29). Gold also found that in Sita's case, while the self-restraint and suffering arising from her subordinate role were seen as the source of her uniquely feminine power, such power was understood as "analogous to the self-restraint and suffering imposed on male ascetics to increase spiritual power" (31). The conclusions Gold drew from her research in Rajasthan mirror mine in Uttar Pradesh, where Sita's persona and inner fire (*tej*) are rendered even more luminous in the crucible of adversity.

Of the three episodes from the Rāmāyanā explored in women's songs, the Fire Ordeal takes precedence. Even for Rāmāyanā enthusiasts, its problematic nature has provoked "creative alterations of the fire ordeal in textual traditions (that) reflect anxious discomfort with the scene" (Hess 1999, 3). So powerful has the preoccupation with Sita's fire ordeal been that it forms a recurring theme in folksongs and ballads, whose heroines' misfortunes often parallel Sita's. In Valmiki's Rāmāyanā, the motif of trial by fire is as much about Rama's test and transformation in consciousness regarding his own divinity as it is about Sita (Shulman 1986, 116). In a similar vein, the grinding song of Satmal presented in chapter 1 offers a glimpse of the anguished mental state of a husband, who, like Rama, must succumb to the censorious pressures of patriarchy instead of protecting his wife against it. And just as Agni in the Rāmāyanā is scorched and extinguished by the greater tej of Sita, who emerges unscathed, so too is this heroine unharmed by the flames as they die down on her entry into the vat. Some have even argued that, "Sita's action is self-destructive and reinforces the feminine identity of dealing with repeated humiliation through an obliteration of the self" (Chakravarti 2006, 227).

Such imagery forms an integral part of folksongs of the region, and given that these motifs are associated with upper-caste proclivities, women's familiarity with them across caste lines is striking. It could be argued that the motifs actually serve to heighten women's perceptions of societal injustice and allow them to create their own spaces within which to critique it. As Cynthia Humes asserts, "The anger of goddesses can thus be appropriated to support the validity of righteous fury against other perceived injustices. After all, the gods ask intervention against those who oppress them" (2000, 148).

If these images succeed in evoking protest at perceived injustices, then, in subtle ways, they achieve another significant purpose, namely, that of challenging stereotypes about Hindu women. In this sense, the narratives discussed here also evoke the myth of Daksha's ceremonial sacrifice and Sati's protest when her husband Shiva was snubbed by her father, Daksha, and excluded from participating in the sacrifice. Sacrifices such as these announce altered states and, like all sacrifices, must be seen as rejuvenative and transformative for the entire social order. According to this logic, transformations effected by the trial-by-fire motifs can be understood as unleashing or giving rise to new beginnings.

THE FIRE MOTIF AND PROOFS OF CHASTITY

The song below enumerates not one but a string of trials for Sita. In retelling the Rāmāyanā with Sita at its center, folksongs depart in significant ways from both Tulsidas' Rāmcaritmānas, the narrative popular in the region, and Valmiki's classical Sanskrit version. The passive stillness of the women at the staging of Tulsidas' Rāmcaritmānas at Ramnagar is in stark contrast to the imagery of Sita's trial by fire, which is a recurring motif in the jatsār, the peasant women's ballads of the millstone anaylzed in chapter 1 and undoubtedly the most tragic genre of Bhojpuri songs. Like Sita, who had to furnish proof of her chastity, heroines of the jatsār are put to various tests by fire.

I

Jab re Sita deī Adit hāthe lihali re
Adit chapit hoī jāī ai
Iho kiriyevā e Sita ham na patiyaibī

Sarap bicharvā ham lebi ai
Jab re Sita dei sarp hāthe lihali re
Sarap baithele phetā māri ai
Iho kiriyavā ham na patiyaibī
Ganga bicharvā ham lebi ai
Jab re Sita dei Gangahi hāthe lihalī ai
Gangahi pari gaile ret ai
Iho kiriyavā e Sita ham na patiyaibī
Tulsi bicharavā ham lebi ai
Jab re Sita dei Tulsi hāthe lihalī
Tulsi gailī sukhāi ai
Aisen purukhvā ke muh nāhin dekhabi
Jini Ram dehlen banvās ai
Phāti jaitī dhartī alop hoi jaitī re
Ab na dekhabi sansār ai

When Sita Devi took the sun into her hands,
The sun set.
"This proof I will not accept, O Sita!
The trial of snakes you'll have to take."
When Sita Devi put her hand into the snake pit,
The cobra sat all coiled up.
"This proof I cannot accept.
The test of the Ganga you must take."
When Sita put her hand into the Ganga,
Ganga dried up into a sandy bed.
"This proof I cannot accept,
The test of the sacred Tulsi plant you must take."
When Sita Devi touched the Tulsi, it dried up.
"Such a being I never wish to set eyes on again,
The Rama who exiled me to the forest.
Let the earth part, let me disappear in it."
UPADHYAYA 1990B, 161

In this version of the Rāmāyaṇā story, Sita must undergo various trials to prove her chastity and yet when she emerges unscathed from each, it is the proofs that are deemed inadequate. Before reaching the moment of Sita's final protest, women are given to explore their preoccupation with their own chastity and the standards against which they must constantly measure themselves. Heroines of the jatsār are arbitrarily subjected to innovative and unexpected proofs, taken from a seemingly inexhaustible list of ways to test women's chastity. The ballad of Satmal, outlined in chapter 1, tells the story of a woman with seven brothers who, suspected of infidelity, takes the ultimate test. In the concluding episodes of the Lorikāyan (see chapter 5), Manjari, the chaste and long-suffering wife of Lorik, who has abandoned her, must nevertheless provide at least three proofs of her chastity. First, she is required to draw out coins from a container of boiling water. In another instance, as proof of her *sat*, the river parts to let her cross. Finally, ready to plunge into a funeral pyre, she is saved just in time.

In another women's ballad, Tikuli, the protagonist, invokes Agni, asking that the fire envelope her before she loses her virtue. The final lines of another ballad evoke the same tragic mood and applaud its female protagonist's decision to avoid shame by willingly taking her own life rather than enter into an illicit relationship. The recurrence of such scenes is striking in women's ballads and might even be said to define them. There may be important psychological explanations for this motif that are worth exploring, but the motif also raises questions about women's own preoccupation with the burden of having to furnish proofs of chastity. Thus even when the narratives are not directly about Sita, it is her trial that serves as their reference point and her humiliation that is evoked and reworked. Such parallels with the Sita narrative seek to explain the misfortunes, struggles, and protests of folk heroines. As Sita's capacity for suffering is almost as powerful as her capacity for resisting injustice, it is the inseparable combination of these two elements that contribute to the potency and appeal of the Sita figure as a metaphor for women's strength.

In this connection, it is useful to recall Shulman's observation that Sita partakes of the symbolism of earth, fire, and sacrifice (Shulman 1986, 116). Sita's birth from the earth and the episode of her trial by fire in the Ramāyanā are the rich backdrops against which the presence of these symbols in the songs of Sita makes complete sense. The Sita songs highlight Sita's extraordinary powers, which resemble the *tapas*, that is, the heat generated from asceticism and yogic austerities. These qualities of Sita remain controlled and restrained, thereby guarding against the devastation that might ensue were their enormous potency to be let loose indiscriminately. Shulman offers the following explanation: "These associations contribute to the sense of an undercurrent of violent power in Sita, heightened and contained by her chastity and constant control (which falls under the rubric of tapas). There are few explicit remarks to this effect in Valmiki, for example, Sita's well-known boast to Rāvana in the Asoka-grove in Lanka: 'It is (only) because I have not been commanded to do so by Rama, and because I wish to preserve my tapas, that I do not reduce you, O Dasāgriva, to ashes by means of my consuming energy'" (Shulman 1986, 116).

While the songs outline the conditions of women's subservience to male dominance, ultimately it is women's superior moral and spiritual power that is evoked in the folk imaginary. Heroines modeled after the chaste Sita have a fiery, fearsome chastity that sometimes causes the spark that lights the pyre to ignite from their persons. Thus the heroines seem to embody the fire, and just as Sita was able to emerge unscathed from the fire and will herself back into the Earth, these formidable folk heroines, in a final act of defiance, summon at-will the flame that will consume them. The action, then, is tantamount to the deification of folk heroines. It would seem that, in these sung biographies, women achieve in death the power that had eluded them in life. Ironically, however, by glorifying their sacrifice, even if it was through a final act of protest, the songs reinforce the very conditions under which such heroism becomes necessary. In contrast to the fierce feminine imagery of these ballads, other songs that have Sita at their center, such as the auspicious songs sung at marriages, explore motifs of conjugality and domesticity.

SITA MANGAL

Purab khojalon betī pacchim khojalon, khojalon Orissa Jagarnāth
Charon bhuvan betī bar eik khojilā, katihen na milen Sirī Ram.

Searched the east, searched the west, as far as Orissa and Jagannath.
In all four directions, daughter, searched for a groom but nowhere did I find
    Shri Ram.

UPADHYAYA 1990B, 122

This couplet captures the contradiction that despite the tragedies associated with the god, it is none other than Rama who can fulfill the role of the ideal groom. Only through many penances, prayers, and good deeds can brides hope to find such a groom. At weddings, however, it is the auspiciousness symbolized by the divine couple Ram-Sita, the respective incarnations of Vishnu and Srī, that is invoked, and it is this image of divinity that is enacted and celebrated. Hence, mangal (auspicious) songs are a way of invoking blessings.

Vidyaniwas Mishra argues that in the folklore of the region, folk sympathies lie with Sita to such an extent that Rama's own compulsions only serve to strengthen Sita's fire of truth (Mishra 2000, 118). I therefore turn my attention to the Sita songs I commonly heard at wedding celebrations in the villages of Benaras and Jaunpur, where I conducted fieldwork, during the wedding season of May and June. I heard most of these auspicious songs of blessing at two separate wedding celebrations in Benaras: one in the multicaste village of Chaubeypur, hosted by an upwardly mobile Yadav household of prosperous peasants where a number of intermediate castes sang the songs of blessing, and the other in the Dalit neighborhood of Churamanpur, hosted by a Dalit household of agricultural laborers. It is the Dalit women of the Chamar caste who are represented in these selections. As the women who sang at these events, identified at the end of the songs below, were also guests, my interactions with them were brief.

Since the song recordings were made while the various wedding ceremonies were underway, I was often unable to include the perspectives of the singers at the time of the recordings. I therefore returned to their various households on other occasions to elicit their views. I heard some of these songs at the brides' haldī (turmeric) ceremonies, wherein the bride's female kin anoint her with herbal oils and rejuvenating scrubs. At both of the weddings, I recorded Mangal songs, the auspicious singing by women of the bride's family also heralded the arrival of the barāt (the groom's party). Many of the songs were thus invariably drowned out by the accompanying brass band. This cacophonous, though customary, singing, so much a feature of wedding celebrations, however, served to create the auspicious environment for the sacred rites that followed.

In the Bhojpuri region, the month of Agahan, popularly believed to be the month in which Sita was married, is considered inauspicious for weddings. Yet, paradoxically, it is the same Sita who is invoked for her auspiciousness at wedding celebrations. Another paradox lies in the ritual wherein prospective brides beseech washerwomen for a pinch of the wedding vermilion. This ritual references Sita's tragedy, as Sita was turned out of her marital home at the complaint of a *dhobī* (washerman) (Mishra 2000, 118). Mishra suggests that the ritual underlines the deep concern within folk consciousness for the tragic wedded life of Sita and Rama. The Sita Mangal songs, however, highlight two distinct aspects of their marriage—on the one hand, the auspiciousness symbolized by the marriage of the divine couple Ram and Sita as incarnations of Vishnū and Srī and, on the other, the struggle and hardship integral to conjugal life (as these were to the union of Ram and Sita), including the "renunciation, asceticism and sorrow [that] mark Sita's largely solitary life" (Zacharias 2001, 35). As we will see below, paradox and contradiction are the hallmarks of these songs and sayings. In the representative collection below, some predominant motifs and structural patterns emerge.

2

Deu na morī maī bāne k daliyā phulvā lorhan ham jāb
Phulvā lorhat bhayalīn dhupahriyā harava gūnthat bhailī sānjh
Ghūmari ghūmari Sitā phulvā charhāve
Siv bābā delan āsīs.
Jaun māngan tūhun māngau Sital dei ūhe māngan ham deb
An dhan chāhe jo dihā Siv bābā, svāmī diha Siri Ram
Pār lagāvain je mori navariyā jehi dekhi jiyarā jurāi

"Pass me, mother, my basket, I go to pick flowers for worship."
She picked flowers until late afternoon, made garlands until sunset.
Again and again, Sita made flower offerings.
Siva Baba gave His blessings.
"Whatever you ask for, Sita, shall be yours."
"Material blessings are fine, Siv Baba, but let Shri Rama be my husband.
Only he can ferry me across to the other world and fill my heart with joy."
MISHRA 2000, 119

As in the couplet that began this section, the bride, in keeping with the cultural ideal in Uttar Pradesh, prays for a groom like Rama. The motif of being ferried across from *this* to the *other* world, namely, of achieving salvation, is a recurrent one with reference to Rama, the savior. Singing Mangal at weddings amounts to both singing about the marriage of Ram and Sita as well as invoking divine blessings. The song also recalls the songs of chapter 3 wherein women itemize the characteristics of a good husband. Such songs are also likely to be heard during the festival of Śivrātri, an important fair relating to Sita's marriage that is celebrated all over the region. During this festival, young women beseech Śiva to grant them good grooms like Rama. The song, familiar to women in the region, exemplifies one of the ways in which the Sita motif is integrated into sung prayers.

3
Rājā Dashrath aisan māngīla sasur ham
Kausilyā nihan hamri sās
Babu Lachman aisan māngilā devarji
Purush māngilā bhagvān

A father-in-law, like Dashrath.
Like Kaushilya, a mother-in-law.
For brother-in-law, none other than Lakshman.
For husband, God himself.

CHINTA DEVI, CHURAMANPUR, VARANASI

The prayers that constitute part of the well-known versions of auspicious wedding songs often feature the above boons. The popularity of this motif cuts across caste lines. Chinta Devi, one of the singers of the Dalit women's version above, explains: "These are the things we pray for and apart from the ones mentioned in the song above, in the longer version of the song, Sita also requests *jauno vidhī hovain* (whatever the mode of worship) for two additional things—a string cot and on that, a lovely infant."

Thus, the auspiciousness of a wedding also makes it an appropriate time to seek other blessings. By emphasizing that not only the groom but also the entire set of new kin must be equally exalted, the song stresses the importance of familial life for the inmarrying bride. Moreover, when the married couple is none other than Ram and Sita, other close kin may bask in their reflected glory. Thus, with the sacredness of the divine couple symbolically transferred to the newlyweds, all who celebrate the nuptials are equally elevated.

4

Patrī Sītā ke patrī kamariyā, lipelī dharma duvariā

Dharam duvariā Sītā līpahī na pavelī, āi parelā Siriram

Pūchi parelā sukumarī se-kekar tū hau dhiyavā e babunī?

Kekar hau bahuver, kavane kulavā me biāhal hau, ke lagelā devar tohār?

Etanā bachan suni bolalī Sītā sukumarī ho

Rājā Janak ke ham bāni ho dhiyavā

Dashrath ke bahuvar, Bharat ke kulavā me biāhal

Lacchman devarā hamār,

Etanā bacan jab sunale Siya, kahelā, Lacchman bulāy dhāi

ke khojā tū nauvā aur bariyā ke le jaī Awadhpur pahuncaī

Slim Sita with her slim waist swabs the sacred space.

She has barely finished when Shriram appears.

He asks the maiden, "whose daughter and daughter-in-law are you?

Whose bride and in whose clan are you married, who is your brother-in-law?"

Upon hearing these words, Sita speaks,

"I am the daughter of Raja Janak,

Married into the clan of Bharat,

Laxman is my brother-in-law."

When he heard these words of Sita, he asked for Laxman

To send for the barber to convey the ritual message of matrimony to Ayodhya.

PRABHAVATI YADAV, CHAUBEYPUR, VARANASI

In this song, and the one below, Sita foretells her own marriage, and it is her certitude that sets the wedding process in motion. But this foretelling is only one of several elements in the song. In the way the song poses its questions about Sita's identity, we learn that a woman is invariably identified first through her father, and then through her father-in-law. Thus, a woman's identity can be said to derive through the male members of her households who exercise various kinds of rights over her. In other words, men who control or provide guardianship to women also define them, so much so that these women scarcely seem to have separate identities. Once a man's ownership over women is thus established, the rest of society is able to assign the women their place in the social universe. Indeed, no exception is made, not even for women of Sita's stature. Through this women's song we learn that even Sita was thus circumscribed and domesticated.

Interestingly, therefore, despite Rama's surprising lack of recognition of Sita as his bride in the opening lines, and despite his ability (as All-Knowing Rama) to easily claim her as soon as he heard about her web of relationships, he still sends for the barber, the ritual specialist associated with the task of carrying formal messages of betrothal and matrimony. On another level, then, the song seems to suggest that the performance of the wedding ceremony, with all its attendant rituals, will not only impart legitimacy to the couple but also serve to locate and firmly circumscribe the woman within a specific social milieu.

5

Asan dasā bābā āsan dasā Muni sab
karson vichār, kahan hoi Sītā biyahavā
Muni sab bole ke rahlin, ki Sītā uthī bolalin
Baba ego patrī bhejahon Ajudhiā, jahān ke rājā Dasrath
Nāhin jāni nagarī Ajudhia, nāhin jāni Rājā Dasrath
Betī kekarā patri likhab a bhejab kahān re?
Ūnch nagar dūr patan, ālhe base chājan
Baba duāre candanvā ke gāch, ūhe he Rājā Dasrath
Sānvar dekhi jin bharmayahon, Tilak chadhavahon
Baba ūhe veer balvān, uhe var sundar
Cācā uhe var vīr balvān, ūhe var sundar

Seated sages, seated the ascetics,
Reflect on where Sita is to be married.
The sages had barely spoken when Sita spoke up.
"Baba, send this horoscope to Ayodhya where Raja Dashrath resides."
"We know not Ayodhya, we do not know Dashrath,
Daughter, whom to write and where to mail the letter?"
"High up, far way in that land to where the birds migrate,
The sandalwood tree at the entrance, that's where Raja Dashrath lives.
Be not dismayed at the groom's complexion, just perform the betrothal ritual.
Father, he is the brave and strong groom and handsome too.
Uncle, he's the strong and handsome groom."

NEETU YADAV, BANHWAN VILLAGE CHANDAULI

Sita's extraordinary power to foretell her own marriage are highlighted once again in the above song, offering a contrast to the quotidian reality in which women scarcely have a say in their own marriages. The reference to the groom's complexion is suffused with irony. Women are routinely warned to avoid, when confronted with the "ideal groom," being side-tracked by irrelevant considerations such as matters of complexion and seeking to deter those conducting the search. This reversal of the ubiquitous emphasis, in the popular imagination, on a potential bride's fairness only enhances the irony. Many songs grapple with Sita's clairvoyance, taking up the motif of the *svayamvar* whereby Sita exercised her agency in choosing her groom. The song suggests the importance of paying attention to the minutest of details when searching for the perfect groom. It also invokes the enormous effort invested, and the involvement of extended families, in the search. At the weddings I attended, such songs functioned like a collective sigh of relief, which seemed especially apt, given that wedding celebrations mark the conclusion of painstaking and often time-consuming searches.

6

Bannī hamār jaisan ho Sītā dulhā lagelā Siriram
Aisan jodi ho khojale na milī jaisan Sita Ram hamār
Bannī ke bābū ho jaisan Janak ji, Dashrath sasur tohār
Gānv ghar nagar ho jaisan Mithilā ke, Ayodhyā nihan parivār hamār
Sab ghar rāj kare hamārī bannī ho, chamkat rahī sansār
Dev-muni sab duvāre par baithi ke sabhi karelā dulār

Our bride is like Sita, the groom like SriRam.
A couple like our Ram and Sita is hard to find.
Bride's father like Janak, Dashrath father-in-law,
Village and town like Mithila, Ayodhya-like the family of ours.
May she reign, our bride, and shine in her world,
As the sages, the guests, shower blessings.

SARALA DEVI KHATIK, CHAUBEYPUR, VARANASI

In this sung blessing, the entire wedding scene is transformed into the idealized wedding of Ram and Sita, thereby partaking of its prosperity. Sarala Devi, explaining the special meaning that Sita Mangal songs have for her, says that she sings these songs so that her daughter's wedded life may be ideal, like that of Ram and Sita: "All young women should be blessed with the kind of conjugal home that Sita had." Prabhavati Yadav, the singer of the first song in this section, offered, "Sita is the ideal woman. So with the blessings of Devi Sita, may our daughter also be beautiful, well-spoken and endowed with virtues. I pray that women display the qualities of Sita." Chinta Devi, of the Camar caste and the mother of the bride at the other wedding where I recorded Mangal, summed up the significance of these auspicious songs thus: "I sing Sita songs simply because in this world, there is not another woman with such a character as Sita's. And I hold my daughter's character to the standards of *satitvā* of mother Sita. For me Sita is the ideal of womanhood—in society women should aspire to emulate Sita's character."

7

Chotī merī Sita re, sab gun āgar
Sītā chale lin phulvarī
Phulvā lodhiyā Sita ghar ke lavatlin
Ram Raghubar dhailen dāhin bānhā
Atanā bacan jab sune lein Rikhaiyā
Baba dese dese lohavā besayā
Ohi lohavā ke dhanush dihalein banāī
Aur maurvā dihalein othanyā
Je ehi dhanush ke nau khand karihen
Ohi se karbo Sita ke biyahavā
Atanā vachan Ram sunah na pailen
Aai mandauvā dhaile thāth
Rovlein ājan rovlein bājan rovein rājan sab log
Pātar Ram pātar karihaiyān kamar lachak jin jāī
Thār bhar lihalin Sita
Candanvā din rāt suruj manaī
Pātar Ram pātar karihaiyan kamar lachak jini jāī
Torelen dhanush karelen nau khand
À bigi dihalein āsmān
Haselen ājan haselein bājan haselen rājan sab log
Sita biyāhī lehi jas.

My little Sita, blessed with the fine quailites,
Sita goes to pick flowers.
She picked flowers and returned,
Shri Ram held her right hand.

When the sage Rikhi heard these words,
The sage looked high and low for iron.
Of the iron he fashioned a bow
And stuck a peacock feather on top.
"Whoever breaks this bow into nine parts
Only he will get to marry Sita."
Ram barely heard these words
He sat down in the sacred space.
All beings cried out!
Slim Ram, what if he were to sprain his waist!
Sita took her position at the sandalwood sacred space,
Day and night entreating the Sun.
"Ram is slim, may he not sprain his waist."
He broke the bow into nine parts.
The skies fell.
Shouts of joy explode as he takes his bride away.

REKHA YADAV, BANHWAN VILLAGE, CHANDAULI

This song creatively integrates the bow-breaking episode into a new narrative, thereby linking the episode with the qualities a groom must demonstrate to win the hand of his bride. Only once Rama has taken Sita by the hand does the sage Rikhi set to work fashioning the bow—the breaking of which will determine Sita's choice of groom. The song emphasizes the orchestrated and prescribed ways in which marriages must be conducted so that the appropriate social norms are observed.

The bow-breaking episode, then, serves to legitimize an existing commitment or attraction between the ideal couple. Despite the groom's considerable attractions, he must first undergo a test to win the hand of his bride—a test through which he must adequately prove himself worthy and deserving. Surprisingly, in this women's song, Rama is not constructed according to mainstream understandings of a mighty warrior hero. Far from dwelling on Rama's physical prowess and strength, the narrative focuses repeatedly on his slender waist and, as a corollary, Sita's prayers are for his safety. Thus, women's prayers for the tests of endurance that men must undergo raise interesting questions about the masculine qualities women consider desirable. The song emphasizes the need to pay close attention to women's perspectives, which are often wholly missing from mainstream masculine discourses about heroism.

8

Gaunvā ūpar baba mandir khanavalā
Mandir parelā lāl maidān
Mandir dekhan chalelen betī ho,
Sita betī, apiran ghunghrū herāi
Unhavā baithe gailen dūlhe Ram
Kanhe suhvā chalelu akel
Aju ke ratiyā, Suhva ehvei gujarihā
Bihāne jaihā apane gāon
Aisan boli jin bolā ho, Ram ji abahi ta bātin kunvār
Jab hamare baba ho dihein kanyādān, tab hoib suhva tohār

At the edge of the village Baba erected a temple,
A temple with a red flag.
Sita sets off to visit the temple.
Daughter Sita loses her anklet.
There Ram, the groom, sits.
"Where are you off to alone, bride?
Tonight spend the night here, go back tomorrow."
"Do not utter these words,
Ram is still a young lad.
When my father perfoms the kanyadān ritual, only then shall I be your bride."

KIRAN YADAV, TIRMAPUR VILLAGE, CHANDAULI

Here, an auspicious song and the sacredness of the occasion serve to harness women's sexualities in the service of the institution of marriage. In this song, the wedding of Rama and Sita underlines an important message regarding sexual codes. The loss of anklets and other items of jewelry such as earrings and noserings is a familiar trope in songs of the region, signifying extramarital or illicit sexuality. The song therefore strikes a note of alarm about safeguarding the virginity of the bride. Kiran Yadav, the bride's mother at the Yadav household celebrating the wedding, considers the song's message crystal clear: "Before marriage or *kanyadān* [the ritual gifting of the daughter to the groom], it is the responsibility of the girl to maintain her sacredness in any situation. Hearing this song, girls would be influenced to follow this advice about maintaining purity [virginity]."

Kiran Yadav's remark suggests that the sacredness of the bride extends to the bride's observance of strict premarital codes and restrictions on women's sexuality. When I inquired about why contemporary social mores are embedded in songs about the ideal couple, Kiran's kinswoman, Neetu Yadav, pointed out that the main message of the song is one of auspiciousness. Then, after reflecting further on my question, she added: "We are simple human beings. How can we compare ourselves with god? We sing these songs simply to bless the married couple and to express our happiness, and not to follow all the deeds of god." Taking the idea of Ram and Sita as role models one step further, Kiran Yadav reflected: "If Sita was a *patīvratā*, so was Ram *ek-patnīvrat* [pledged to a single wife] and therefore this, too, is our idea of the ideal couple." Kiran and Neetu Yadav explained that, through these songs, ideal models of behavior are necessary and reinforced. They concluded by emphasizing the continued relevance of these songs to their community.

9

Gao mana cita laya gao surata samaya Sita ka mangal gāiye
Kaune sāgra khudai hai kinane bandhā hai palā
Kauna kahāra pāni bhare
Sita baithi nahāy lado baithi nahāy sita ka mangal gāiye
Dasrath sāgar khūdai hai Lakshman bandhi hai palā
Rama kahāra pāni bhare
Sita baithi nahāy lado baithi nahāy Sita ke mangal gāiye
Palī thī beti palī hain kacā dūdh pilāy dahiyā bhatā khilāi
An ganvā ka chokrā le jāi rath bithalāy sita ke mangal gāiye
Jo main janati betī hoengī parāi, lado hoengi parāi
Aga dhātura main letī khāi
Letī garbha girāy sita mangal gāiye

Sing heartily, the song of Sita, keep her image in your heart.
Who got the lake dug out, who set the sail?
Which kahar filled the water?
Sita, ready for her bath, dearest ready she is, sing her praise.
Dasrath got the lake dug out, Lakshman set the sail.
Rama's kahars filled the water.
Sita ready to bathe, dearest ready she is, sing her praise.
I raised her, raised her on milk and pure foods.
A lad of another village takes her away on a chariot, sing her praise.
If I had known she would belong to another, become another's,

I would have consumed the *dhatura*
And aborted the womb, sing the praise of Sita.

SRIVASTAVA 1991, 296

The song above articulates a mother's grief and unbearable sense of loss at bidding farewell to her beloved daughter, Sita. In a song ostensibly about blessings, it is interesting to find a mother's grief at her daughter's impending departure at her wedding slipped in at the end. The last stanza evokes the mood of pathos found in similar songs sung by mothers at their daughters' departure of brides, as in the following excerpt from a song I discussed in chapter 3:

Were a daughter's birth foretold, a concoction of chillies I'd have consumed, or smoked chillies to abort, to escape the unbearable sadness.

These lines evoke the various strategies women adopt to get rid of unwanted pregnancies, but here, as in other songs of the same genre, we learn that the sadness derives from the departure of a beloved daughter for her marital home. It is at the moment of a daughter's final departure that her mother must confront and articulate the trauma of this parting. These songs appear to emphasize the sorrow of this impending parting and offer at least one reason why the birth of a daughter is rarely celebrated with the same exuberance as that of a son.

Given the tragedy of Sita's life, one can understand the anxieties inherent in the following intriguing and rare wedding song, which articulates an alternative viewpoint to the one advanced in hundreds of songs sung across caste divides, all of which celebrate nuptials by evoking Rama and Sita as the ideal couple.

10

Tilak carhhāi Bābā ghare cali alien, Ama dehariyā dhaile thār
Kahū kahū Raja ho Ram ke suratiyā, kavnā nacchtare avtār ho
Kā ham kahin Rani Ram ke suratiyā, Ram sūrajvā ke jot
Ram ke jyoti dekhin adit chapit bhailen, mohi rahlen Pasurām
Pheri avaou Baba tilak ke dinavā, balu ham rahbon kunvār ji

The engagement settled, father returned home, mother waited at the door.
"Tell us about Rama's beauty, under which auspicious star did he take divine birth?"

"How shall I describe Rani, Rama's beauty, his countenance the rays of the sun
    itself.
The sun was made in Rama's likeness, none other than Him that Parasuram
    adored."
"Break off the engagement, Father, I'd much rather stay unmarried."

Was it Sita's tragic fate and impending ordeal that prompted her unusual request to break off her engagement with Maryada Purushottam
Ram, "most exemplary among men"? The reference to the sage Para-
surama evokes the moment in the Rāmāyanā when Rama won both the
hand of Sita as well as the blessings of the sage who arrived on the scene,
roused from his meditations by the thundering noise caused by the breaking of the bow. Given that most songs seek out and celebrate the qualities
of Rama in the groom, a song that questions this stereotype is both
unsettling and rare. Thus, songs that appear to break from the norm pose
unresolved puzzles in their refusal to endorse the received wisdom. This
song asks listeners to reflect on why Rama should be considered the ideal
groom, when indeed Sita suffered such humiliation and sorrow. What,
then, are to be the standards against which to measure the ideal groom
and, more so, what qualities should individual women search for in
prospective grooms? In other words, are women's expectations about conjugal fulfillment at odds with those of the society? Similar anxieties and
misgivings permeate the next song, in which Sita reflects on the unknown
future that was to follow her first meeting with Rama.

11

Ram Lakhan duno van ke aheriā ho
Van baithī khele lan aheriā ho
Khelat aheriā ho
Lagi gaiel madhur piyās piyās
Nahī dekhlen tāl ho, nāhi dekhi pokharvā ho
Na dekhi nīcak gaun ho
Ahre nirkuchavā van me, koi nahi apnā
Ram morai piyāsal bhailein
Apne rasoiyā se nikalein Sital devi
Hathvā gharilvā judai pāni
Lehu na Ram, piavahu judai pāni
Baithā kadamb jude chāhi

Kekar hau tu nātin panātin
Keker janmal bhatīj ho
Kaune kul me biyāh racal
Kekar hi kul ujiyār ho
Raja Janak kul mein janam bhaīl
Dasrath kul mein biyāh ho
Ram kul hoihe ujiyār
Aur Ram hauven svāmi hamār
Atanā bachan Ram suni pavale ho
Ban paithī candan katāi
Candan katāi darvā fanvale ho
Doke doke lāge lan kahār ho
Jau mohi janati Ram bairī hamār hoieba
Nāhi baithati jude chāhi,
Na piyāvatin thandā pāni

Ram and Lakshman are off to hunt.
In the forest they hunt.
Then a strange thirst rises.
Not a lake or a pond is seen,
Not a single village,
"In this deserted forest, not a soul we know.
My Ram is thirsty."
From her kitchen emerges Sita devi
Holding a pot of water.
"Here, Ram, drink this cool water.
Sit under the shade of the kadamb tree."
"Whose grandchild are you?
Where were you born?
In which clan were you married?
Whose clan will you illuminate?"
"Born in the clan of Raja Janak.
Into Dashrath's clan I married.
Ram's clan will be illuminated.
And Ram is my husband."
Ram scarcely heard the words,
He sent for the cutting of sandalwood

To fashion the carriage
And appointed kahar carriage carriers.
"Had I known that Ram would become an enemy,
I would not have invited him to rest in the shade,
Nor offered him cooling water."

DHANAWATI YADAV, BANHWAN VILLAGE, CHANDAULI

In this equally intriguing song, Sita's last lines make a riddle of all that preceded them. As Sita offers Rama shade and cool water, it is clear that she has recognized him, and yet Rama still does not know who she is. Thus, the song shifts between recognition and nonrecognition, between actions that merely follow other actions and events that have been foretold. If Sita invited Rama to share the shade because she could foresee that he would become her husband, then why did she not also foresee the rest of her life? Could it be that Sita had to live her life according to a prearranged script? In other words, predictions, like memory, appear to be highly selective. Thus, in the last lines of the song, Sita is at pains to point out that she did not foresee her ultimate separation from Ram and the related tragedies at this first meeting. In this way, the tragedy of Ram and Sita is an endless source of unresolved conundrums about which we might speculate. In the section below, I set such riddles aside to dwell more fully on the conjugal life of Ram and Sita. These songs focus more directly on the nature of the struggles that characterized their union.

CONJUGALITY AS SITE OF STRUGGLE

While a number of songs glorify Ram-Sita as the ideal couple, wedding songs also underline the difficult transition the wedded couple is to make. Like the lives of Rama and Sita, the songs strike subtle notes of warning. They suggest that far from being a bed of roses, domesticity can be a journey punctuated by hardships and many tests along the way. Sita Mangal, these auspicious wedding songs, are celebratory in nature but also hint at dark possibilities. Suddenly, and for no apparent reason, everything might go horribly awry. Four themes—namely, control, vigilance, empathy, and bearing witness—surface repeatedly in marriage songs. These dilemmas and their resolutions appear to both define and illuminate conjugal life.

12

RESTRICTION

Sāsu tabahūn na lauten pardesiyā ho nā
Phar gaiyīr nimiyā, lahasī gaiyin dariyā ho nā
Are Ramā ghorvā charhala āvai bidesiyā ho Ram
Are Rama bīti gail bārah barisvā ho Ram
Are Rama ghorvā charhala āvai bidesiyā ho Ram
Kekeri haiyun tuhūn dulāri ho Ram?
Are Rama kaune Raja ke hayu tu patohiyā ho Ram?
Are Rama kekari haiyu patari tiriyavā ho Ram?
Are Rama kekari re lagaayī nimi bahāraun ho Ram?
Raja Janak ji ki bāri dulāri ho Ram
Are Rama Dasrath ke hai ham patohiyā ho Ram
Are Rama Ramchandra ke bāri biyahau ho Ram
Rama unahin ke lagāī nimi baharaun ho Ram
Rama kekare re adar nikriu baharvā ho Ram
Rama sāsu ji ke adar nisare baharvān ho Ram

Mother-in-law, still the traveler did not return.
The neem tree has flowered, the branches are laden, O Ram!
O Ram! Then riding a horse, returned the wanderer.
O Ram, twelve years passed and he returned.
"Whose beloved are you?
Of which Raja are you the daughter-in-law?
Whose slim bride are you, O Ram?
Who planted the neem tree you upkeep, O Ram?"
"Beloved of Raja Janak, his daughter I am, O Ram
Daughter-in-law of Raja Dashrath.
I am the bride of Ramchandra.
I care for the neem tree planted by him."
"At whose orders did you step out of the house?"
"At mother-in-law's orders, I stepped out."

MUNRAJI AND SUBHAVATI, BARSARA 2002

The above excerpt offers an unexpected ironic twist in its last lines about a wife who was married so young that she is unable to remember the moment that transformed her life into one of anticipation of union with the traveler. The chance encounter in the field with her long-absent husband turns out to be merely a conventional reassertion of male authority and control. The wife's endless wait and anticipation, then, produce a poignant anticlimax that captures the condition of wives abandoned by their migratory husbands. This song seems to weigh the years of loneliness and lack of companionship against male dominance, highlighting both the interrogation that reestablishes the relationship and the irony of its necessity. In women's songs, as we saw in chapter 2, migrant husbands are presented as callous, insensitive, and indifferent to the needs of the wives they left behind, and, in most cases, forgetful of them entirely.

In an unexpected twist, however, this song ends up being about Sita, and its warning note is sounded by none other than this ideal wife, who hints at the patriarchal restrictions in store for her with the return of her long-awaited husband. Even the exemplary Rama, the ideal husband, is stereotypically domineering the instant he returns.[4] To make its point, this song about the idealized mythic couple must depart considerably from the mainstream Rāmāyanā story, which only adds to its irony.

The use of the English word *order* is noteworthy not only for its contemporary feel but also, and more importantly, for how it illustrates Narayan's argument that folksongs evolve in response to changing and contemporary realities rather than representing timeless, self-contained, village traditions (Narayan 1993, 177–204). In the colonial context, peasants' familiarity with authority and the issuing of orders are to be expected, but the everyday usage of English words is also underlined.

13

RESISTANCE

Na jaiba Ajudhia, na jaibe ho
Mori mahatāri na jaiba ho, mātā mori na jaiba na
Guru ji aīhen āihen ho
Mori sakhiyā ho sakhi morī re, kavan lota mein paniyā deba
Sakhiya mori kauno lota paunva parai parva
Ban chorabe na, nāhin jaibe na ho Ajudhiya, nāhin jaibe na
Tohre aihen hain guruji
More sakhiya re sakhi morey, sonvā ke lota mein ho paniyā
Lāvo paniya, lota pani jamuna tīrai, lota pāni lāvo re

Paunvā dhoān munir
Caran dharī, dihein asīsā, asīs dehein guruji ho
Ab na jaibe re Ajudhiya, na jaibe Ajudhiya

Shall not return to Ayodhya, no, never!
My mother, I shall not go, mother mine, I shall not go.
The sages come to take you back.
My friends, my dears in which pot to offer them water?
Which pot for the ritual washing of the feet?
I shall not leave the forest, not go back to Ayodhya, no.
The sages come . . .
My dear friends, friends of mine, do fetch some water in the golden pot.
From the Yamuna river, do fetch the water.
To wash the feet of the sages.
To bow at their feet and receive their blessings.
But to Ayodhya I shall not go, not go back to Ayodhya, oh no!

DALIT SINGERS, CHURAMANPUR, VARANASI

Powerfully articulated, the song stands out as a model of resistance within folk registers, as the singers appear to be saying a vehement "no" to injustice of all kinds. On no account will the Sita of this song be persuaded to return to Ayodhya, wherefrom she was exiled. Yet staying within the parameters of her culture is equally important to her, as her concerns about appropriately honoring guests and spiritual teachers and receiving sages' blessings reflect. The Dalit women who sang this song, danced to it with gay abandon, fostering a mood of unrestrained revelry. The occasion was the celebration of a male birth, but, as the singers pointed out, the song is very popular at weddings, too, owing to its catchy and rhythmic beat. In fact, an acknowledgement of resistance offered by Sita's story is found in a number of congratulatory birth songs.

An upper-caste version of this song, included in Krishnadev Upadhyaya's two-volume anthology on Bhojpuri folksongs (1990b), also highlights the motif of Sita's respect for the sages who Rama had sent to fetch her. Here, Sita refuses to return, but out of respect for the sages who have come at Rama's behest, she does take five steps in the direction of Ayodhya. It is striking that such messages about taking a principled stance against injustice are found embedded within congratulatory songs, which render them even more potent because of the mundane, albeit celebratory contexts, into which they are slipped.

The inner worlds of the bride and groom revealed in wedding songs underline the difficult transition the wedded couple must make. Here, the conjugal bed itself becomes a metaphor for the trials of marital life. The song below illustrates, in particular, how women internalize vigilance and control.

14

ETERNAL VIGILANCE

Anganā me ratulī palangiyā
Obariya mein dasavelī ho
E sāsu, nānhen vidhi likhle lilār
Kaise ke sejiyā dasabi ho
Ram sūtele, Sita jāgeli
Beniyā dolāveli ho
Ai Sita, kāhe uthelu tu karvatiyā
Nīndariyo nāhin āvelā ho
Nāhin ham pet bhari khainī
Nīndariyā bhari sovelī ho
Ai Ram, ban hi ke din niyarailen
Banhī raurā jaibai ho
Jāhu Sita pet bhari khaibu
Nīnariyā bhari soibu nu ho
Ai Sita, Lachuman lākh manaihen
Banhi nāhin jaibū nū ho
Jab Sita bhari pet khailīn
Nīnari bhari sovelī ho
Arai sūtal Ram uthā bane gailen
Kehu na jāgelā ho
Aagi lāgasu ehi nagare
T avarū Ajodhiya mein ho
sūtal Ram bane gailen
T kehu na jāgelā ho

The cot is ready in the courtyard.
Yet how to decorate my bedchamber?
Mother-in-law, what is to be my fate?

How to decorate the bedchamber?
Ram sleeps, Sita stays awake.
Gently moving the fan.
"O Sita, why do you toss and turn so?
Are you unable to fall asleep?"
"I never had a hearty meal
Nor ever a full night's sleep
Because Rama's days of exile approach
And to the forest he will go."
"Go Sita, have a hearty repast
Have a restful night."
"O Sita, despite Laxman's thousand entreaties
To the forest, you should refuse to go."
But after Sita had a hearty meal,
Had plunged into the deepest slumber
Oh! That's when sleeping Ram awoke and went off to the forest.
Then, not a soul was awake.
A curse on this city,
And on the city of Ayodhya.
That Ram awoke and went on his path of exile
While not a soul was awake!

UPADHYAYA 1990B, 420

This song is a complex meditation on vigilance that must be understood on many levels. It illustrates the Rama-Sita story's potential and malleability in conveying deep truths about women's existential realities. The motif of Rama leaving for the forest in the dead of night when all are asleep, a detail that starkly deviates from the Ramāyanā narrative wherein Sita is his constant companion throughout his hardships, raises questions about folk perceptions. Rama's stealthy exit echoes both the actions of many folk heroes and heroines and women's and men's fears about separation. The heroine tying the hero to the nuptial bed with a red string, to prevent his escape in the middle of the night, is a recurring motif in tales of the region (as in the Lorikāyan, see chapter 5). Alas, the string is fragile and the heroes invariably escape! The song speaks volumes in Uttar Pradesh, where women appear to have been otherwise silenced or at least made invisible, in various ways, within public discourses.

Sita's shock at discovering that Rama left while she was asleep echoes the theme of bearing witness. Her remorse that Rama left while the entire city slept might serve as an indictment of indifference to the plight of others. Her deep pathos evokes the incomparable magnitude of an event such as Rama's departure. In questioning how such a thing could come to pass, the song appears to invoke a social conscience. Other songs develop a similar mood of empathy by questioning quotidian existence in the light of an occurrence such as Rama's exile.

The following song enumerates the many witnesses, both human and animal, to Sita's abduction by Ravana in his chariot. In bearing witness to Ravana's crime and in delineating the route to Rama, caste specialists and a range of creatures all secure for themselves a hallowed place in the universe, all, that is, except for a pair of Cātak birds. So engrossed are these birds in their lovemaking that they are completely oblivious to the abduction. Consequently, the birds are unable to inform Rama about the direction in which Ravana's chariot headed.

15

Lakari cīrat tuhūn loharvā chokarvā
Eihi rahihe dekhuvā Sita ho jāk
Hamahun to selī Rama Sita ke palangiyā
Sita ke Ravanvā hari le jāk
Kaparā dhovat tuhūn dhobin bitiyā
Eihi rāhi dekhuva Sita ho jāk
Hamahun to phichiõ Rama sita ke chunariyā
Sita ke Ravanava har le jāk
Eihi pār jatva ho, oh pār jataiyā
Eihi rahihe dekhuva Sita ho jāk
Hamahun to rahin Rama apanā Chakuvā jarai
Ham nāhin dekhuva Sita ho jāk
Din bhar chakva ho joriyā milhiyā
Sānjh beriyā rahihā ho chipāi

The woodcutter's son, fashioning wood.
"Along this road, I saw Sita being taken away."
"I sewed Sita's cot."
Saw that Ravana abducted Sita along this road.
The washerman's daughter washing clothes,

"I, who wash Sita's cunari shawl,
Saw Sita abducted by Ravana."
On this side, Jat and the other side Jatni,
Saw Sita being abducted along this road
"So engrossed was I in my Cakvā
I didn't see Sita go by."
So, all day long the Cātak birds may pair
But at dusk must pine for each other in vain.

MEENA DEVI AND MOTHER-IN-LAW, MISRAULIA CHHAPRA

The birds' indifference to Sita's plight, even as an oversight, is a lapse for which they must pay a heavy price. The last stanza announces the curse of separation that the species will bear for eternity. The song puts a different spin on the cries of the Cātak birds, who, distracted by love, must remain separated at night, thereby paying the price for their distraction. Ignoring the Divine leads to misfortune, and indifference to Sita's plight to eternal yearning and separation. The judgment the song pronounces appears to be a cosmic sentencing.

EMPATHY

Of the long list of tragic episodes connected with Sita's idealized persona in the Ramāyanā, her exile in the forest is one of the more major injustices she must endure. Folk narratives provide a range of alternative explanations for Rama's compulsion to exile Sita. In the classical Valmiki version, Rama's provocation for sending Sita into exile was the chance remark by a dhobī, who, doubting Sita's chastity during her many years in captivity, questions Rama's compromised honor, reminding him of a king's moral duty to lead by example. The provocation remains equally arbitrary in the songs, highlighting the inherent injustice at the root of Sita's exile. Indeed, these episodes in Valmiki's Ramāyanā concerning Sita's exile in the forest, rather than Tulsi's Ramcaritmānas, engender the greatest empathy for Sita. While a trial by fire might address particularly upper-caste concerns, Sita's abandonment and childbirth, episodes connected with the second phase of her life, allow women of all castes to relate to Sita's biography. The song below picks up the story at the moment Sita is sent into exile.

16

Khoincā mein le le sarsoinyā
Chitat Sita nikselī ho sarson
Ehi rahiyā lavatihen devara Lachhman
Kadariyā toori khaihanī ho
Awadh nagariyā se Sita dei re calalī
Rāhe bāte bole kāga boliyā ho Ram
Kāg ke bachaniyā suni Sita manre jhurbe
Kāhe devarū nayanā mor pharke ho Ram
Ghorvā ke veg devarū pavan samanvā
Sehu ghorvā pāv-pāv calelā ho Ram
Toharo suratiyā devarū suruj ke jotiyā
Sehu kāhe dhūmil ho gailī ho Ram
An ban gailī dūsar ban lavalī
Tīsare Brindavan ailī ho
Devarū, ek būnd paniyā piabvahū
Piasiyā se biākul ho
Baithahu na bhaujī candan tare
Candan birichh tare ho
Bhaujī, paniyā ke khoj karai āīn
T toharā piāīn nū ho
Bahe lāge juruin bayariyā
Canan chhori chhaiyan ho
Sīt bhūniyan pare kumhlāī
Piasiyā se byākul ho
Tor let patvā kadam kar
Donvā banavalī ho
Tangale lavangiyā ke dariyā
Lakhan cale ghare orai ho

In a bundle she took some mustard seeds,
Stepped out scattering them along the way.
"The mustard seeds, this way he'll return,
Brother-in-law Lakshman, by then, they'll germinate for him."
And Devi Sita left Ayodhya city.
On the way the crow called, O Ram!
Hearing the crow, Sita had misgivings.

"Why does my eye twitch so, brother-in-law?
The horses, brother-in-law, always sped like the wind.
Then why do they move so slow, O Ram!
Your countenance, brother-in-law, always like sunshine
Why has it clouded over, O Ram?"
They crossed one forest, then the next.
The third they came to was Brindavan.
"Brother-in-law, just a drop of water
I crave, the thirst unbearable."
"Rest, sister-in-law, under the sandalwood tree,
Under the cooling sandalwood.
I go to search for water.
Then, I shall bring you some."
Cooling winds began to blow.
The sandalwood boughs gave shade.
On the earth lay Sita wilting,
The thirst unbearable.
First, he picked kadamb leaves
Fashioning them into cups,
Then hanging up the clove basket,
Lakshman turned back homeward.

ROY 2056 VIKRAMI, 87

Several elements in the song establish Sita's proximity to nature and remind us of her origins, while the image of Sita being cradled by the earth to which she will return adds to the pathos. Despite the somber nature of Sita's journey, her magnanimous act in her hour of trial, calculated to assure prosperity for her affines, emphasizes women's social conscience. Folk beliefs embedded in the narrative, such as the twitching of eyes foretelling misfortune, enhance the moment's poignancy while rendering Sita's sorrows intensely human. The details allow listeners to domesticate Sita and claim her as human, as "one of us" whose sorrows and trials resemble those experienced by peasant women across time and space and beyond the divides of caste and class.

As Sita is at once Earth, Nature, Field, and Nurturer, ecofeminist ideologies have mined the Sita metaphor to argue for a return to nature and its pristine glory in the face of industrialization's onslaught. Vandana Shiva, for instance, has influentially argued that women are the natural protectors of the environment. Since the 1980s, those who struggle against widespread depredations of the environment in the name of development have celebrated nature as Prakritī, the feminine principle. Women serve as representatives of this principle, and their power in collective struggle has been seen as *strī-shakti* (Rajan 1998, ws 36).

Ramchandra Gandhi's *advaita* (nondualist) perspective on the separation of Rama and Sita is instructive. He writes, "The ecologically educative separation of Rama and Sita by mutual consent became distorted into the sexist banishment of Sita by Rama for suspected infidelity in Lanka" (Gandhi 1992, 21). This separation of the divine couple, he argues, is "the price that has to be paid for the ecological violation implicit in the killing of the demon deer Marica by Rama at Sita's instigation" (21). This theme is present in the Ramāyaṇa's earliest episode, where the death of one of a mating pair of *kraunca* birds by a hunter's arrow is an ecological violation of such cosmic magnitude that it prompts the observer Valmiki to express himself in verse (20).

Gandhi discusses the Sita tradition within Hindu, Jain, and Buddhist folklore, where it is often overlooked and where it counters the militant masculinity of the Hindutva movement. Here, too, women are associated with nature, nurturing and motherhood, and preservation and pacifism (Rajan 1998; Gandhi 1992). The emphasis on Rama within Hindutva doctrines, Gandhi suggests, may serve to efface many elements of the Sita lore.

"The values of steadfastness, firmness, fidelity, and the devotion of the wife to the husband [the seed giver] for the sake of progeny" form the subtext evoked in the songs, and hence Sita's construction in these songs reinforces the ideology of seed and earth (Dube 2001, 123). Self-denial and sacrifice are key components of the sustained contribution the mother makes through her procreation and are found in abundance in these songs. The implications of this ideology are far-reaching since, by equating the woman's body with the field or the earth, the process of reproduction is equated with that of production and the rights of children with rights over the crop (140).

Empathy with Sita, then, is a value peasant women understand and experience deeply in their own lives. In wedding songs that celebrate the marriage of the ideal couple, Ram and Sita, and describe scenes of Sita's devotion and domesticity and even in the pedagogical jatsārs, it is the peasant women's own selves that stand reflected. Hence the unique opportunity the Ramnagar Ramlīlā provides women, as "spectator-pilgrims," to silently and spontaneously express their solidarity with Sita could be described as affirming, even transformative.

In this chapter I have argued that the persona Sita belongs to no single category; rather, she embodies a plurality of voices and viewpoints. Despite her relevance as a role model for chaste upper-caste Hindu women, Sita's persona and lore have enabled the emergence of alternative models that have validity and significance for peasant women of lower strata as well. The Sita that emerges from the folklore and oral traditions suggests peasant women's nuanced and complex relationships with this figure. Given that her story is one among many within the oral folk traditions of the region, and that folk narratives are open to multiple interpretations, women of many castes can claim Sita.

Were Sita's chastity and trial by fire the only aspects of her persona valorized by peasant women, then her relevance for upper-caste women would tend to overshadow her meaning for other castes. It is owing to the flexibility of the Sita metaphor that women are able to use her narrative to reflect on their own struggles. Women's songs of Sita encompass an astonishingly diverse repertoire of experiences, voices, approaches, understandings, solutions, and expressions.

In the words of Hess, "social forces create and are created by cultural artifacts" (Hess 1988; 253); as such, one could argue that singing about Sita amounts to singing about peasant women's own lives. That Sita's persona and lifestory mirror those of peasant women becomes apparent when we consider the diverse solutions to and interpretations of life events that the songs offer. Thus, in addition to the fact that women "experience nurturing and empowerment through female divine imagery or the worship of female deities" (Hiltbeitel and Erndl 2000, 17), these songs suggest that women identify with Sita on several levels. They also show that women's identification with Sita rarely amounts to an unquestioning or uncritical acceptance of her persona and actions.

The songs evoke Sita as symbolic of strī-shakti, the power of women, which, unlike Western understandings of power as the exercise of control and domination (Hiltbeitel and Erndl 2000, 19) or of agency, remains somewhat in the realm of potentiality, manifesting itself only in moments of provocation. Further, as women sing together about their lives, they create new forms of the Rama and Sita story. Nilsson notes, "They tend to emphasize the human frailties and human aspects of the divinity they sing about" (2001, 141). Rao has argued that the contents of the women's Rāmāyaṇā songs do not, in themselves, make the singers feminists; women sing these songs because it is the womanly thing to do. Further, the same women who sing these songs also participate in the public, often male-dominated Rāmāyaṇā performances and recitations with great devotion, as we saw at the Benaras Ramnagar Ramlīlā, which began this chapter. As Rao argues with regard to Brahmin women of Andhra Pradesh, "Perhaps the value of the songs consists precisely in the absence of conscious protest. The women who sing these songs have not sought to overthrow the male-dominated family structure; they would rather work within it. They have no interest in direct confrontation with authority; their interest, rather, is in making room for themselves to move. It is the internal freedom that these songs seem to cherish. Only when such freedom is threatened by a power exercised by the head of the household do the women speak up against him, even when subverting his authority rather than fighting openly against it" (Rao 1991, 133).

CHAPTER FIVE

⟿ When Marriage Is War

The "meaning" of this or any other epic is not purely or even primarily determined by the text. Meaning, significance and especially the power to reproduce social groupings are a function not of text but of context—that is, of culture and history.

WILLIAM S. SAX, *DANCING THE SELF*, 95

Today, dowry, gifts, conspicuous consumption, and the enormous expenditure bride-givers incur are understood as the hallmarks of north Indian marriage celebrations. How can we supplement a gendered understanding of marriage, both its logic and celebratory aspects, with sociological insights obtained through folk narratives? In what ways do oral narratives serve to balance our undue reliance on scriptural and textual evidence when seeking to explain the nature of marriage as a form of exchange (Dumont 1966, 1970; Trautmann 1982; Inden and Nicholas 2005)?

Among north Indian ballads, the Lorikāyan, known for its rich descriptions of the various aspects of marriage and articulating the values, aspirations, and motifs of dominance and subordination, offers extraordinarily rich insights into this rite of passage. One of the most popular *gāthā* (ballads) of the Bhojpuri-speaking region, as a mas-

culine performance tradition it complements the feminine song genres I
have analyzed so far.

The Lorikāyan's martial, masculine focus and hero-centered narrative,
concerned predominantly with the nature of power and physical prowess
in a geographically vast and socially complex universe, is the context
within which we explore how gender is socially constructed by caste
patriarchies (see Flueckiger 1996). Here, masculinity is delineated as a
public social status striven for and maintained in specific social contexts,
rather than as an innately present quality (O'Hanlon 1997, 3). In addition
to marriage, this chapter also seeks clarity on other themes and issues of
contemporary relevance raised by the text—for example, the consolidation of caste patriarchies and mechanisms for establishing and maintaining control over women.

The Yadavas, a broad caste group comprising several allied subcastes
that are historically concerned with issues of identity and seeking upward
mobility and together constitute one-tenth of India's total population,
claim the ballad as their own, and as such it offers insights into processes
relating to intermediate castes (Rao 1979, 123–241). Specifically, the Yadava category comprises cognate castes such as Ahirs, Gopas, Goalas, and
Abhiras, all of whom claim descent from the Yadus, the dynasty to which
Krishna is said to belong (124). While Yadavas occupy several regions,
they are concentrated in the Ganges plains, where they account for 10
percent of the population. They form one of the largest caste groups in
Uttar Pradesh and Bihar, respectively constituting 8.7 and 11 percent of
the population according to the 1931 census[1] (Rao 1979; Jaffrelot 2003,
188). The assertiveness of the Yadava caste, which constitutes the upper
crust of the Other Backward Classes (OBC) category, in the Bhojpuri-
speaking belt after Independence heighten the significance of the ballad, which reflects the aspirations and values of this large and upwardly
mobile caste group. Since the 1980s, the Yadavas have been rapidly replacing Brahmins and Kshatriyas as the dominant caste in the countryside.[2]
Since Independence, the caste has doubled the amount of land it controls
by systematically investing the wealth it gained from dairying and government service in land. The post-Independence land reforms, which
benefited mid-level castes in particular, helped the Yadavas consolidate
their economic and political base (Jaffrelot 2003). The rise to power of

the Samajwadi party in Uttar Pradesh and of the Janata Dal in Bihar are representative of this trend. The consolidation of Yadava strength is reflected not only in the power structure but also at various levels of administration, including the district, *tehsil* (block), and village levels. Owing to a state policy that supports both reservations and affirmative action, the Yadavas are now recognized as an educated class often employed in government and police bureaucracies (field notes; Jaffrelot 2003). Details provided in an article published in Patna's newspaper, the *Telegraph*, on 2 October 2002 contextualizes the contemporary appeal of the hero, Lorik, claimed by the Yadavas as belonging to the Yadava caste.[3]

According to the popular understanding, the wealth of the Yadava caste is attributable in part to the industrious nature of Yadava women, who in the past contributed their share of labor to the caste's dairying as well as agrarian production. Today, however, the withdrawal of women from work in the fields for the purpose of "status-production" is a distinctive feature of Yadava upward mobility (Papanek 1989; Srinivas 1962). Upwardly mobile groups' typical undervaluation of women's labor and their consequent "hiring in" of labor for agricultural tasks are trends that also characterize the Yadavas (Jassal 2001, 49–63). We find a graduated scale of women's work, with women's complete withdrawal from agriculture, in imitation of the Kshatriya model, being the approved norm. For women, these trends translate into other kinds of seclusion as well, such as restricted mobility and visibility in public spaces, in conformity with the veiling norms for Kshatriya women.

This chapter is divided into four sections: The first section identifies the features of the *birahā* singing tradition to which the ballad belongs for the purpose of appreciating how the epic reproduces, and is in turn reproduced by, the Yadava caste. The second section provides a broad outline of the ballad's plot, followed by a discussion of its treatment of marriage and how it imagines this rite of passage as a battle that ends in the redressing of power between two opposing groups. The third section focuses on the ballad's construction of gender, exploring specific caste patriarchies, followed by a discussion of women's agency. The last section attempts to locate the ballad within historical processes that concern the Yadavas, such as their ongoing struggles to achieve Sanskritization[4] and greater power and visibility.

THE PERFORMANCE CONTEXT

The Lorikāyan is sung at celebrations ranging from betrothals (*Tilak*) to festivals and, as the renowned professional birahā singer Hiralal Yadav of Benaras points out, "this is the singular and typical form of entertainment among Yadavas." Hiralal Yadav says that he rarely performs the entire epic from beginning to end and usually sings only the most popular segments, such as the episodes dealing with Lorik's marriage. His comments confirm Joyce Burkhalter Flueckiger's observation that Indian oral epics are "performed episodically, with popular episodes being performed most frequently and sometimes, with considerable interaction from audiences that are likely to have a general knowledge of the epic" (Flueckiger 1989b, 428). Such audiences are also more likely to seek connections with the epic's emotional or devotional content rather than with developments in its narrative per se. Flueckiger found in Chattisgarh, for instance, that men are also more likely than women to "identify genres with the wider communities of which they are a part, such as village or region, rather than with the more limited group of performers only," likely because women enjoy a comparative lack of mobility (Fleuckiger 1996, 181).

When asked to explain the meaning of birahā, Hiralal Yadav waxes lyrical: "To simply sing out the cry of separation is birahā: the separation that the cowherdesses experienced when they were separated from Lord Kirshna; the agony Sita experienced when separated from Ram. Birahā emerges from *virah* (separation). To experience a defeat is birahā, to be abducted is birahā; pining for god, for one's guru, the music that emerges from all these separations is birahā" (Hiralal Yadav). At the invitation of Hiralal Yadav, in 2001 I attended a birahā performance at Tengra Mor on the outskirts of Varanasi, where I first heard him sing an excerpt from the Lorikāyan. The audience at this particular performance was largely working-class or self-employed. Many were petty traders, rickshaw pullers, drivers, and sundry other specialists employed in the city of Varanasi. As a guest of this noted birahā singer, I was delighted to be seated right in front, but I soon found that I was the only woman present and therefore extremely conspicuous! However, a few hours into the concert, my host politely asked me to leave, as the audience was becoming restive in anticipation of the bawdy and sexually explicit singing to follow. I was reluctant to leave since the music was so delightful and entertaining, but I could see that the audience around me was getting dangerously tipsy, and upon realizing that my informant and escort for the evening was also high, my maestro host called an auto-rickshaw and summarily had me packed off home!

Luckily, this was not before I had heard at least four of the teams competing that night, each representing a distinct *akharā* or musical style associated with a particular guru. The singing took the form of a challenge to the rival group, which in turn had to respond musically. Like those of women, men's singing traditions forge strong community ties. The popularity of men's wrestling akharās has been documented, but these were modeled upon and drew inspiration from the musical akharās that promoted the growth of distinct musical traditions and styles under the direction of accomplished gurus (Marcus 1989). Through akharās and their affiliation with a common teacher and his teachings, groups of men were bound to each other.

The audience at Tengra Mor repeatedly interrupted the performance as individuals approached the stage with small offerings of money between Rs.5 and Rs.10. The protocol of the concert demanded that the singer recognize the patrons as they made their offerings. This meant that the singer was forced to stop singing in order to call out the individual's name and often also the sum he had offered. While the format allowed not only for the expression of appreciation but also for the recognition of the audience in the public arena and for the momentary basking of the patrons in the singer's glory, the interruptions were frustrating to me. Unlike in radio song request programs, where the names of those requesting the song are announced before or after the song, these steady interruptions came during the singing itself, which tested my patience and prolonged the entire show interminably. However, the audience hardly seemed to mind and appeared to be prepared to camp out for the entire night.

The singers sang standing up, sometimes resting on a *lāthi* (staff), a feature of the biraha Yadava tradition.[5] The most thrilling aspect of the event was that the lyricists, who were seated on stage along with the musical orchestra as part of the team, composed the stanzas on the spot. The singing involved a vast amount of theatrical expression, and the singer sometimes stepped forward, practically enacting the mood and character of the song, much like one would see in a Western opera. The many percussionists kept the beat very lively and entertaining, and the entire team maintained their steady improvisation in response to the mood of the audience.

Hiralal Yadav explained that the Lorikāyan is an integral part of this birahā singing tradition of the Yadavas. He points out that the conventions of the tradition are a legacy of nineteenth-century musical duels that appear to have been significant in the socialization of male youth. Evoking the spirit of the duel and competitive wrestling matches between contesting teams, belonging to an akharā appears to be an important, though under-researched, aspect of masculine folk singing in north India. Affiliation with an akharā ensured the continuity of singing traditions (paramparā) as well as the teachings of the guru on which the akharā was centered, yet, as the ballad delineates, it also appears to have forged ties and sensibilities that were in opposition to ascriptive, hierarchical, caste-based ones (Brass 2003; Marcus 1989).

During my fieldwork in the region, I found that the notion that musical challenges could help to deflect real conflicts was something of a popular wisdom. The following section outlines the main plot of the Lorikāyan, which I variously refer to as an *epic, ballad,* and *chronicle.*

THE PLOT: TWO WEDDINGS AND AN ELOPEMENT

First, I must stress that there is no single text that can be called the Lorikāyan, since "living epic traditions are not static but continue to change and respond to the communities in which they are performed" (Blackburn et al. 1989, 7). Indeed, in some regions the epic is known as the Chanaini, after its heroine, and it was also the inspiration for Maulana Daud's Chandayan, a medieval Sufi literary text (Hines 2007). For the purposes of this chapter, I draw on the translated and written Bhojpuri version of the ballad recorded by S. M. Pandey in the 1970s and 80s (Pandey 1987). This version is based on the recordings of the singer Sivnath Chaudhuri, made in 1966 and constituting 48 hours of audiotape.[6]

The Lorikāyan gāthā, or chronicle, traces the main events of the life of its hero, Lorik, who undertook extraordinary travel adventures, at least three romantic interludes and marriages, and innumerable feats of heroism on the battlefield. Lorik's divinity is hinted at; he is understood as a godly incarnation tasked with rooting out evil, and hence his lore parallels that of the mythical Krishna, who was also a Yadava. The personification of bravery, Lorik gained his superhuman qualities and extraordinary battle prowess as gifts from the goddess Durga who appears to assist the hero, her devotee, at every turn.

The ballad begins when the young Manjari, inspired by a divine intervention, announces that her marriage must be settled with none other than brave Lorik, the cow-herder from Gaura. In fact, she goes on a *satyāgraha* or hunger strike until her marriage is arranged. In foretelling her marriage, Manjari proclaims the name of the hero who will liberate her caste of cowherds from the tyrannical king of Agori, according to whose ruling all young women of the territory are to be handed over to him for his harem. The narrative establishes early on that the hero has been incarnated to save the honor of this herding and dairying caste. By extension, and as processes of Sanskritization have illustrated in other contexts and periods, it comes as no surprise that Lorik will achieve this in part by preserving the honor of the women of the caste, as well as establishing stricter controls on them.

When the Nai (caste of barber) and the Brahmin priest (in accordance with folk traditions) arrive at Gaura carrying the marriage proposal sent by Manjari's father, we meet Chanaini, the femme fatale of the ballad. Chanaini tricks them and leads them to her home to settle Manjari's marriage with her brother in place of Lorik. The raja of Gaura then threatens to kill all those who participate in Lorik's marriage to Manjari. After innumerable hurdles and the crossing of many rivers, mountains, and forests, the *savā lākh* (huge) marriage party, comprising 360 *carvāhas* (herders) clad in battle attire and joined by increasing numbers, arrive at Agori to solemnize the marriage. The marriage party, encamped in the surrounding thorny fields, resembles an army at war.

The hero marries Manjari, and the bride and the groom both receive elaborate gifts and prestations. The last and final hurdle before the newlyweds can leave is the war that must be fought with the king of Agori and his numerous Kshatriya allies. This is a righteous war fought by Lorik and his enormous army and, ultimately, an emancipatory one as the oppressive king is killed. The episode ends with the newlyweds and the entire marriage party moving to Gaura. A second marriage is celebrated shortly after, that of Lorik's elder brother to Satiya, the daughter of a Kshatriya king.

The central character in the next episode is Chanaini, the daughter of the Ahir king of Gaura, Lorik's native village, and the woman who attempted to divert Lorik's marriage proposal to her own brother. In this episode, Chanaini shows even more pluck and resilience as she manages to escape from her impotent husband. Traveling alone, she is pursued by Bathwa, a lower-caste Chamar, who attempts to seduce her. After she rejects his advances, the wily Chamar then attempts to terrorize all the inhabitants of her village by polluting the village wells. Lorik is summoned to fight Bathwa and defeats and kills him, but he is filled with remorse when he discovers that Bathwa was his *gurubhaī* as they shared the same guru at their akharā. The episode raises interesting questions about the ability of akharā affiliation to transcend caste rigidities.

Chanaini is now desperate to meet Lorik, and her chance soon comes at a banquet her father hosts and to which he invites all Yadavas.[7] The seduction of Chanaini by Lorik is a fascinating tale involving the construction of a sturdy rope by which Lorik gains entry into her chamber, Manjari's eventual discovery of the clandestine affair, and the circumstances surrounding Chanaini and Lorik's elopement. The lovers escape to far-off lands and have innumerable adventures on the way. Manjari, Lorik's chaste wife, forgotten and abandoned by her husband, falls on hard times. This episode offers a tantalizing glimpse of the agency of women. The episodes that narrate the elopement and the couple's flight from Gaura offer a robust, entertaining tale in which the hero and the heroine are well matched.

In the last section of the ballad, Lorik learns that the Kols, the Chandals, the Turks of Gajangarh, and the people of Paranpur have mounted a four-pronged attack on Gaura and made off with his family's cattle and wealth, after killing Lorik's brother. Saddened, Lorik returns to Gaura and reunites with the now impoverished Manjari. In the final episodes of the ballad, Lorik's mother and wife, robbed of their cattle, are reduced to selling yoghurt in the bazaar. In the last episode, Lorik commits suicide, and while there is no victory or kingdom to be won, Lorik's dignity and honor are restored. In the section below, we sidestep several of the epic's important themes and issues to focus on what it might have to teach about marriage. In subsequent sections, I tease out the significance of sociological elements and motifs relating to the construction of gender by caste patriarchies.

The genius of the folk epic lies in its operation as a prototype for contemporary marriage celebrations in north India. Upwardly mobile groups appear to model their marriages after the one laid out in the ballad. The destabilization of power between opposing groups, which is at the heart of all north Indian marriages, is a significant insight that emerges from the opening sections of the gathā. We learn about the struggles and strategies wife givers and wife takers use to achieve a state of equilibrium between their parties, given the powerful shift in the usual status of these groups that has transpired. In the ballad, once the groups have collectively agreed to the marriage, profound shifts begin to occur in the physical and social universe, shifts that require immediate resolution through the deployment of a range of resources, both economic and noneconomic—for example, wealth, clan, caste, and village support—as well as other virtues such as physical strength, fearlessness, and intangibles such as wisdom, wit, and the ability to make decisions. It would appear that marriage provides the singular occasion to test the strength of the economic, social, and cultural capital of each member of the two groups arrayed against each other in the transaction. The orchestrated way in which the destabilizing as well as the constructive aspects of marriage are worked out and resolved in the folk imaginary call for layered understandings of this rite of passage.

It is necessary, here, to revisit the precise moment—in the chain of events from which the symbolic significance of the action may be inferred—that Lorik accepts the proposal of marriage to Manjari, brought to him by the barber and Brahmin from the bride's natal home in Agori. To complicate matters, there are other contenders for the groom's hand, lacing the situation with heartache and conflict from the very start. Lorik turns down each of these proposals. In retaliation, the rejected parties, in this case the powerful king Sehdev of Lorik's own village, who had offered Lorik his daughter's hand, prevents Lorik's barat from leaving the village to solemnize the wedding. Lorik rightly laments, "we've only begun and here is the first hurdle." But in the epic as in life, every restriction is ultimately an opportunity to be seized headlong, and in this as in others of such magnitude, we find Lorik's father literally rising to the occasion with a leap and declaring, "now you have a chance to see my masculinity."

The barāt, comprising savā lākh members, is like an army charging into battle that "runs by day and walks by night." After two days of grueling struggle, they rest, staking out, it would seem, territories of support as well as planning their subjugation of resisting kings. On reaching the territory of a powerful king, the groom's father, Kathait, devises a strategy calculated to disrupt and provoke fear in the local populace and stir in the local ruling king speculation about the comparative strength and power of this unknown visiting army. The motif of the Ahirs/Yadavas challenging Kshatriya dominance is introduced here. Faced with his next hurdle, the groom prepares for battle with his "electrifying" sword while the king aims his arrows. In a series of dazzling sword fights, the hero cuts down the enemy like "peasants threshing wheat," the barāt (army) moves on to its next challenge: crossing the Son River, on whose banks the enemy forces are positioned to prevent their passing into Agori. A friendly boatman of the Mallah caste (one of the many lower castes who prove worthy allies) defies his orders and ferries the army across the river while Kathait, the groom's aged father, demonstrates his agility and masculinity yet again by rowing himself across.

On arriving in Agori, the barāt is met by the bride's mother's brother who plays an excellent go-between, carrying messages between the groom and the bride with great efficiency. The first message he delivers is an inquiry from the bride's mother about where the party is to set up camp. Now comes the moment for the bride's mother to show her power, and she does so by suggesting they camp in a thorny field filled with overgrown vegetation. Far from the subservience one would expect from the bride's mother in contemporary times, here in the folk imaginary we find a stunning example of an ingenious and powerful shrew who takes every opportunity to humble her opponents, the bride-takers, daring them to beat a retreat should they find themselves outwitted by the challenges she hurls their way. What ensues next is a battle of wits, rather like a chess game in which each move is undercut by a countermove. When offered the thorny field, for instance, the groom's inveterate father slashes away the thorny growth, clearing the field in no time.

The battle of wits continues as the bride's mother then sends the barāt a ration large enough to feed an army, with the condition that not a grain of rice must be left behind. The bride-takers eat what they can and dump the remaining provisions into the Son River, evoking the conspicuous consumption of today's wedding celebrations. The bride's mother then sends her daughter's future father-in-law some chaff with which to fashion a rope, which proves to be a key prop in her next elaborate bid to embarrass the groom's party, but Kathait counters this request by demanding an inverted sieve with which hold the water for moistening the rope. These highly symbolic games continue long after the marriage ritual has been completed. Among these games is the groom's mother's fashioning of a golden water goblet for the barāt—a goblet she then orders stolen with a view to causing uproar among the guests. How the hero and his brother, disguised as yogis who carrying on a symbolic conversation with the galaxies, cross even this hurdle constitutes another layer of this fantastic tale.

These episodes highlight the ingenuity of women and their own battles for power. From the start, the epic celebrates the strength and ingeniousness of women and their demonstrations of power, much of which would likely remain unknown, were it not for such ballads. Even the minor female characters in the ballad of Lorik are towers of strength, imaginative and enterprising and ready to challenge the male order. For instance, the series of traps that the bride's mother lays to embarrass Lorik's marriage party are devices through which she conducts an elaborate symbolic conversation with the groom's father, who rises to meet all the challenges and contests she throws his way, with great aplomb. That the bride's mother is the initiator of these mind games is itself remarkable; that she is also the one who judges their handling of these challenges raises interesting questions about gender expectations among peasants.

Āju bhāi dhani dhani na paniyāh, paun tīrath kai
Jehavān k hovai maradvā ba budhī re mān
Āju bhāi bār bār na argar hamre dālī
Samadhiy kātiya karat bārein khay re kār
Ohi din sunah re haliyā Kathait ke
Bolt banāh laramvāh, kai re boleu
Āju bhāi bār bār aygarvā je samdhi dālen
Kāti keni hamhyun na kailīn khay re kāur

The bride's mother said, "Glory to the waters of that sacred land
Where the men are so intelligent.
Ever so many obstacles and riddles I laid out,
Yet the groom's father found solutions to all."
Now listen to what happened next with Kathait.

He said, "Grave and important problems were raised by the bride's mother
And now I have a riddle of my own for you."
PANDEY 1987, 60

Lorik's father, displaying ready wit, presence of mind, and foresight, is
able to skillfully outwit the bride's mother and emerges victorious on
behalf of the marriage party. The episodes, like knots or riddles that must
be untied before transformations can occur, serve as hurdles the party
must overcome before it can move on to the next stage (see Hasan-Rokem
and Shulman 1996). Just as Yudhishthira, at the end of the Mahabharata
war, was called upon to answer Yama's questions, the bridegroom's party
is subjected to tests of wit before the prize, the bride Manjari, can be
claimed. Handelman, describing these ritual games as "Traps of Transformation," has highlighted the ritual aspect of these exchanges at rites of
passage, their purpose being to effect changes and transformations in the
results by introducing paradoxes into the predictable course of action
(Handelman 1996, 37–61).

These episodes resonate with insights into marriage transactions; the
heightened sense of rivalry between and solidarity within groups the
marriage context engenders; and the need to manage the potential conflicts and conflagrations that the close proximity of, and extended period
of interactions between, the two rival groups might engender. We see
that, as in warfare, both sides must be as well matched as the couple
entering into matrimony. This insight is significant, owing precisely to
the nature of the interactions. The ballad details these exchanges with a
precision reminiscent of a cricket match commentary.

The sense of spectacle, theatrics, and high drama culminates in the
bride's seemingly bizarre, last-minute requests, which the members of her
natal clan must fulfill before she condescends to mount the bridal carriage
and depart for the groom's home. This moment in the proceedings appears
to be a potentially rich one for the bride, who can demand the fulfillment of
otherwise impossible requests. It is the bride who, at this moment, strongly
demands her dowry. If this scene is representative of ongoing traditions,
then the sanction and legitimacy that the bride's demands appear to
receive raises questions about women's rights to the wealth and property
of their natal homes, a right they would have had to forgo, especially if
their marital homes were geographically far from their natal ones.

We know from the sociology of upper-caste marriage networks that the logic behind arranging upper-caste marriages between geographically distant households was in part aimed at thwarting any claims outmarrying brides might have over their natal property (Jassal 2001; Berreman 1993). Lorik's brother explains this convention using a simpler logic.

Aju bhāi karab bibahvā na hamare gaunvā
Dinvāh din kai hoi re kal re kaunau
Kaunau gharī khātire āpdhva hoī re jaiheun
Selahiya dhāngai duarvā re hamāur
Ohi din marab bhuvanvā je hoi re jaiheun

I shall not marry within the village,
For any day, on some pretext or other,
At any time, should a misunderstanding occur,
My mother-in-law might cross over my threshold,
And that would spell doom in my own home.

PANDEY 1987, 34

It is interesting that the Lorikāyan, a folk text concerned with the aspirations of upwardly mobile groups seeking affirmation of the Kshatriya lifestyle, emphasizes the enormity of this distance by asserting that it took the marriage party three months and nine days to cover the distance between the bride's natal and marital homes.[8]

Biti gayal tīniya mahinvah, ter re rojai
Teserke ailī na handaiyā, re pahunci
Ohi ghari nauāh babhanvān je bel re vai kai
Cauk cannan na thikvāh, hoi re gainau

When three months and thirteen days had passed,
On the thirteenth day, the wedding palanquin returned.
At that moment, the Barber and Brahmin were sent for,
And the courtyard anointed and cleaned.

PANDEY 1987, 34

While this description evokes the metaphor of the battle and the return of the victorious army with its spoils, it also subtly draws attention to another fact asserted at different points in the text, namely, the unlikelihood that the bridal couple will ever return to the bride's natal home.

In chapter 3 and elsewhere, I have explored the implications of this sever-ance from the bride's natal homes in terms of its implications for women's land rights (Jassal 2001, 22–25).

In his analysis of martial epics, David Shulman provides a highly abstract but convincing argument about the "battlefield [as] an arena in which life is dissolved back into the chaos from which it emerged. The battle also reproduces the originally agonistic structure of the sacrifice as a contest in which two parties vie for the life won from death" (Shulman 1986, 124). Shulman develops the twin ideas of marriage as sacrifice and of battle as marriage based on Tamil myths. He points out, "Again, there is a creative side to the destruction wrought in both these forums: the chaotic forces released in sexual union, on the one hand, and in battle, on the other, ultimately serve to replenish and sustain the ever-vulnerable forces of life" (Shulman 1986, 124).

If indeed, as Shulman so persuasively suggests, the disorder of the battlefield is a metaphor for life, the battle itself represents the oppor-tunity to restore order to chaos and to secure the triumph of virtue, purity, limitation, and control (124). In the wars Lorik fought, the central drive appears to be the will to assert the new reality of Yadava supremacy over the prevailing Kshatriya dominant order. While the success of the wars Lorik fights in terms of achieving these aims is inconclusive, the search for order, control, and limitation emerge conclusively as goals. For instance, it is possible to argue that through Lorik's marriage to Manjari, who personifies upper-caste values, the ballad seeks to reconcile the re-leased chaotic energies and harness them in the service of greater pa-triarchal order, restriction, and control. Also, Lorik's own death, staged as an act of sacrifice, suggests transformation and renewal.

As I pointed out above, and perhaps reflective of the nature of medi-eval wars, an extraordinary feature of Lorik's biography is that mar-riages become the pretext as well as the occasion and site for the conduct of warfare in the interests of caste mobility. The groom's marriage prepa-rations and *barāt* processions resemble those of armies marching into war, and, invariably, the marriage sites are transformed into battle-fields complete with bloodshed, the clash of steel, and the separation of the victors from the vanquished. The ballad confirms D. D. Kosambi's observation that women and wealth were the two main causes of war (Kosambi 1975).

However, in the context of the ballad, another reason acquires equal validity. By defeating the ruling dynasties, the Yadavas, under the direction of Lorik, subjugate and lay claim to the kingdoms of the wife-givers, thus re-enacting an original sociological truth—the *anuloma* axiom that wife-takers are superior to wife-givers. According to this rule, daughters must marry up, and, since in this case the wife-takers are of a lower caste than the wife-givers, it is possible to restore social equilibrium only by vanquishing the bride's people. Hence, the superiority of the wife-takers can only be demonstrated in battle and can only be established by winning that battle. The structural inequality between wife-givers and wife-takers thus provides a convenient rationale for the ensuing warfare, though the text also provides a host of other more convincing reasons. Victory in such wars, then, serves as the means for a group to assert and proclaim its status as well as to establish alternate centers of rule. If a group's claim to rulership had to be preceded by its earning the right to claim kshatriya status, then proof of victory through war might have been only the first step in that direction.

WOMEN'S AGENCY IN A MALE BALLAD

The extraordinary illustration of women's agency in the opening chapters of the ballad, namely, the young Manjari's announcement of the name of the person she has decided to marry and her undertaking of a hunger strike to underscore her decision, elevates personal action to the realm of the political. This politicization derives from the fact that, although her insistence is based on a metaphysical revelation, the husband she is demanding to take in marriage has been incarnated as the savior of the entire caste. In today's rural context, where scarcely any young women have even the remotest say in this matter, this lends a fantastic element to the ballad and also parallels Sita's *svayamvar* (self-decision in marriage).[9] The feminine power whose ubiquitous and significant presence easily identifies this ballad as a warrior epic is the power of Durga, which, used in the service of male warriors, "ironically denies to women the very sense of embodied power that the male ideology asserts they possess" (Caldwell 1999, 31).

The resourcefulness of the bride's mother is another example of female power. Yet another is Chanaini's flight from her impotent husband. As she approaches the forest near her natal home, she encounters Bathwa Chamar, who tries to seduce her. Her response is to evoke her chastity, through which she hoodwinks the Chamar and escapes. At the expiatory feast given by her father, Chanaini, also referred to as Chanva or Chanda, flirts with Lorik, initiating a clandestine affair that eventually becomes public, and the two plan to elope.

Jharokhvā se Canvāh ankariyāh bāi re phenkat
Ahirā ke girtī patilvāh par re banī
Jauno dhari lotāh na leikahu, bir re Lorikāh
Sojhai piyat Caniyāh, re nirikhī
Canvāh kholi kai ancharvāh, bai dekhāvat
Ahire ke carhal na citvāh, bai re jāteu

From the window, Chanva threw pebbles
That landed on the Ahir's leaf-dish.
While he drank from his water-pot, the brave Lorik
Gazed at her nonstop.
Chanva was slowly unveiling herself.
She was entering into the Ahir's heart.

PANDEY 1987, 251

The ballad struggles to reconcile the willful, enterprising character of Chanaini, who is prone to breaking societal rules, with the demands of caste patriarchy in which women are not only strictly controlled by men but also wholly lack spunk or sexual initiative, except to demonstrate their chastity. Meanwhile, Manjari, owing to her extraordinary and exemplary quality of sat, the form of women's chastity that holds the husband as divine and worthy of worship, has a premonition of the impending elopement, but is unable to prevent the elopers from setting off for the town of Hardi. On the way, Lorik has other minor adventures and battles but the lovers finally settle in Hardi, where the hero rises to the position of a "Raja."

Since women's agency might be perceived as potentially disruptive to the social order, it comes as no surprise that at different points in the narrative we encounter various references to women's agency and the need to fear, denigrate, channel, and control it. The incestuous nature of the relationship between Lorik and Chanaini is also hinted at, given they are from the same village and their relationship is therefore a prohibited one, which provides another rationale for their elopement. Throughout the ballad, Chanaini's wayward ways are also occasionally seen as spelling havoc for the societal order. As the couple is eloping, even the trees pass judgment.

Avarāh pharal na pervā je dekh re bāy
Aju kahen beseh na jatiyā je hau Canaini.Bessā havvāh sakhārav je pali re vāur,
Ihe bhai biyahā na bijri me chori re dehlen
Urharī leiaku Hardiya je bāi re jāt,
Âj pheri bolal avara je puni re bāi
Ohi din bol na besva je ba Canaini
Saiyyāh manbāh, kahanvāh re hamārAwarāh ke debāh, na jariyā tu dahli re āi
Ohi din bolal Ahirvā ba bir re Lorika,Āju kāhaen sunbeh n dhanvā je tū biyahaiyā
Deh deh toi jhagarvā re chali macāval, kaha lahan Lorikah gaihei na tar revāri

The avla tree was flowering.
The tree said, "Chanaini is by caste a Vaishya, her entire clan is of Vaishyas.
She has left her wedded husband.
With the man of another, she is on her way to Hardi."
The tree again repeated these words.
Vaishya Chanaini said to Lorik,
"Listen to me love, take out your sharp sword and strike that tree to the
  ground."
Brave Lorik chided, "Dear, you go about picking quarrels on the wayside.
Why should Lorik have to pick up his sword again and again?"
PANDEY 1987, 285

It is possible that in the attempt to establish full-bodied marital traditions, caste mores that were less restrictive for women were denounced, which also contributed to the attempts to control women's inherently disruptive tendencies in judgments such as those voiced by the Awla tree in the above lines. Further, in accordance with upper-caste patriarchies, it is the women who must be controlled in order to assert a high status. Toward the end, Chanaini emerges as an example of the havoc that can be let loose in society when women have the freedom of choice or the ability to voice their own preferences, especially in the realm of marriage and the choice of marriage partners.

As the character of Chanaini embodies the relative freedom available to women of her background and their lack of dependence on the male order, the ballad cannot refrain comment, lest it seem to endorse women's freedom of choice. From time to time, the text appears to manage and control the threat to the patriarchal social order suggested by the freedoms Chanaini represents. Further, as Flueckiger points out, elopement implies a freedom of choice for both individuals, made on the basis of their personal feelings. And since such freedom threatens both caste endogamy and the maintenance of strict caste boundaries, it also threatens the idea of the social control of women that is to follow in later episodes (Flueckiger 1989a, 46).

Chanaini's wholly earthy, unpredictable, fun-loving, and erotic persona serves, in the ballad, as a good match for the hero and as a foil to Manjari's controlled, long-suffering one. For instance, she is the first to intercept Manjari's marriage proposal to Lorik and bring it to her own brother. In addition, apart from her exercise of agency in escaping a problematic marriage, Chanaini, keeping herself well hidden, attempts to catch the attention of the hero by throwing pebbles at him during a banquet. Ever watchful, she also intervenes just in time to save Lorik from mistakenly consuming poison. She scarcely forgoes an opportunity to tease, even in seemingly tense moments such as when the hero is clandestinely poised to climb the rope to her chamber. By playfully refusing to catch the rope he throws up, she risks embarrassing and exposing him. Likewise, during the tense moments leading up to the lovers' point of rendezvous before their elopement, she heightens the sense of expectation and adventure by hiding behind a tree and prolonging the hero's anxiety, emerging from her hideout only when Lorik is on the verge of giving up and turning back. She also confronts Manjari in the bazaar, where after picking a fight with her, she settles down to eat some greens, recovers her strength, dusts herself off, and then heads home.

In striking relief are Chanaini's ingenuity, resourcefulness, and capacity to adequately protect herself. However, as pointed out above, practical commonsense is no match for the virtue of chastity in terms of serving the interests of patriarchy. The ballad also presents another alternate femininity in addition to the intermediate-caste persona of Chanaini. The very Manjari who, we are told, changes her apparel many times a day, is now dressed in tatters.

Ab parī gailī bipaityā Manjari ke
Ohi jau nagar Gaurva lei re gānvau
Ab kahain javāni Majariya cal re khete
Ghantāh ghantāh kaparvā re badauli
Dhiyavā ke aiseya bipatiya pari re gaileen
Uhnva bhayal na dasiyā re harāmau
Tab kahahin dhurvā na dhurvā ka dekh re lattā
Jori jori paharati pevanvāh, dhan re bāy

Now such misfortune struck Manjari
In village Gaura;
Where once that Manjari had walked the fields,
Changing her clothes hour by hour,
Such misfortune struck the wife,
Such was her state,
That the clothes she wore were tattered and torn.
She darned and wore them, did the wife.

PANDEY 1987, 324

Manjari and her friends, not knowing that Lorik has returned, go to sell yoghurt at a bazaar Lorik has set up outside Gaura's city walls. However, the river is too high for them to cross to reach the site. Manjari then appeals to the river to part, and the river miraculously obeys, owing to Manjari's *sat*—once again, her penance and vows of austerity.

Javan bahiā sattai dharamvā je bāncal hoihen
Ā phuni hoi jāh na nadiyā aihi re pārau
Ohi din pargat durugvā je hoi gailīn
Bīceh deileni na dalvāh dūi kankarī
Āju banhi gayal na dharāv je dunon ballī, bīceh radki kankalī na may re dān
Ab chali gali na Bohva je dhani Majariya

If sat and righteousness still flow within me,
Then may I cross the river to the other side.
That moment Durga appeared.
She erected two sets of stones.
On either side the flow of the river came to a halt.
Manjari crossed over to Boha with her basket.

PANDEY 1987, 348

This episode is preceded by one in which Manjari must prove to her mother-in-law, and lay to rest all suspicions, that her seemingly sudden wealth was not ill gotten. To prove that she did not obtain the wealth in her basket through unchaste, illicit means, Manjari is called upon to take the test of chastity, which involves putting her hand into a heated vat. These episodes evoke the numerous examples of the sati and Sita motifs featured in women's songs, particularly those examined in chapters 1 and 4.

Jo ham aikei na bapvā se hob na bitiyā
Ke pher aikei purusvā bai re yārei
Jab okre satei dharamvā par re hobai
Pher carhi lebei rupiyā ho nikāli
Ohi dhari dālai hathavā dhan Majariya
Kari bani rupiyā eik re tohi
Onkeu tanih na dagiyā nahin re lāgal
Sabkani gayal re manvā re baith

If I am that worthy daughter of that father
And chaste, known only to one man.
If sat and righteousness are within me,
Then I shall take out the coins from the fire.
Then she put her hand in, that great Manjari.
She felt the rupiya with her hand.
Not a stain was on her hand.
Everyone's heart was deflated.

PANDEY 1987B, 347

Scarcely is this episode over that Manjari, believing Lorik is dead, prepares a funeral pyre to commit sati. From a distance, Lorik and Chanaini, in disguise, watch paralyzed by growing disbelief. The scene forces Chanaini to reflect for the first time on her own position as the other woman, the eloper. Just as Lorik has reason to regret his actions, this scene provides Chanaini with an opportunity to reflect.

Ā jekri biyahiyā je janghvā ke jarlī
Ā keke tanikav daradiyā je nāhi re bāye
Āju bhāi orhi orhariyā ke kavan re gintī
Haman kelieye pachtavā je deib re bai

Uhvan se dankal ahirvā je bir re Lorikva
Jiakeni cecur dhailvā je dekh re bai
Manjari ke dhaike ceculvā ja khince re lehlen
Thokare se marlini na agiyā je gai cchitarāi

The one whose wedded wife is burning,
He feels not the slightest pain or remorse.
Then why would he value the one he eloped with?
For me, why should he care?
But lo, from there leapt the Ahir, the brave Lorik,
Caught the wrist of Manjari
And holding her thus dragged her away.
Kicked the pyre and scattered the fire.

PANDEY 1987B, 351

Despite the fact that Manjari is saved so valiantly by the brave Lorik and thereby spared from death, her attempted sati elevates her status and, by association, that of her entire caste. By thus enacting an upper-caste Kshatriya norm, Manjari not only reminds us of the restrictive practices that constitute upper-caste women's identities but also fulfills the aspirations of the entire caste. As Yadavas claim the epic, the women of the caste adopt Manjari's actions as their own code of behavior, perfectly in line with Kshatriya norms.

The relative ease with which Manjari subjects herself to not one but a series of trials in quick succession underline her elevated divine status, thus lending luster not only to her caste but also to the hero Lorik, who, by saving her, has the opportunity to once again act heroically. It seems to matter little that Lorik had abandoned Manjari; what is underlined here is his return. In keeping with the requirements of patriarchy, it is the hero who must be convinced of his wife's chastity before he decides to return, never mind that by then he is on to his third wife. Indeed, as "for a married woman, this power derives from her faithfulness to her husband, and, hence, in part from male control and protection" (Fleuckiger 1989a, 44–48), Manjari's quality of sat refers back to and glorifies the heroism of the hero who controls her.

In the end it is Manjari's particular brand of sat and chastity that somehow saves the day, assuring the return of the chastened hero, marked by due remorse and regret. But it is the other woman, the eloper (*uraharī*)

Chanaini, who must take the blame. Hence, despite her being so irresistible to the hero, when hard days come round, it is only the lowest status and condemnation that is reserved for her. In denigrating Chanaini and her insistence that he leave Gaura without considering the needs of his caste brethren, Lorik is able to place his misfortunes squarely and conveniently at the doorstep of the other woman. The very agency of women like Chanaini, who can be branded as elopers and thus of easy virtue, serves to absolve the hero of excess blame.[10] Freedom, agency, and uncontrolled action here represent danger and deserve only condemnation in women, even as they are celebrated and extolled as virtues in the hero.

Toward the end of the ballad, the women's agency we observed in the opening episodes—with the young Manjari demanding to be married to none other than Lorik and with the robust character and escapades of Manjari's mother and then Chanaini—dissipates into familiar patterns of conformity to strict upper-caste norms and standards of behavior. The promise of women's agency as embodied by Manjari dwindles to dependence and conformity, and instead it is her chastity and sat, loosely defined as the "truth of one's being," that is valorized. In the last episodes of the ballad, we witness the valorization of the passive instead of the active woman, as well as a shift from endorsement of defiance, as represented by Chanaini and even Manjari's mother, to the more compliant traits represented by Manjari.

Since in the early sections we are afforded insights into a universe of extraordinary gender parity, it is disconcerting to find that toward the end of the ballad the feminine strength that is valorized is of a qualitatively different kind, deriving from the quality of sat or chastity. This is the chaste wife that has been described as "an empowered figure in (Hindu) myth who functions as a means of taming or domesticating the more fearful aspects of woman's sexual appetite" (John and Nair 1998, 17). However, the Lorikāyan's genius lies in its willingness to both explore and absorb the polarities represented by the two female characters, Manjari and Chanaini. Finally, by showing how the characters perceive the world and their places within it, the ballad raises questions about its social milieu. The concepts, values, and problems the ballad addresses are significant, since they not only refer back to the social milieu that gave rise to them but also anticipate contemporary trends in north India.

LORIKĀYAN AND YADAVA MOBILITY

In contextualizing the epic within a specific historical and sociocultural milieu, we see that the Lorikāyan serves as important source material for the values and concerns the Yadava caste has about upward mobility. To what extent, then, is it possible to connect the singing of the Lorikāyan, on the one hand, and documentary evidence of Yadava values and efforts to achieve social mobility over the course of the last century, on the other? If the nineteenth century was characterized by efforts of various castes occupying the middle rungs of the caste order to achieve social mobility, to what extent were the values the ballad projects, especially those regarding women, actively endorsed by pastoral and cattleherding castes of the Shudra varna who claimed Kshatriya status and sought to adopt Kshatriya practices? While it has not yet been possible to establish the exact relation between a particular group's singing and claiming of the ballad and their social practices, do the ballad's motifs nevertheless suggest a blueprint for action and practice? In this section, I seek answers to some of these puzzles in the contemporary social history of the Yadavas.

It is worth beginning this attempt to locate the ballad within the society that produced it with a note by the nineteenth-century colonial administrator, Colonel Oldham, who described the "martial races" of the Bhojpuri region, particularly the Bhojpuri Ahir caste, as "predisposed" to turbulence. Oldham writes:

The Bhojpuri Ahirs (the cowherd caste) are specially noted for their daring and skill as thieves and burglars, the more law-abiding people in other parts regarding them with terror. . . . During widespread disturbances in 1917, which broke out without previous warning in the district, and threatened to involve the neighboring districts in grave communal strife, I had to call in a large force of military and armed police (about a thousand in all) to quell promptly and effectively the lawlessness abroad.

Raheja quotes Oldham:

Several proverbial sayings might be cited as exemplifying these characteristics. For instance, there are some very popular verses in praise of their favorite weapon, commonly called the "Song of the lathi," telling of its uses in crossing a stream or a ditch, in dealing with human or canine enemies, and how necessary it is to carry one, even if you have a sword hanging by your side. There is a well-known proverb that says, "Don't go into Bhojpur; if you go, don't stay; if you stay, don't eat; if you eat, don't go to sleep; if you sleep, don't feel for your purse; if you should feel for your purse, don't weep!" (i.e., you will not find it!). . . . Then we have a proverb that means, "if hit, hit back and don't stop to consider whether you are committing a sin or virtue." And there is a delightfully terse and suggestive saying, especially quoted of the Bhojpuri as representing his attitude toward others. The words mean simply "is the dish thine or mine?" A Bhojpuri is supposed to ask this question. If the person addressed answers, "Mine," a blow of the lathi at once settles the proprietorship, the clenched fist for an enemy; "the powerful man's lathi hits the very middle of the forehead," and so on. So much for the mere joy of fighting. (1930, 323–24, quoted in Raheja 1996, 502)

In these ways, the colonial state appears to have naturalized the Yadavas' rebellious spirit. The communal strife referred to above appears to have been a consequence of the severe dislocation of social and economic relations of colonialism and a move on the part of the caste to secure higher status in the 1901 census by asserting Hindu orthodoxy. What is left out of Oldham's account is the organized struggle against colonial government, zamindars and moneylenders. In other words, Oldham seems to be providing a justification to quell the "naturally" violent caste instead of the revenue demands that prompted the unrest in the first place (ibid). Raheja explains that people's own proverbial speech was deployed to essentialize caste characteristics, and to reinforce notions about the necessity of colonial rule, in turn providing the foundation for much of the anthropological and historical understandings of the region. The extent to which a ballad such as the Lorikāyan would have served to reinforce these very notions, is an important question that needs further investigation.

While the ballad's motif of the resemblance between marriage and warfare immediately springs to mind, evidence suggests that the colonial state naturalized the Yadavas' rebellious and martial spirit in diverse ways. Gloria Goodwin Raheja has shown that from the second half of the nineteenth century onward, "proverbs were repeatedly wrenched from the social practices in which they figured, and interpreted not as situated commentaries but as abstract and literal renderings of caste proclivities" (Raheja 1996, 508). If, as Raheja explains, the Yadavas' proverbial speech was deployed to essentialize characteristics of the caste and to reinforce notions about the necessity of colonial rule, then, like so many proverbs about the Yadavas, the Lorikāyan appears to have provided abundant source material for the colonial construction of caste. Hence, popular ballads are likely to have provided ballast for much of the prevailing anthropological and historical understandings of the region. However, as colonial accounts were always selective, it pays to attend to what they leave out, in this case, the abundant evidence the Lorikāyan presents about caste parity in the middle reaches of the caste order.

The historical evidence on the colonial period suggests that in emulating Kshatriya practices and claiming Kshatriyahood as Yadava Kshatriyas, Yadavas faced considerable opposition and conflict with upper castes through the 1920s. Their efforts to claim Kshatriyahood have been documented in numerous accounts (Pinch 1996, 111; Frankel 1989). We learn, for instance, that Yadava caste reformers were attempting to reconfigure an upper-caste patriarchical vocabulary within the new grid of hierarchical norms and possibilities that the colonial context offered. By the 1920s, caste *sabhās* (councils), which persistently pressed for caste claims to higher status, had emerged. These caste councils focused on social reform and on developing political agendas to organize caste members to assert the caste's economic and political demands. Caste members' involvement with processes of redefining community equipped them with a new language of politics. Here were sown the seeds for what came to be known in the postcolonial era as identity politics.

In the nineteenth century, the Yadava movement emerged as an extremely successful response to the opportunities the census provided to upgrade caste status. The Yadava movement had a wide inter-regional spread and attempted to merge regional caste identities, such as those represented by the Goala, Ahir, Ahar, Gopa, and so on, in favor of the generic term *Yadava* (Rao 1979). Thus a number of pastoral castes were subsumed under the Yadava category in accordance with decisions made by caste councils at the regional and national levels. The Yadava caste, comprising a number of subcastes known locally by various names, became the first among shudras to gain the right to wear the *janeu* (the sacred thread), a case of successful Sanskritization that continues. The success of the Yadava movement also lies in the fact that among the *jati sabhās*, the Yadava sabhā was likely the strongest and its journal, *Ahir*

Samachar, acquired a national spread. As an epic claimed by the Yadavas, then, it is worth exploring the extent to which the Lorikāyan played a role in this reimagination.

Certain themes suggest themselves for further inquiry. For instance, E. A. Gait, the census commissioner, noted as early as 1911 that "the Goalas of Bihar have resolved inter alia to give up infant marriage and to prevent their women from selling milk or going to market" (Gait 1913, 392). As outlined in the preceding pages, the Lorikāyan associates declining fortunes with women's peddling of milk products in the marketplace, a practice seen as humiliating for the entire caste. By the nineteenth century, among those practices recognized as markers of lower status were the sale of milk and cowdung cakes by women, and upwardly mobile Yadava women were debarred from frequenting bazaars (*hāts* and *ganjs*). Similarly, attempts were made to curb women's productive labor in the fields. The injunction against women working in the fields stemmed from the assumption that the women of cultivating castes who labored were liable to be exploited or abused. Such vulnerability was seen as making laboring women less chaste than upper-caste ones.

Caste patriarchies considered women in general to be unsafe in public spaces, a fear fuelled by the engineering of a horror of fairs. In the north Indian rural context, village fairs or *melās* have always been associated with legends, saints, pilgrimages, and festivals. Particularly for women and irrespective of caste, fairs were occasions for periodic, seasonal recreation and leisure. From the nineteenth century onward, however, a number of tracts appeared suggesting that danger lurked in fairs, where women might easily be molested or abducted (Gupta 2001, 96). A tract popular in the nineteenth century, *Melā Ghumnī*, went so far as to suggest that women who visited fairs were "prostitutes and sensuous creatures with no qualms or morals" (96). By devaluing women's forms of entertainment and cultural expression, reformers sought to reorder culture and leisure while also achieving respectability for certain castes.

Further, in the eighteenth and nineteenth centuries, marketplaces such as hāt (a local periodic market), *bajār* (a permanent market for general merchandise), and ganj (the wholesale market for bulk goods) "were seen as central knot(s) in the social fabric, closely tied to both political, economic and religious interests" (Urban 2001, 1086). At this time, the marketplace served as a microcosm for the world of power as a whole, since the material, religious, and social exchanges that occurred there were inextricably intertwined. Marketplaces that began by selling ritual commodities attached to religious or sacred sites were often supported by political establishments and came to signify both political authority and material clout. These spaces were a "metaphor for the worldly authority of the ruling elite" (1088). It is in this capacity that the caste reformers' prohibitions against upwardly mobile women trading in marketplaces tie in with the restrictive norms for women outlined in the later sections of the Lorikāyan.

Moreover, as the marketplace also functioned as a potential space for the subversion and critique of the dominant order (Urban 2001, 1088), this particular restriction on Yadava women would also have implied a lack of freedom to speak frankly and critically. And all the more so, since, as Bakhtin has argued, performances in the marketplace rendered these spaces potentially threatening to the ruling powers, especially since the lower classes could express themselves openly there and circulate subversive discourses among themselves (Bakhtin quoted in Urban 2001).

Furthermore, since the songs and plays composed and performed by women were largely popular events that took place out in the open in streets, marketplaces, fairs, and festivals, the "moral police" of caste patriarchies stepped up their campaign against these forms of female expression as well (Banerjee 1989, 157). Given the growing ominous and even subversive connotations that circulated around marketplaces and periodic fairs of all kinds, it appeared in the nineteenth century that women, as custodians of the honor and purity of entire caste groups, would need to be protected from such spaces. The reformers' anxiety about the women's folksongs addressed in chapter 1 of this volume thus went hand in hand with the alarm about women's use of public spaces and the campaign to restrict their access to them in the interest of protecting them.

In addition to drawing on proverbs and ballads to construct its understanding of Yadavas, the colonial state likely drew on, and fuelled its anxieties with, the Lorikāyan, particularly the ballad's representation of wedding celebrations, a central concern of this book. The colonial state's concerns about the upper castes phenomenal expenditure on wedding celebrations, a practice common among the Kshatriyas and other landed groups, dovetails with the Lorikāyan's themes. If colonial anxieties indeed originated, at least in part, in the people's own oral texts, then it is conceivable that the colonial state drew much of their understanding of, and anxiety about, wedding celebrations from the Lorikāyan.

Again, it is not possible to directly relate the singing of the Lorikāyan to the actual evidence of conspicuous consumption observed among upwardly mobile peasant castes in the nineteenth century. However, the archival evidence points to the immense anxiety this consumption generated within the colonial state, which was concerned that its own revenue demands might not be met. These revenue concerns alarmed the colonial state and prompted its concerted moves to curb such consumption among the landed gentry, among whom excessive expenditure at weddings was the norm. In the twelve districts of Awadh, for instance, the British India Association (BIA) appears to have persuaded the local ruling elites to put these curbs into effect. The following excerpt from a letter on the subject, written by the Secretary of the BIA to Chief Commissioner Oudh on 25 March 1963, spells out the logic behind the intervention: "It is astonishing that taluqdars should consider the fame and dignity of their houses prompted by a prodigality that must bring ruin to them. Another such celebration of marriage as has just taken place at Dera will be the ruin of that noble and loyal family, an event that would cause the government deep regret. The example set by the taluqdars is imitated by their humbler Kurmies, small proprietors driven to mortgage and sell their properties to provide funds for a marriage, and it is truly sad that a Rajput will throw away his birthright to celebrate a marriage" (Jassal 1989). This letter explicitly cites the tendency of upwardly mobile castes such as the Kurmis (and, no doubt, the Yadavas, as the predominant cultivating caste) to emulate Kshatriya marriage practices. The document appears to confirm efforts among the cultivating castes to emulate the marriage practices of the Kshatriyas in order to advance their claims on a higher status.[11] How much of the colonial state's understanding of marriage practices derived from folk forms such as the Lorikāyan needs to be explored further in light of the arguments made in this chapter about the social construction of gender. As the Lorikāyan illustrates, upwardly mobile groups routinely emulated upper-caste practices and Kshatriya codes of honor for women, which provided familiar models and a blueprint for those who aspired to rulership. The ballad's illustration of how these norms were upheld to regulate the lives and attitudes of women continues to be relevant to our understanding of similar processes not only in colonial times but also into the present day.

While the Lorikāyan could be read as a text about caste identity and its evolution, possibly from medieval times, its contemporary relevance lies both in its continued function as a defining text for the assertion of an overarching Yadava identity in north India and in its significance for this community's vision of its past. The ballad's sociological motifs, though associated with the upwardly mobile caste of the Yadavas, are also relevant to other upwardly mobile caste groups.

This chapter focused on a masculine ballad to show that the gendered musical world is separated not only spatially but also by genre, narrative texts, performance styles, and concerns (see Sax 2002; Schechner 1977; Blackburn and Ramanujan 1986). Beyond the gender-exclusive, caste-inclusive nature of musical akharas and their potential for forging community, containing conflicts, and bridging caste, communal, and religious divides, we can also question the akharas' demarcation from women's musical traditions and the continued efforts to safeguard these spaces from feminine influence. We find that in the nineteenth century the popularity of akharas coincided with the withdrawal of women from public spaces such as fairs and markets and the attempt to suppress women's folk music traditions such as the wedding *gālīs* (abusive songs) explored in earlier chapters, which reformers and upwardly mobile caste patriarchies considered obscene. The social universe of caste cooperation glimpsed in the Lorikāyan delineated the akharā as an alternative to the milieu of caste separation.

The epic's conflation of marriage with warfare provided a point of entry for apprehending the influence of caste patriarchies in the construction of gender. In place of hypergamy, the anuloma custom of maintaining the structural inequality between wife-givers and wife-takers accepted as an axiomatic characteristic of upper-caste marriage patterns, the Lorikāyan brings to light a lesser-known, perhaps more widely practiced, norm among the intermediate castes, that of parity and equilibrium. Through the wit and innovations of the bride's mother, the Lorikāyan underscores the strength of the wife-givers, far removed from their posited inferiority. In fact the text takes great pains to highlight the unique mettle and strength both of women and of the wife-givers, who, if not superior to the wife-takers, at least balance the structural inequality the marriage transaction effects. In providing such details, the Lorikāyan serves as a rich account of the sociology of the intermediate caste order. A gendered reading of the text suggests the subjugation of lower-caste norms in the process of consolidating and forging a ruling class ethos.

While the hero's interactions with the other female characters add depth and dimension to his character, leading him to embark on adventures and challenges and to develop a fleshed-out, robust masculinity both in the battlefield and in life, in the end, these risk-taking women are chastised and must lose out to the upper-caste norms of chastity, which are prioritized.

It is only against the ample evidence of the power and skill possessed by women from a range of servicing castes that the disappointingly limiting upper-caste qualities of sat and pativrata emerge triumphant, to the exclusion of all other traits. The many episodes that highlight the wit, wisdom, skills, and extraordinary prowess of women force one to reflect on the sociological and historical eclipse of these very qualities in women, as the values of chastity take over and women's dependence on men is valorized. The helpless, dependent woman who is reduced to tatters when her male protector abandons her reinforces the values of saintly inaction and women's waiting in piety and grief for her protector to return. The practical life skills of resourceful women are condemned as threatening. It is clear therefore that upward mobility has meant the eclipse of a range of women's skills. Thus the construction of a new masculine identity deriving from the control of land and territory requires that women become men's property. Finally, while the Yadava past outlined in the text is posited as an age of glory, the ballad also illustrates that women were crucial to, if ultimately sidelined by, the processes of forging a new caste identity and refurbishing patriarchy. These inherent paradoxes and ambiguities, however, make it possible to argue for the multiple perspectives the ballad presents.

CHAPTER SIX

⟿ Taking Liberties

If Hindu culture puts a premium on the unassertiveness of women,
on Holi the reverse is entirely appropriate. Likewise, if Hindu culture
ordinarily proscribes open displays of sexuality, on Holi, sexuality is
one of the dominant and most obvious motifs of the day.

JOYCE BURKHALTER FLUECKIGER, *GENDER AND GENRE
IN THE FOLKLORE OF MIDDLE INDIA*, 51

During my travels by public transport through north
India in the weeks before the Holi festival, I heard a
specific genre of song exploding and spilling out of public spaces, markets, buses, and auto-rickshaws. Described
as *phūhar* (sloppy) and *ashlīl* (obscene), this genre of
Bhojpuri songs emerges on audiocassettes each year in
great abundance around Holi, the spring festival characterized by a temporary suspension of gender and caste
hierarchies. Publicly characterized as obscene, or more
appropriately transgressive, the dominant motif in these
recordings is the joking relationship between a woman
and her younger brother-in-law. This chapter explores
how themes and forms characteristic of folk traditions
change with their means of communication. The cassette recordings hint at the existence of women's spaces
within the culture of Holi. However, the appropriation

of a genre that originally served as a space for rural women's innovation and improvisation has modified women's song traditions and commercialized them in such a way that monetary rewards accrue to the appropriators while the women remain silent objects of the male gaze. The recordings allow us to inquire into issues of culture and social change, gender constructs, kinship norms, lower-caste assertions of identity, and a range of other caste, class, and gender concerns.

This chapter utilizes Holi cassette music as the source material for an inquiry into a range of issues of interest to scholars of contemporary social change and public culture. Of particular interest are the linkages between rural- and urbanscapes and the transitions and transformations that occur when forms and ideas travel between rural and urban milieus. As traditional forms, such as festival songs expressing kin and caste sensibilities, including classificatory kinship terminologies, are appropriated for the fashioning of popular culture, taste, and consciousness, the sociological relevance of these categories in both their old and new contexts becomes significant. This chapter seeks to further our understanding of the gendered impact of technological advancements through which oral traditions are reinterpreted and reworked to address contemporary caste, class, and gender concerns. Issues of patronage and consumership, as well as how these affect the content of an existing genre, are significant lines of inquiry these recordings open up (see also Blackburn and Ramanujan 1986, 29).

In recent years, scholars of gender have re-examined the field of folklore to understand the devices available to nonliterate societies for transmitting dominant values over generations, including the social construction of gender. The analysis of oral traditions and of women's speech genres and knowledge systems has proved a fertile field of investigation in unearthing women's consciousness. For instance, Lila Abu-Lughod shows how women's strategies of defiance were excluded from commercial recordings of Bedouin culture (Abu-Lughod 1990b, 24). In his pathbreaking book, *Cassette Culture*, Peter Manuel (1993) has explored the contradictions and challenges posed by the introduction of new cassette technologies in India and the revitalization of local subcultures and community values due to the decentralization of cassette production. Where possibilities of multiple interpretations exist and where traditions are rich and varied—but also continually being reworked, as in the Bhojpuri-speaking region—the challenge is to understand how, why, by whom, and in whose interest existing genres are being appropriated and the purposes served by the appropriation.

THEMES AND MOTIFS IN CASSETTE RECORDINGS

This chapter singles out one such folk genre, Holi songs, to reflect on those features that lend themselves to adaptation and the logic by which traditional genres are transformed. The popular and mass appeal of these recordings, including the messages they contain, within the sociopolitical milieu of contemporary Uttar Pradesh and Bihar complements our understanding of political and social change in the region. This appeal is thus eminently worthy of sociological attention.

The supposed incestuous ties between a woman and her husband's younger brother is a recurring motif of these recordings and one of the puzzles I seek to solve in this chapter. The dyad of a woman and her younger brother-in-law is utilized to express a range of emotions, from separation and longing to the explicitly erotic, from veiled innuendoes to the recounting of overt sexual encounters. Is this just an extension of the age-old joking relationship or is the relationship undergoing dramatic change?

Occasionally melodious, often haunting, but for the most part aggressive, abrasive, flippant, bawdy, and offensive in their insistence, especially when heard in public spaces, these recordings enable an interrogation of the realm of familial ties and the changes therein; the reassertion of patriarchal values that appear threatened by the obvious visibility of women in public spaces; and contemporary processes of cultural production. Deriving inspiration from folk genres, though not quite from traditional folk music, the songs are reframed and reinvented in accordance with contemporary tastes and markets.

If tacking new urban lyrics onto a familiar, though primarily rural, folk song genre is about reinventing tradition or reframing the traditional, then what those lyrics say throws new light on contemporary concerns in north Indian society. The chapter thus echoes Blackburn's and Ramanujan's concerns with investigating how themes and forms characteristic of folk and classical traditions change when the means of communication change (Blackburn and Ramanujan 1986, 25).

Today Bhojpuri popular prerecorded cassette music (of which the Holi songs are an important example) competes with Hindi film music, contributing to the peculiarly cacophonous quality and chaotic character of north Indian mofussil towns and semirural- and urbanscapes. In contrast to the film songs that constitute popular culture all over the country, Bhojpuri song genres are regionally specific, inspired by the folk melodies and songs of eastern Uttar Pradesh and Bihar. The heavy truck traffic on the Grand Trunk Road, the major highway connecting the mofussil towns of these large and populous states, is the channel for this music, transmitted largely through truckers, its primary consumers.

Undoubtedly composed and recorded by men, and mostly sung by men even when a women's point of view is being portrayed, these songs are obscene to the extent that, taken out of context, they attempt to titillate and usurp spaces traditionally available to women. Interestingly, Joyce Burkhalter Flueckiger (1996, 50) has observed that within the ritual context of Holi celebrations among unmarried girls in central India, songs that had been taken out of context were considered bad. In much the same spirit, when, during fieldwork one winter in Barsara village, Jaunpur, I asked one of my favorite singers, Munraji, to sing a kajlī the song of the rainy season explored in chapter 2, she replied that it would be "embarrassing" to do so, out of season.

In varying degrees the adoption of brash, lewd, carefree, permissive, and licentious tones adds to the heavy sexual and erotic content of these recordings, which has resulted in their being uniformly branded as *ashlīl* or obscene. However, it might be more appropriate to describe the genre as transgressive. The relationship that is being transgressed, however, is not just one of the traditional gender hierarchy, but also one of caste hierarchy. Much depends on the social context in which this joke is expressed (see Douglas 1968).

HOLI AND JOCULAR SONGS

Finally comes the indecency which is a distinct element in the observance [of Holi]. There seems to be reason to believe that promiscuous intercourse was regarded as a necessary part of the rite. CROOKE, *AN INTRODUCTION TO THE POPULAR RELIGION AND FOLK-LORE OF NORTHERN INDIA*, 392

Phāgun mein Bābā devar lāge.

In the month of Phāgun, even an old man may seem like one's younger
brother-in-law.

Are holiyo me āja bāur bhail ba tamanvā sajanvā ho
Kab le khepī hoī baiganavā sajanvā ho

Oh! Return in the Holi season, crazy one, that's my wish.
How long will you stay this time, my uncaring love.

HOLI SONGS AND SAYINGS, FIELDNOTES, JAUNPUR, 1999–2002

Holi is celebrated all over north India on the full harvest moon, exactly
a month after the spring festival of Basant Pancamī. The festival evokes a
joyous mood of color and camaraderie. The celebrations involve a carni-
valesque subversion of established hierarchies of status, caste, and gender
—enabling society, after each such release, to go back to its original functioning through the restoration of order. H. Bergson's (1956) metaphor of
the safety valve for releasing pressure in a way that is nonthreatening to
the system is an apt description of the festival and its strong cathartic
component. Further, as Bergson suggests, only those who share common
norms and values weep or laugh together, and only those who have a
claim to group belongingness may partake of the humor. The more rigid,
complex, and layered the social inequalities and hierarchies, the more the
need for ritual festive release and role reversal.

Many scholars have investigated how role reversal reinforces hierarchy
and the authority of rural elites. M. N. Srinivas's (1952) and Ranajit Guha's
(1983) accounts are particularly insightful. Srinivas found that among the
Coorgs, an oracle from the Banna caste, considered highly polluting,
conducts the ceremony of ancestor worship. This grants him the license
of speech. However, it is the temporary and ritual character of the role
that not only underlines but also perpetuates existing structural cleavages.
The impure caste of Poleyas are similarly compensated for their normative exploitation by the momentarily prominent place they are afforded
in certain Coorg festivals. When they revert to their position in Coorg
society as the most disenfranchised of its members, the rituals serve to
reinforce the distance between upper and lower castes (Srinivas 1952).

Ranajit Guha emphasizes the element of predictability in calendrical festivals like Holi, which serve to affirm, rather than overthrow, rhythm, order, and hierarchy: "The saturnalia, the systematic violation of structural distances between castes and classes, the defiance of rules governing interpersonal relationships between members of the family and community, the blatant undermining of private and public morality, all of which feature in this ceremony, add up not to a disruption of the political and social order in the village, but to its reinforcement" (Guha 1983, 34).

However, even if these inversions do not threaten existing relations of domination and subordination within society, they do offer a space that, though momentary, is nevertheless crucial to those involved for the ritual enactment of release and subversion. While in some regions the aggression is physical—as in Barsaana in western Uttar Pradesh, near the birthplace of Krishna, where women wield clubs against men—in the Bhojpuri-speaking belt, women's aggression is verbal and takes the form of cathartic abuse. Licensed speech, sayings, songs, and prescriptive rebellions serve as insurance against the genuine article (Guha 1983, 45).

In villages across Uttar Pradesh, as in Rajasthan, men, often led by a crowned jester and accompanied by drumming, conduct a noisy procession through the streets, indulging in mocking, ironic, and violent horseplay (see also Gold 2000, 219). Such processions of folk clowns are a recurrent motif in folk festivals in other parts of the country as well. Shulman (1985, 201) argues that the clowns at the Mariamman festival in Tamil Nadu draw inauspicious forces (such as the evil eye or *drsti*) upon themselves, thereby deflecting these forces from others. In the Mariamman festival, the clowns bring into play creative energies that normally lie dormant, or are subdued or excluded, thus challenging the ordered domain of social life. In exactly this sense, clowning imparts a crucial dynamism to Holi, and the element of slapstick may be seen as expressing the "immediate liberation of suppressed forces" (201).

There are other interpretations of Holi, too. With some regional variation, the Holi myth also narrates the burning of a demoness, Holika, and the saving of the infant Prahlad, the symbol of truth and virtue. From Ann Grodzins Gold's description of the festival, we learn that in Rajasthan, exactly a month before the festival, a dead tree branch symbolizing the demoness who is to be burned on Holi eve is planted in the ground. This marks the beginning of a month-long taboo on the movement of women between their natal and marital homes (Gold 2000, 213). While in popular understanding the taboo serves to protect women from the rowdy atmosphere of Holi, Gold alerts us to the element of ritual danger involved, especially in rituals where female power is recognized as demonic and therefore, both dangerous and divine. In Holi celebrations in Rajasthan, for instance, women effectively claim for themselves the role of rescuers and life-givers, highlighting female worth and community, while also diffusing the divine/demonic, benevolent/dangerous dichotomies of male-authored discourses.

Based on the observations I made during my intermittent fieldwork in Jaunpur district in Uttar Pradesh between 1999 and 2002, the preferred norm in this region appears to be that, at the onset of the month of *Phāgun*, characterized by the singing of *phāg* or *phaguā*, families send any visiting daughters back to their marital homes, just in time for the Holi celebrations in which both genders have contrasting roles to perform. In enacting the Holi myth, "men will beat down the demonic female whereas it is woman's part to rescue the child with all its potentiality" (Gold 2000, 217). The taboo also appears to have much to do with the agricultural cycle, since the month preceding Holi is the time for harvesting the *rabī* crop. Unlike *kharīf,* the time available for harvesting rabī is very short, and the crop must be harvested quickly. The restriction on women's movement during this period ensures minimum disturbance to the labor process.

Characterizing the mood of this month is the phāg musical tradition, associated with lush green fields, flower-scented breezes, the excitement of ripening mangoes, the sap-dripping, intoxicating *mahuā* trees, and the melodious songs of the *koel* (cuckoo). Phāg melodies primarily evoke the mood of *shringār* (love) and are resplendent with desire, teasing, aggression, and unrequited love. In familial contexts, phāg lyrics explore themes like the resistance of newlywed brides to leaving their natal homes for their marital ones; new brides' wedding night nuptial anxieties; women's desire for jewelry and ornamentation; and so on.

At the start of Holi festivities, it is customary to strike a spiritual note by singing of the deities Rama, Krishna, or even the ascetic Shiva engaged in the play of Holi, such as the following easily recognized lyrics sung all over north India in the phāg melodic style, as popularized through Bollywood films:

Horī khelein Raghuvira Awadh mein, Hori Khelein Raghuvira
Kekre hānthe kanak Pichkārī
Kekre hānthe abirā
Hai, kekre hānthe abirā Awadh mein.

Rama, (of the Raghu dynasty) plays Holi in Awadh
Who holds in his hands the golden water-squirter
In whose hands the rose-powder
Oh, whose hands are filled with rose-powder in Awadh

However, the mood steadily shifts to more earthy and physical realms, and the songs and melodies keep pace with the shifts. In rural contexts, the easy transition to and deployment of imagery and symbols common to both agricultural and human fertility is startling. D. D. Kosambi's (1970) insight that Holi rites were designed to promote and encourage procreation are borne out effectively in the following song, which also evokes the regeneration of the earth, a return to the womb, and a celebration of the seed, of contained energies, and of creation in its pristine stage (Jassal 2006, 309).

Kohiyā aibo bhaiyā ho, agutāil bīyā bhaujī
Lāgol hāvā phāgun ke, paniyaīl bīyā bhaujī
Pahile rāva chuā he se rahe barā harkat
Ab to biyā pāni le kar apane se dharkat
Kākohi hamrā se lasiyāīl bīyā bhaujī
Lāgol hāvā phāgun ke, paniyīl bīyā bhaujī
Pahlo gavnā taunā ghare rahe dudha danvā ho
Bākir ab cuāil bāte colī ke khajanvā ho
Ab ke īhe dehiyā se pakthāīl bīyā bhaujī
Lāgol havā phāgun ke, paniyāīl bīyā bhaujī
Gudu ho bujhatā garmāīl bīyā bhaujī
Lāgol hāvā phāgun ke paniyāīl bīyā bhaujī
Kohiyā aibo bhaiyā ho agutāīl bīyā bhaujī.

When will brother return? The seed has ripened sister-in-law,
With the winds of the Phāgun season, the seed laden with sap
At first, just a touch was a big deal,
Now the ripened seed tumbles with its own weight
Shall I say I made it even juicier, sister-in-law

With the winds of Phāgun, the seed laden with sap?
First there's marriage, only then milk and grain in the home,
But this time, the bounty within the blouse drips!
This time the seed ripened within the body
With the winds of Phāgun, the seed laden with sap
Maybe a baby boy, the warmed up seed, sister-in-law
With the winds of Phāgun, the seed laden with sap
When will brother return? The seed has ripened, sister-in-law.

CASSETTE RECORDING BY GUDDU RANGEELA, "BHATAAR HOLI," T-SERIES, 2000

Women's dependence on their brothers-in-law, namely, the *devar-bhābhī* bond and the other dominant motif in the song, is explored in a later section. Over the month of Phāgun, the mood builds and reaches a crescendo on the morning of the festival, when the splashing and drenching of everyone in sight with colored water is the norm. Intoxicants are freely consumed, and dancing, singing, drumming, celebratory eating, and the exchange of sweets infuses the mood with revelry, merriment, and magnanimity. The melodies switch to the more boisterous *dhamār* style, and the bonhomie extends to embracing members of other castes such that the element of physicality is very pronounced and in your face. This physicality is always combined with plenty of teasing, tricking, and playfulness and the breaking of caste-based commensality taboos. Aggressively competitive verbal exchanges between the sexes in the *jogīra* melodic style add a punch to the festivities.

Gold has persuasively argued that practices involving sexuality and female power and the associated jokes and rituals are, in fact, a response to mortality. Based on her fieldwork in the Rajasthan countryside among a "population who cared obsessively about getting children by means of processes divine and organic," Gold argues that the dances, jokes, and worshipful stories suggest "a life-affirming sexuality on the part of women offered a bountiful replenishing of the human community faced with death's losses" (Gold 1988, 304). Gold concludes that "just as cyclical natality and mortality underlie other concepts of death, so the fertility motif in village religion, with its playful and serious, bawdy and esoteric expressions, seems to penetrate most aspects of religious life" (Gold 1988, 306).

Of significance to the issues discussed here is the fact that traditionally women used the occasion to indulge in ritual and spontaneous verbal abuse and developed fairly elaborate songs and sayings to channel and vent their resentment. The potential to improvise in abusive songs is particularly great for those so inclined. During fieldwork in village Ramnagar, Jaunpur, for instance, I found that there were always a few talented female singers who appeared to compose the rhymes and ditties on the spot and lead the rest of the group. Their singing was accompanied by the often-hysterical mirth of others, who joined enthusiastically in the chorus. Gold cites the following verse as an example of the genre sung in Rajasthan villages, particularly during the days preceding Holi: "The potter woman's vagina's like a broken jug's rim: a rolling mouth, all that's left is the hole" (Gold 1988, 130). In addition to the secluded Rajput women, Gold observed women from Brahmin and Mahajan castes mingling with those of peasant and artisan castes, all of them singing such songs together. In a footnote, Gold explains that these songs "include barbs at numerous castes (in terms of their sexual attributes) but are sung communally by mixed-caste groups of women with great esprit de corps. They display a sexual imagination that is little credited to South Asian peasant women and evoke an eroticism that is explicitly linked to fertility, if also to infidelity" (Gold 1988).

Among the agricultural castes of Ramnagar village, Jaunpur district, including Telis (oil-pressers), Mallahs (fishers and river-farers), and the numerically preponderant Yadavas (cultivators and middle-peasants), I found considerable social interaction around Holi. Among the various intermediate castes in the village, the teasing songs are sung within earshot of the men and are meant to be mildly embarrassing but not outright offensive; and, of course, in keeping with the spirit of the festival, to take liberties or "get your own back" and thus subvert the system is socially sanctioned. As the joking consists of playing with meaning, attempts to alter meaning in unexpected ways are common (Zijderveld 1983, 7). The jocular element is foregrounded, and to take offence would be simply ridiculous. The only option is to retaliate in kind, but during fieldwork, I found that men were mostly silent. Sheepish spectators, they were forced to hear myriad variations of such songs several times, over several days, leading up to the festival. In this context, therefore, Susan Gal's insights about women's special verbal skills as strategic responses to their positions of relative powerlessness are especially relevant (Gal 1991, 182).

Traditionally, therefore, Holi songs offered a realm of gender interaction wherein women got the chance to reverse roles and to experience a sense of empowerment, if only momentarily. My presence in the field during part of the festival confirmed my hunch that the jovial and good-humored possibilities these songs offered helped to release pent-up tensions and to defuse resentment and animosities, as well as allowed for the rejuvenation of collectivities and cathartic healing. Women always appeared to be strengthened by the festivities and celebrations and in better form during and after them. Women's careful attention to grooming and their attire the day after Holi further emphasizes the mood of freshness and newness heralded by the festival.

The next section contextualizes some concrete examples of cassette recordings in circulation in the Holi season during my fieldwork between 1999 and 2002 in the Bhojpuri-speaking region.

HOLI SONGS AND THE PRERECORDED CASSETTE INDUSTRY

The popularity of the songs and their ubiquitous presence in the form of recordings need to be contextualized not only within a burgeoning music industry but also within an urban folk tradition of avid musical consumption. The technological breakthroughs that made the production and circulation of music on a large scale possible over the past twenty years also greatly revolutionized musical consumption, accessibility, and tastes. The variety and range of recorded music in shops and bazaars, lanes and markets small and big, all over the towns of north India, and the ever-increasing demand for it, is itself a phenomenon worthy of sociological investigation.

The region boasts of a range of musical specialists, practitioners, balladeers, and epic singers, both professional and part-time or seasonal. Research on the astounding range of folklore traditions alive and thriving today in the Bhojpuri-speaking belt confirms the musical sensibility of the region (Marcus 1989; Servan-Schreiber 2001). Like the *gāthā* or folk ballads that reflect the vitality, strength, and specificity of the urban cultures from which they emerged (Servan-Schreiber 2001), these recordings are undoubtedly an urban phenomenon.

It is against this thriving backdrop that the popularity of the recordings must be contextualized. While the music is produced and recorded in studios in Delhi under the brand name *T-Series*, it is heard mostly on the highways of Uttar Pradesh and Bihar in north India. The recordings are sold from small stalls at bus terminals and found especially in market towns dotted along the Grand Trunk Road. However, the cultural practice of playing music loudly in public places ensures that the recordings are heard by all commuters, and as such they do not remain the sole possession of the purchaser but instead reach the entire spectrum of castes and classes in north India.

The vast population of town dwellers, shopkeepers, service providers, migrant workers and laborers, semiskilled workers in industries, and those engaged in the transportation of goods and people are the most visible consumers of the recordings, which can be heard all the way from Delhi eastward to Gorakhpur, Varanasi in Uttar Pradesh, and Patna and beyond to hundreds of small towns in Bihar. As such, there are unmistakable parallels between the consumers of these recordings and those of the gāthās, oral epics of an earlier era, whom Servan-Schreiber identifies as "rickshaw-vālās, coolies, boatmen, Baniyas, cattle-sellers, themselves wandering and moving people, listening to wandering and moving singers" (Servan-Schreiber 2001, 45).

The songs also closely resemble the genre known as gārī or gālīs (abusive songs) (Raheja and Gold 1994; Gupta 2001; Marcus 1989) explored in chapter 3, a form of legitimized ritual abuse sung by the wife-givers at the conclusion of the wedding ceremony to embarrass the wife-takers. This ritual precedes the departure of the groom's party from the wife's natal home with the new bride. Through the gālīs, the significant relationships within the patrilineage are ridiculed and among these, the tensions at the core of the devar-bhābhī bond are particularly exposed. In this sense, too, the Holi songs evoke the mood of the gālīs.

The Holi song genre is also closely associated, both in narrative and in musical style, with the folk genre known as birahā (separation) discussed in the previous chapter. Where literacy is low and the thirst for information and knowledge high, the prerecorded birahā cassettes have come to occupy a significant niche. The theme recurs in a range of folk songs gathered under the generic term birahā. The birahā genre lends itself most effectively to the transmission of news-based information and sensational narratives of contemporary relevance and interest (Marcus 1989). The versatility of the genre became evident in recent times, when, only a few weeks after the murder of the famous Bandit Queen, Phoolan Devi, a cassette narrating in song and verse the tragic life of the runaway child bride-turned-dacoit-turned-Member of Parliament hit the market. Several other versions followed in quick succession, surfacing in bazaars all over north India. Likewise, cassettes telling the story of Princess Diana's life and the dramatic circumstances of her death were immensely popular.

A brief detour through the production of cassette recordings and their widespread dissemination would not be out of place here. During my years of fieldwork, the Bhojpuri folksong market was dominated by T-Series, a company known for film music as well as thousands of recordings in every imaginable genre and Indian language. T-Series, established nearly twenty years ago, is now a diversified group with a US$90 million core business of consumer electronics, CDs, and audio-video magnetic tapes and cassettes. With an ultramodern recording studio and laboratories in the New Okhla Industrial Development Authority (NOIDA) in Delhi, the company has rights to over 2,000 video and 18,000 audio titles comprising over 24,000 hours of music software. The company claims to have built the first music bank in the country and scouts for talent in lyrics, voice, music composition, and artistic creation through its website. While the scale of the company's operations suggests that it relies on a widespread sourcing network for songs, it is also instrumental in shaping tastes and musical trends.

The recordings I examine below point to the women's spaces that existed within the culture of Holi and that have now been appropriated for purposes far removed from those originally intended. Derived from and inspired by the folksong genres, the recordings in their modified form merely hint at the rich and vibrant tradition of verbal exchanges between sexes that form the core of the Holi festivities. While it would be useful to study how these recordings are consumed within the original setting from which they derive, I have not been able to perform the kind of extended participant observation required for such a study. Instead, I have investigated other sets of concerns and the possible ways in which themes, frames, and content are reworked in the commercial process.

My sample consists mainly of Holi songs adapted to the easily recognizable phāg and dhamār melodies. One obvious and puzzling feature of these recordings is the predominance of male voices articulating women's defiance of sexual mores. This in itself is suggestive of male anxieties within patriarchy. Musical exchanges in the form of clever verbal feats by teams of men and women in the *jogīra* style also show up on different cassettes, but these are rehearsed and orchestrated with the voices remaining predominantly male. However, as Manuel suggests, quoting Kakar, "the parallel for the adoption of female persona by males already exists within the Bhakti tradition where the human soul is feminine in relation to the divine. Bhakti is preeminently feminine in its orientation, and the erotic love for Krishna (or Shiva, as the case may be) is envisioned entirely from the woman's viewpoint, or at least from her position as imagined by the man" (Manuel 1993, 205).

While I found several songs that were based on familiar film tunes, the ones I present here are by far the most representative and reflect the themes and melodies most characteristic of the genre. The openly assertive sexuality is of course the most striking feature of the genre, but a closer listen reveals other common distinguishing traits. Songs like the one below definitively embody the male gaze.

Man kare gorī tahār jobanā nihār ke, Ja jhār ke
Rang lagaitī ughār ke, ja jhār ke
Dehn sughraitī bhari ekvār ke.

I wish I could stare at your bosom, go dust off the color
Smear your naked body with color, go shake it off
To envelop you in a tight embrace!
CASSETTE RECORDING BY GUDDU RANGEELA, "CHATKAAR HOLI," T-SERIES, 2004

The following song, an exploration of women's consciousness within patriarchy as well as male anxieties about women's fidelity, is more complex. The assertive female sexuality suggested here is startling to find within a dominant patriarchal culture that prescribes strict monogamy and, indeed, enforces it. The brash, carefree, and upbeat mood of abandon that the song cultivates stands in stark contrast to the reality of segregation between the sexes and the ideal of limited, visible social interaction between men and women, especially in public spaces. Here again the voice is distinctly male:

Kolo kolo bhatār badlaiya sakhī
Kolo kolo bhatār badlaiyā
Na cāhe aincā na cāhe paincā,
Na cāhi hamrā batohiyā

Kolo kolo bhatār badlaiyā sakhī
Kolo kolo bhatār badlaiyā
Na bahumat bā torā re, na bahumat hamār ho
Âo banā lo eho sakhī, milī julī sarkār
Majā leve ke ehi upaiyā
Kolo kolo bhatār badlaiyā sakhī
Kolo kolo bhatār badlaiyā
Na culhā upās rahī
Na Gudu ke ās rahī
Mor mardā torā lāge
Tor mardā morā pās rahī
Hoi duno ke dāl faraiyā
Kolo kolo bhatār badlaiyā sakhī
Kolo kolo bhatār badlaiyā.

Tomorrow let's swap husbands, friend.
Swap husbands.
I don't want this one, nor one like that.
Nor is it the traveler for me, let's swap husbands, friend.
Swap husbands.
Neither your views will take priority, nor mine.
We'll have a shared government this way.
A recipe for fun.
Swap husbands.
Neither cooking nor fasts.
No waiting for kids.
My husband will seem like yours.
And yours will be near me.
We'll cook their goose, both of them.
Let's swap husbands.
CASSETTE RECORDING BY GUDDU RANGILA AND SAPNA AWASTHI,
"KHARE KHARE LAGĀLAU," T-SERIES, 2003

Male preoccupation with women's sexual transgressions, albeit in parodying, jocular, and lighthearted tones, is reflected in diverse ways in the songs below. Their humorous twists reflect a need to manage these anxieties such that threats to the established gender hierarchy are channeled in other ways.

Yār ke cūmā develū udhāi ke udhaniā
Bhatrā ke tū garāvelū nathuniā
Bhatrā ke tū carāvelū cuhaniā
Yār khātir seb santarā sab re laganiyā
Bhatrā ke delu sukhale sukhaniyā
Yār aihen kām jable rahī tū dulhaniyā
Bhatrā ji sab din ke vo thaganiyā.

You're off to kiss your lover under draped covers;
For the husband, you fashioned a noose.
And sent him off to graze, the husband,
For the lover, servings of apples and oranges,
Just dried leavings for the husband.
The lover is of use as long as you're a bride;
The husband, a deceiver for all your days.

Âr cāhe hokhi bhatrā se mār
Bhabharī chikhaibo yār ke
Âr patiyā pathāi ham lihabo bulāī
Âr ho jahiyā holiyā dhamār ho
Bhabharī chikhaibo yār ke
Âr dhansal ba karejvā mein ohi re suratiyā
Bhabharī chikhaibo yār ke
Âr cāhe hokhi bhatrā se mār

Oh, so what if I'm in for a thrashing from husband dear?
I'll offer my lover the treat to taste.
Oh, I'll send him a letter to call him.
Oh, this Holi will be rollicking.
I'll offer my lover this treat to taste.
Oh, his image digs deep into my heart.
I'll give him the treat to taste.
Oh, so what if I'm in for a thrashing from husband dear?

CASSETTE RECORDINGS BY SUDARSHAN YADAV, "HOLI KE BOKHAR," T-SERIES, 2002

In keeping with the spirit of the Holi festival, the suspension of restrictions of all kinds, including those pertaining to the women's sexuality, predominates, but in jocular and ridiculing ways. The innovation, such as it is, lies in the lyrics, which can be very suggestive, while the melodic structure remains recognizably consistent. Hence, it is not unusual to hear spiritual and uplifting pieces sung in the same melody as ashlīl ones, serving to further emphasize the latter's transgressive nature.

By thus parodying male anxieties and identifying them with the ritual subversion inherent in the Holi festival, the actors ensure that real transgressions that might threaten established gender equations will not occur. In fact the more outrageous and bawdy the content, the better it fulfils the traditional requirements of the festival celebrations:

Satuā khā lo bhatār, satuā khā lo bhatār
Dahī ceurā khoihen iyarau
Holi ho, holi ho
Bhūiyan sūto bhatār, bhūiyan sūto bhatār,
Palang par suteihen iyarau
Holi ho, holi ho
Dālo upre bhatār, dālo upre bhatār
Nichvān se daleihen iyarau
Holi ho, holi ho
Cumā le lo bhatār cumā le lo bhatār
Bāki māja mareihen iyarau

Eat the *satuā*[1] husband, eat satuā;
Curds and puffed rice for lover.
It's Holi, it's Holi!
Sleep on the floor, husband, sleep on the floor;
The bed is for loverboy.
It's Holi, it's Holi!
Lay it on top, husband, on top;
Lover will put it from below.
It's Holi, it's Holi!
Take a kiss, husband, just a kiss.
Everything else, loverboy will enjoy.
CASSETTE RECORDING BY GUDDU RANGEELA AND SAPNA AWASTHI,
"KHARE KHARE LAGĀLAU," T-SERIES, 2003

To the extent that the lyrics reflect the male gaze in their preoccupation with *jobanā* (breasts), male sexual imagery such as *mūsarvā* (pestle), *ajgar sāp* (huge snake), the physicality and double entendre of *rang dālo* (smear color) and even the play and sport of Holi, women's voices are muffled, if not silenced outright. As in the *rasiyā* recordings Manuel analyzes, women are portrayed as "libidinous and potentially unfaithful," a portrayal that is then used to justify the harassment and heckling to which they are subjected (Manuel 1993, 204).

In sum, the subtexts of these songs underline and reinforce the assumption that women's sexuality, if left unchecked, would wreak havoc with the normative structure of patriarchy. While both these recorded songs and women's spontaneous songs in the traditional Holi context ultimately end up reinforcing and reaffirming patriarchy, they achieve this in quite different ways. The fact that the recorded songs, far from the fleeting expressions of women participating in personal rituals of festive release, are available to be played and replayed repeatedly removes them from any association with an authentic women's voice. Here again, Flueckiger's insights from central India parallel my findings:

"It is no longer an acceptable, empowering tradition of initiation for lower or adivasi-caste women but has shifted to reflect a male representation of women, whose sexuality must be bound; it is this representation that identifies the *dalkhāi gīt* as *burī* (bad or vulgar)" (Flueckiger 1996, 75).

Ironically, a genre that originally served as a space for rural women's expression has been appropriated for the commercial gains of men while the women derive no monetary or other advantages thereby. Like African American musical genres in the United States, the songs have been dissociated from their original contexts. As Perry Hall notes, "as the innovations become dissociated from the experiential context in which they arise, they begin to lose their functions as statements of affirmation and humanity relative to those contexts" (Hall 1997, 49).

HOLI SONGS AND THE DEVAR-BHĀBHĪ BOND

The central and most striking motif in this genre of recorded Holi songs is the relationship between a woman and her younger brother-in-law, namely, the devar-bhābhī bond. In fact, the recurrence of this motif suggests that it is only through this relationship that it is possible to give voice to erotic themes.

Gori jobanvā hilāve parāpāri
Devarā bhatār mein karāve mārā māri.

The fair one shakes her fulsome breasts
Igniting a war between husband and his younger brother.

CASSETTE RECORDING BY GUDDU RANGEELA, "CHATKAAR HOLI," T-SERIES, 2004

E Bhaujī, e Bhaujī āī hai holiyā bahār, cunariyā tohrī sarke
Rang debe coliyā tohār kevariyā bandh kaike
Bāraho mahinvā ham lālsa puraibe
Manvā ka tohre piyasvā bujhāibe
E bhaujī ! rang debe coliyā tohār kevariyā bandh kaike
E devar ! rang jaihen coliyā hamār sajanvā jehiyā aihen
Â jehiyen holiyā bahār sajanvā jehiyā aihen.

"O sister-in-law, Holi is here, your stole is slipping
Slipping, sliding, revealing.
I'll color your bodice, locking the door.
Quench your desires of the entire twelve months.
Slake the thirst of your heart.
O sister-in-law, I'll color your bodice with the door locked."
"O brother-in-law, my bodice will be colored when my husband returns."
The gusts of Holi will be felt when he returns.

CASSETTE RECORDING BY VIJAY LAL YADAV AND ANITA RAJ,
"RANG DEBE CHOLIYA TOHAAR," T-SERIES, 2003

Jaldī se chuttī leke āja more Rajā
Holi mein jobanā garam bhail bā
Jaldi se chuttī leke āja more Raja
Devarā barā besaram bhail bā.

Hurry up, take leave and come, my love
In Holi my breast is warmed up
Hurry up, take leave and come, my love
Younger brother-in-law is acting shamelessly.

CASSETTE RECORDING BY GUDDU RANGEELA, "CHATKAAR HOLI," T-SERIES

The ubiquitous deployment of the devar-bhābhī joking relationship
to explore women's sexuality and consciousness within patriarchy as well

as to express sexual abandon, unrestrained by everyday gender and caste hierarchies, is the most striking feature of this song genre. Moreover, in the rural context, one might speculate that as a kinship category, the term *bhābhī*, as well as its synonym often used in the songs, "*bhaujī*" can be applied to any woman of a certain generation without causing undue offence, by virtue of the fact that it establishes the woman's husband as one's elder brother. At least in the region where I conducted my fieldwork, the term *devar* could be appropriately applied to all bachelors in a woman's marital village. The rationale for the easy familiarity that lies at the heart of this bond, so explicitly stated in the song below, is worth exploring:

Devarā ki cāl hamrā lāge barā būra ho bālam
Dāle rang uthāke phurhūra ho bālam
Kobo hātho colīye me dāl deitā pūra ho bālam
Dāle rang uthāke phurhūra ho bālam.

Brother-in-law's ways I find most annoying, beloved.
He tosses handfuls of color and then disappears, beloved.
Sometimes he puts his hand right into my blouse
Tosses handfuls of color and just disappears, beloved.

CASSETTE RECORDING BY GUDDU RANGEELA, "BHATAAR HOLI," T-SERIES, 2000

The devar-bhābhī bond traditionally contained all the ingredients of a typical joking relationship, which A. R. Radcliffe-Brown in his classic essay "On Joking Relationships" characterized as relations between persons in which one party is entitled to take liberties toward the other, who must, in turn, tolerate and bear it (Radcliffe-Brown 1959). In contrast to wives' avoidance relations with their *jeth*, their husband's elder brother, who as the senior member of the patrilineal clan is second only to the father-in-law in degrees of avoidance (see chapter 1), a woman's relationship with her devar (her husband's younger brother) is less restrictive, much more congenial and familiar, and requires no symbolic avoidance such as veiling. Faced with a hierarchical and sometimes hostile environment in their new marital homes, women looked to their devar as an ally in times of need. In return for the support he provided, a man's younger brother could expect to take liberties and enjoy favors from his elder brother's wife. The element of teasing and jesting thus disguised a mutually advantageous bond—one that eased the difficult transition for a woman into her marital home through the bestowing of affection and indulgences on her husband's younger brother. On the other hand, this bond meant that the incoming bride of the devar would encounter a potentially difficult situation fraught with jealousy, owing to the already present rival for her groom's affection—the bhābhī, the elder brother's wife. The suggestive overtones of the commercially recorded songs, the hints of favors and familiarity, obscure the pragmatism involved in cultivating an ally within the husband's clan and reduce the alliance to a merely sexual relationship.

In parts of north India and among certain intermediate and agricultural castes, which in principle permitted widows to remarry, the bond extended to an unstated understanding that, should the woman face early widowhood, the younger brother-in-law would marry her (Chowdhury 1990, 259–74). In this sense, as Prem Chowdhury has argued, among non-Brahmin castes, levirate marriage provided an alternative to the ideology of sati or self-immolation at the husband's funeral pyre. In other words, widow remarriage was clearly prohibited only among Brahmins and the martial Rajputs. Recent research on women's rights to land has confirmed that in Punjab, this custom, called *karevā*, preempted the potential threat to the unity of the patriclan posed by the subdivision of patrilineal property—if, for example, the widow remarried outside of the clan—and ensured that the patrilineage would remain intact (Agarwal 1995; Jassal 2001). The possibility of a widow's remarriage, which threatened the property of patrilineages, could only be contained by ensuring that the widow would not move out of the clan.

The same cultural logic promoted the varying degrees of easy familiarity between these two relatives as the accepted societal norm in other parts of north India, too. In any event, a woman's friendship with her younger brother-in-law was accepted, legitimized, and encouraged, in some cases to the extent that the former was expected to replace or fill in for the husband in contexts where the latter was likely to be absent. This is precisely the dimension of the relationship that has contributed to the joking, teasing, and sexual undercurrents as seen in the last line of this song:

Holi mein lutai da lahār, bhaujī rang dāle dau
Pore pore bhaujī tohār carhal ba javānī

Dekhi tohe muhvā se giratāve pāni
Māre joban upkār bhaujī rang dāle dau
Holi me lūte da lahār bhaujī rang dāle da
Upar nīce sagaro dāle da bhaujī rangavā
Colī, dorhī, rāl na corve kauno angavā
Āju ho būjhi la bhatār bhaujī rang dāle dau.

Let me abandon myself to the Holi mood, sister-in-law, let me color you,
Every bit of you, bursting with the abundance and glow of youth.
Just to look at you is mouth-watering.
Youth is so kind to you, sister-in-law, let me color you.
Let me abandon myself to the Holi revelry, let me color you,
Your blouse and knees, leaving no part,
Today, consider me your husband; let me color you.

CASSETTE RECORDING BY GUDDU RANGEELA, "CHATKAAR HOLI," T-SERIES, 2004

BROTHER-IN-LAW DEPENDENCE AND MALE OUTMIGRATION

I now turn to a song I heard performed by a group of women of the Mallah (fishers and river-farers) caste during my fieldwork in the Jaunpur village of Barsara. It is a classic of the jocular genre. The song belongs to the *kahrauā* genre of songs sung by the caste of Kahars or water-carriers. Here women's reliance on their brothers-in-law for assistance in running errands and for keeping women's secrets, and the rewards expected in return, are significant motifs that allow it to capture the essence of the devar-bhābhī bond. The song clearly suggests that Holi was by no means the only context within which such songs were sung. Rather, the easy familiarity found here, by no means caste-specific, could find expression in a range of contexts. It is, however, not surprising that the theme is so boldly articulated by women of the Kahar caste, who are known to have enjoyed fewer restrictions since their caste functions of fetching water and laboring in the fields allowed them relative freedom of mobility. Kahars are considered a "clean" servicing caste, traditionally allowed entry into the inner courtyards of upper-caste homes, where they assisted upper-caste women in household chores, including washing dishes.

Mandavā dhovan gaye bābā ke sagarvā
Morā tīkavā ho girelā manjhedār

Morā devarvā ho mor tikavā girelā manjhedār
Hāth torā jorūn devarā gor tohre lāgun
Mor devarvā ho Ganga me bovāide mahājāl
Eik daiyān dāle bhaujī dūsar daiyān dāle,
More bhaujiā ho tīsre me ghonghiyā sevār
Hāth tora jorūn . . .
Morā devarvā ho pheri se bovāide mahājāl
Eik daiyān dāre bhaujī dūi daiyān dāre
Morī bhaujiyā ho tīsare mein tikavā tohār
Hāth tore
Morā devarvā ho bhuiyān se tikavā la uthāi
Bhuiyān se tīkavā bhaujī le uthāi
Hamarā ke debau kau dān
More devarvā ho lāhurī nanadiyā toharā dān

"Took my washing to Baba's lake,
My forehead ornament fell into mid-stream.
Dear brother-in-law, my ornament is in mid-stream
I plead with you, brother-in-law, cast the big net into the river."
"Sister-in-law, I cast the net once, then the second time,
The third time nothing but snails and small fish."
"I plead with you, brother-in-law, cast the big net again."
"Sister-in-law, the first time, then the second
The third time, sister-in-law, your ornament appears."
"I plead with you, brother-in-law, pick up the ornament from the ground."
"For picking it up, sister-in-law
What will be my reward?"
"Dear brother-in-law, your own younger sister, that will be your reward."

SUBHAVATI, BARSARA, JAUNPUR

This song may be understood simply as one of jokes between the devar-bhābhī dyad, but since it is so loaded with sexual innuendoes and hints at the horror of incest in the last line, it is also suggestive of sexual transgressions between the two relatives and the sexually charged ties underlying the bond. In folksongs, where the loss of ornaments such as earrings, toe-rings, and the forehead ornament, all symbols of matrimony, signify loss of chastity, the recovery of the ornament by the brother-in-law leaves no doubt about where this chastity might have been lost, especially since a reward in the form of a bribe is expected. Historically, the region most likely to have fuelled the pragmatism of this relationship and kept it alive is the setting of my fieldwork, the states of Uttar Pradesh and Bihar. As explored in chapter 2, over the eighteenth and nineteenth centuries, the region witnessed male outmigration on an unprecedented scale. Beginning in 1834, as liberated slaves refused to work on sugar plantations, the resulting labor shortage fuelled the large-scale colonial recruitment drives for indentured labor to Mauritius, British Guyana, Trinidad, and Jamaica (Kumar 2001, 53). Areas where long spells of drought and famine had pauperized agriculturists and were driving peasants out of villages in search for work proved to be the ideal recruiting grounds for indentured laborers. Between 1845 and 1917, about 143,900 Indians were brought to Trinidad (with a total of over 500,000 to the Caribbean) (Niranjana 1998, 114). Ninety percent of those migrating to the Caribbean hailed from the Ganges plain, that is, the United Provinces, Central Provinces, Oudh, Orissa, and Bihar (Niranjana 1998, 115). Prabhu Mohapatra (1995) has argued that the importation of labor peaked in the 1870s and 1880s and that most of the recruits in the prime age group of between twenty and thirty years were drawn largely from the United Provinces and western Bihar.

The colonial planters' reluctance to permit the migrants to establish a permanent community made for a gender imbalance, such that only 23 percent of the emigrants were women (Mohapatra 1995, 231). Hence, for over two centuries, the migration of older male siblings, either to the shores of Calcutta to seek their fortunes in the sugar colonies or into Calcutta's emerging industrial centers, meant that the countryside was systematically depleted of young able-bodied males.

In the context of absentee or migratory husbands, who were sometimes gone for years at a stretch, the role a younger brother might have been expected to perform, as well as the duties and responsibilities he might have been expected to shoulder, can only be imagined. The existing devar-bhābhī bond sanctioned by folk and patriarchal traditions would have thus developed greater complexity and evolved other multi-layered dimensions in response to rising demands and expectations. Grounded in patriarchal anxieties about young women left behind and societal anxieties about the monumental changes migration triggered, there emerged an enormously rich repertoire of traditional folk songs dealing with the devar-bhābhī theme in the context of the husband's absence (Jassal 2006, 306–11).

While the repertoire of yearning songs that hint at the relationship between devar and bhābhī reflects the history and continuation of migration from the region, it was the Holi festival that provided the space within which the jocular element and the taking of liberties was justified, legitimized, verbalized, and given full-blown expression. Even within the commercial reframing of the folk song traditions, this motif remains a recurring one:

Are kaute phāgūnā bitī goile re, porodesiyā na auilen
Are desiyā na auilen, porodesiyā na auilen
Are gahānā tīkhāla me goroile re, porodesiyā na auilen
Bhītere bhītere bhaujī ranī haī gāch ho
Piyā sange rangavā khelā mohā chahāt ho
Are māja kīrākīrā kari koile re porodesiyā na auilen
Are kaute phāgūnā bitī goile re, porodesiyā na auilen
Are jethe jīke dekhe ho ā gaile marad
Are dekhī dekhī dilvā me hotā hamrā dorad
Are pāpi hamrā dāya tuhūn kaile re, porodesiyā na auilen
Are lāgato ki khisī lauike cithiyo re bochale
Are Motiya ke betvā re domī ito kochale
Are kauno sauvatī bāre koile re, porodesiyā na auilen
Are kause phāgūnā bitī goile re, porodesiyā na auilen
Are Gudu khātir sālo bhar se asrā lagāi ke
Are rākhelā ranīha chati Vipin se lukāi ke
Are kohiyā le khātir rakhī dhoile re, porodesiyā na auilen
Are saute phagūnā bitī goile re, porodesiyā na auilen

Oh how many Phāgun seasons passed, since the dweller in foreign lands returned?
Oh the traveler never returned.
My jewelry remained locked within the cupboard and the traveler didn't return.
Deep inside my breast, I nurse a huge wound.
My heart desires to frolic with my husband in Holi.
Oh he spoilt all the fun—the traveler, he didn't return.
Oh how many seasons since he returned?

Oh, the elder brother-in-law did return.

Seeing this my heart is pained.

Have mercy on me, sinner, my husband did not return.

Sometimes I think, just out of spite I'll send off a letter.

That Moti's son is pressing his attentions on me.

If he has a new mistress who is she? The traveler did not return.

For the sake of Gudu, I've been in wait for a whole year,

Shielded my modesty from the gaze of Vipin.

Tell me, for whom did I guard all this? The traveler never came

How many Phāguns has it been?

CASSETTE RECORDING BY GUDDU RANGEELA, "CHATKAAR HOLI," T-SERIES, 2004

In this region, women's songs of separation have become synonymous with phāg renderings. The songs also explore a gamut of conflicts and contradictions that acknowledge both the normative gender hierarchy between men and women and relationships that are more egalitarian in nature, even those wherein married women are either sexually more experienced or older than the bachelors in question, such as their younger or other classificatory brothers-in-law:

Naram bā anganā cūtī ho rang
Jan sagarī dālou ho devarā
Dāle ke dālo na bichvā me
Eik kagarī dālo ho devarā
Noikhe māno rangavā se sāra angavā būr dau
Ihe nihorā ba eiko alangavā bhaiyā khatir chor dau
Māro pickārī bhale dhorhī me satā ke
Ūpar māja le lo bhītarī bacā ke
Colī uthāke na hātho lagāke na ragarī dālo na devarā
Dāle ke bāto na bicavā me eik kagorī dālo na devarā.

The courtyard is soft, dripping color.

Don't put the whole of it, brother-in law;

If you must put it somewhere, then place it in the center.

I wish my entire body to be drenched in color.

Leave aside this part, saved up for your brother.

Squirt the colored water, up close by all means.

Enjoy the externalities, save the secret parts.

Raising my blouse, paint on the color with your hands, brother-in-law
And if you must, place it in the center.
CASSETTE RECORDING BY GUDDU RANGEELA, "CHATKAAR HOLI," T-SERIES, 2004

The multiple expressions and interpretations the genre affords add to its immense appeal for listeners and audiences. Suggestive, veiled, and ambiguous as well as blatantly forthright, the layered quality of the texts adds to the nonelitist nature of the recordings. Although continuously evolving, the recordings nevertheless maintain some continuity with the earlier forms, especially in terms of theme, melody and style. Their popularity appears to be on the rise, and as Peter Manuel suggests in the case of *rasiyas* or songs based on the motif of yearning between Radha and Krishna,[2] these recordings, too, might have a role to play in reconstituting the boundaries between private and public musical life (Manuel 1993, 218).

To conclude this section, I turn to the popularity of folk forms known as "chutney" brought to Trinidad by indentured laborers from rural north India, especially of genres performed largely by women in prewedding ceremonies. The movement of these songs, with their explicitly sexual and humorous themes, from the secluded private sphere of the home to public venues has become a bone of contention for the Indian community's leaders in Trinidad, who see these cultural forms as degraded or vulgar. These concerns parallel earlier anxieties about rural Creole women's sexual and economic independence. In the Carnival in Trinidad in 1996, the surprise hit sung by Sonny Mann was a Bhojpuri chutney song, "Lotay La," about a man seducing his sister-in-law (Niranjana 1998, 127). The complex mix of ethnic, cultural, racial, and gender issues in new sites of modernity occasioned by geographical displacements is an important theme for future research but one that cannot be explored here.

HOLI SONGS AND CASTE MOBILITY

By the twentieth century, the Indian elites themselves trained their attention on the sexuality of lower castes and classes as detrimental to the health and well-being of the nation. MARY JOHN AND JANAKI NAIR, INTRODUCTION TO *A QUESTION OF SILENCE?*, 19

It comes as no surprise that the reform movements of the last century targeted the singing of folk songs as obscene and unworthy of chaste women. For instance, the soiling of the *cunarī* or bosom cloth, in folk-songs a metaphor for an illicit relationship, acquired commonplace usage. For social reformers of the nineteenth century, it was lower-caste women's sexuality and the failure of lower-caste men to control it that was deemed to be partially the cause of the lower castes' impurity (Rege 1995, 33). As Gupta (2001, 26) points out, social reformers conflated chastity with upper-caste practices. Both the Arya Samaj and the Sanatan Dharma movements were against the "bad customs" of women singing obscene songs and participating in Holi celebrations. Gupta demonstrates that owing both to colonial perceptions and to the efforts of social reform movements, the air of obscenity linked to Holi revelries became associated in public consciousness with lower-caste practices or at least with Hindu degeneracy (Gupta 2001).

In the preceding chapters, I have enumerated the range of restrictions that caste reformers spelled out for women, perceiving women's social and economic behavior as the sphere through which to effect change with a view to elevating the status of the entire caste (Jassal 2001, 48–63). Sanskritization, as a strategy embraced by a range of upwardly mobile caste groups throughout the first half of the last century, meant the adoption of restrictive social codes for women. In addition to proscribing women's rights to participate in *melās* (fairs), attend the theatre, and bathe semi-nude at public *ghāts*, other culturally popular practices such as the singing of ritual songs (*gālīs*) at weddings and at Holi were severely condemned. The implications of Sanskritization varied for men and women.

In this context, it may be fruitful to analyze the resilience and popularity of the Holi song genre, an expression of lower-caste femininities that is today being replaced by the assertion of lower-caste masculinities in defiance against Sanskritization norms, as well as to note the continuing relevance of its structural logic. To further probe questions of caste, class, and gender in contemporary north India, I reference two encounters I had in the field, both of which throw into sharp relief the importance of "Negotiating the Serious Import of Humor," the title of Joan Emerson's essay (Emerson 1969), and of women's inability to reclaim their voice once the genre has been appropriated by men and appears in the public domain.

In the first encounter, I observed a woman request to change a particularly sexually suggestive music cassette, which was playing in a public space. Her request was refused on the plea that it was "only a joke" and, as such, an integral part of the seasonal festive mood. The situation confirmed Gal's insight about the function of irony to allow men to "disclaim the intent if it results in challenge or threat" (Gal 1991, 183). In the second encounter, a less offensive cassette was interrupted midway, ejected, and swiftly replaced by an obscene Holi cassette, just as a group of middle-class women entered the public space. In both cases, the women present were the intended targets of the lyrics, the women's obvious discomfort only enhancing the men's voyeurism, a mild form of harassment understood in the contemporary Indian context by the euphemism "eve-teasing."

These encounters resemble Peter Lyman's account of masculinities, in particular, the role of sexist jokes in forging male group ties and the channel joking provides for men's anger (Lyman 1987, 148–63). Lyman suggests that where aggressive conduct is valued, it must be in accordance with the power hierarchy and must serve authority, not challenge it. The very fact that the aggression is channeled through music mutes its edge. Further, the cultural legitimacy the devar-bhābhī bond provides frees it from individual aggression and turns it into a form of group solidarity. Similarly, Lyman has argued that male bonding requires an "eros of aggression," wherein, for example, collective obscene talk that might be witnessed by unfamiliar women produces a high level of excitement and arousal.

In his analysis of the contradictions and vulnerabilities young men feel about their relationships with women and their responsibilities at work, Lyman focuses on three elements of joking relationships: the content of the jokes, the eroticism of the rule-breaking, and the projected image of strength and being "cool," all of which are pitted against their dependence on both women and work (Lyman 1987, 157). Thus, even while individual men may recognize the songs as vulgar, they serve the purpose of strengthening male bonding.

One possible explanation for the phenomenon discussed above is the increasing polarization of upper and lower castes and the place of gender in these processes. The space that lower castes occupy within a hierarchical structured order is similar to that occupied by women within patriarchy, and hence the lower castes' experience of powerlessness might be compared to women's lack of power. Women, perceived as being closer to nature, represent the chaotic elements over which patriarchy must impose order and structure. At the same time, patriarchy draws from these elements, which it first structures. If the space occupied by lower castes in this structured universe is the same as that occupied by women, then the appropriation of this genre by lower-caste males must be understood as "an attack on the social order" and their chance to subvert it. In this sense, it also parallels and echoes women's subversive role in the Holi festivals described earlier. Hence the lower caste or class appropriation of the genre and the visible and public assertion of this appropriation can be likened to attempts to relax the rigidities and thus feminize the masculinity represented by the hierarchical caste order.

The images of women these songs evoke also hint at the unease and hostility that exist between upper-caste women and lower-caste men. In no small measure, the middle-class women's movement, on the rise in towns since the 1980s, and the growth of NGOs committed to women's empowerment have contributed to the visibility of women's issues and their aspirations for gender inequality. Images of powerful and educated women on national television in recent decades may, in turn, have contributed to the assertion of masculinities.

Since the control of women's sexuality has always been a significant concern of caste patriarchies, intercaste relations in the north Indian countryside lie at the heart of the changes we are discussing. Music's inherent ability to transform and synthesize is precisely what contributes to its effectiveness. It fuses ideas together, serving as a nonviolent means of communication and of breaking down walls and hierarchies. Because of its association with femininity, hyperpatriarchal structures fear this form of expression; hence the banning of music by regimes such as the Taliban. Black and protest music has shown that when hierarchies cut too deep, music has the potential to heal the wounds.

In north India, the widening economic gulf between the upper and lower classes and the lower castes' thirst for political enfranchisement provides a fertile ground for the synthesizing work of music. The use of song at a public festival to critique and parody a behavioral norm so fundamental to patriarchal and caste order is tantamount to a mild form of consensual social protest on behalf of the disenfranchised. While the Holi songs parody the social order on one level, on another they reinforce the very order they seek to subvert. Indeed, as Michele Mitchell shows in another context, the "longing of black men to seize the prerogatives of manhood denied them by the larger society could and did stultify black women's own desires" (1999, 17).

This chapter analyzes the gendered impact of technological change by focusing on the genre of song recordings associated with the Holi festival. By focusing on recordings specific to this spring festival, I was able to explore a gamut of interlinked phenomena, ranging from the questioning of gender hierarchies to what constitutes the erotic and the purpose it serves in upholding the social order.

As Holi represents a liminal state that exists in time rather than in space, the application of fluid new rules offers breathing space and a release from society's corrosive and destructive elements. In allowing the social body to be reborn and rejuvenated, the festival serves a similar role to that of collective sacrifice in ancient civilizations, where the integral violence had a purpose. In challenging the existing hierarchy and exploring the many dimensions of gender relations, the recordings hint at widening cleavages and gulfs and point to all that is simmering under the surface, urgently seeking resolution.

Equally, however, the recordings serve to reinforce established hierarchies and gender stereotypes. Yet, while the traditional Holi song genre was nonthreatening to the social order, the recordings tend to usurp the space that was traditionally available to women for engaging in role reversals and spontaneous expressions of their discontent.

The songs illustrate how ideas and messages travel between rural- and urbanscapes. In the commercialization of Holi songs today, and in their ready availability and accessibility in the form of music cassettes, we find the sensibility of Holi, the elements that constituted its inner logic, and its purpose as a means of release considerably altered. Now, it is not the women who articulate and direct their insults toward men, but the men who sing what were once women's songs; as such, the element of role reversal so empowering and crucial to women's spontaneous song sessions is lost. In this attempt to evoke the mood of bawdy revelry characteristic of Holi, it is the feminine gender that becomes the butt of sexual jokes.

Further, the devar-bhābhī bond, already an easily identified cultural space where men can take liberties with and tease women, appears to lend itself most readily to the message of bawdy licentiousness today's new cultural entrepreneurs seek to promote. And since the new songwriters are men aiming to appeal to an audience at a bazaar, the new songs tend to contain stereotypically demeaning images of women, wearing the jocular guise of the bhābhī (sister-in-law). In the name of meeting public demand, the new cultural entrepreneurs create their own definitions of public need and taste. While the songs focus on the licentiousness of the devar-bhābhī relationship in particular, the fact that the presence of a younger brother-in-law is axiomatic for married women across caste and class lines means that the songs ultimately conflate all women with those who are permissive or who occupy degrading roles.

In short, the commercially recorded songs simultaneously transgress established gender norms, appropriate women's autonomous spaces, recast women as objects of the male gaze, and express lower-caste masculine resistance to Sanskritization. All this is accomplished through the opening Holi provides, even as the genre ultimately reinforces the existing order. Nevertheless, the song texts are available to multiple readings, which accounts for the recordings' immense popular appeal.

Each is invariably memorable, a perfectly worked-out expression of skilled composition, though often disarmingly simple. These *catus* have appealed to, and shaped, the taste of generations of people. . . . They bring to mind, in addition to aesthetic judgement, a host of literary, political, and cultural contexts, indeed, a whole world view.

VELCHERU NARAYANA RAO AND DAVID SHULMAN,

A POEM AT THE RIGHT MOMENT, 4

The songs presented in this book are complex poetic forms through which their singers convey "provocative interpretations of themselves and their society" (Briggs 1988). As vital oral resources that reinforce the existence of competing statements in any context, these songs impact listeners and singers in diverse ways. While the songs analyzed in these pages could be seen primarily as a source of pleasure, they also lend themselves to new contexts and are remembered and recalled to recreate and imagine older contexts (Rao and Shulman 1998, 3). Thus, in addition to offering endless amusement and critiquing male dominance, they also serve to induce feelings of solidarity, to develop and nurture the skills of interrogation, and to sharpen women's powers of negotiation.

In village settings, therefore, the singers with the most varied and extensive repertoires were respected in their communities, who regarded them as the village memory or conscience keepers. These singers set the tone for ceremonies, work, and informal gatherings and enriched each of these contexts by teasing out and bringing to the surface emotions appropriate and desirable to the collective. Such abilities might be said to parallel the expertise of those ritual specialists who instinctively know when to chant the most appropriate Sanskrit mantra required for a Hindu ritual, for instance. In this sense, the singers attempted to interpret the traditions and social settings they engaged, that both might be transformed during the performance. Since different singers remembered different songs their community had collectively produced, each of their song collections was integral to their particular community's overall repertoire. It is no wonder that interested singers were keen to enlarge their repertoires and that collecting and swapping songs through oral circulation remains a pleasurable pastime for many.

The manner of such oral transmission suggests a profound awareness of the grammar of poetics. If it is the meter of a song that facilitates its remembrance, then those songs most widely circulated reflect the community's acceptance and endorsement of their enormous appeal. In turn, the songs' poetic qualities further shape their audience's sensibilities. Hence, what Rao and Shulman concluded in regard to the Telugu verses holds true for our songs as well: "Through the domain of desire, social commentary, the articulation of cultural values, and critical taste, these interlocking stanzas embody an entire education, an expressive vision of life and poetry" (Rao and Shulman 1998, 250).

The songs of the preceding chapters confronted and grappled with a gamut of women's emotions and experience. As emotions are cultural artifacts and culturally embedded phenomena, these songs offered a point of entry into the ethnographic analysis of emotions, allowing the fullest exploration even of those emotions that must remain suppressed in the interest of familial life. Competing voices and dialogues between daughters and fathers, mothers-in-law and daughters-in-law, sisters and brothers, husbands and wives, sets of sisters-in-law, upper-caste women and lower-caste lovers all enrich our understanding of multivocal and contrasting perspectives.

As discourses of emotions, the songs also offered complex and nuanced insights into "the multiple, shifting, and contested meanings possible in emotional utterances and interchanges" (Abu-Lughod and Lutz 1990, 11). Through focusing on both the practices and the meanings of collective singing, I was able to investigate how emotions as forms of social action are informed by cultural values as well as how they affect the realm of the social as idioms of communication. The songs demonstrated that emotional talk is not only about internal psychological states but also about social life and power relations. Hence, chapters 2 and 3 in particular charted how emotional discourses are shaped by the political economies in which they arise. Songs sung on the occasion of marriage, for instance, provide an outlet for the intensely contradictory emotions relating to the departure of a daughter that can scarcely be articulated in ordinary speech. At wedding ceremonies, as women remember and relive their own departures, the songs serve as tearjerkers, thereby effecting the public displays necessary to induce the appropriate emotions. It was possible to retrace the affective emotions of at least some of the songs, especially those that move people to tears and are, in this sense, also experienced bodily.

The ability to choose the most appropriate song for any given context, much like the ability to choose a "poem at the right moment" (see Rao and Shulman 1998), had the potential to enhance the drama and significance of that moment, elevating it from the mundane to the memorable. Moreover, since the songs also evoked associations and cultural interconnections in singers and listeners alike, each of this volume's chapters sought to highlight their importance as means of effective social communication among those who share common bodies of knowledge and value systems. In this regard, the intertextual resonance allowed us to hear the competing voices that, over time, have imbued the songs with their layered nuances. Far from treating each song individually or in isolation, therefore, I have attempted to highlight the interconnections between the songs and genres. As each song echoes others, each is best appreciated as part of the whole and as integral to the totality of the oral tradition.

Moreover, the music to which these songs were set served to induce the appropriate moods, and the melodic variations ranged from the dirge-like quality of the grinding songs and their grim messages to the upbeat, flirtatious banter of the kajlī. Some melodies oozed sexuality and playfulness, while others conveyed innocence or injustice. In songs that raised questions about existing power relations, the harmonies appeared to serve as the background for the interrogation or protest we were about to hear. Thus, like clues embedded in the performance, the formal structures that framed the songs were almost as meaningful and important to my analysis as the content and the words.

Songs also lend themselves to different interpretations as a function of context. Thus, as texts, their meaning is by no means fixed but is constantly evolving and shifting, as are the interpretations they make available. It is the meaning that the singers themselves attach to their songs that gives these songs their enormous fluidity and allows for a range of interpretations to be made. Taken together, the songs reveal just how audience sensibilities have been shaped by the insights, wisdom, and sheer poetry of the songs. From cautionary advice and social commentary to reflections on cultural values, bargaining, negotiation, interrogation, and insights into the realm of desire and intimacy, the songs offer a vividly expressive and integrated vision of life. Above all, the songs reflect women's interdependence and cooperation, in the spheres of both work and ritual.

While themes and language occasionally offered clues about the historical origins of a particular song or genre, as in the case of the migration songs, this aspect proved elusive. Despite the disconcerting sense these songs provide of the social milieu's coherence and homogeneity, the fact that they are used to illustrate ongoing social processes confirms their historicity, making these texts a "constellation or conjuncture of both past and present" (Niranjana 1993, 321). As source material for the anthropologist, then, the songs' timeless or static quality may be attributed to the process of transcription or translation that appears to fix them in time. Rather, since songs work like social commentary, most singers attempt to invoke or remember songs appropriate to an occasion precisely to express a particular interest or viewpoint.

For instance, Sita songs, while making sense of the present also reflect the dynamism and vitality of the past, thereby providing a bridge between shared textual traditions and the uniqueness of the present. In this sense, far from merely repeating timeworn traditions, my fieldwork experiences demonstrated how songs also help to create and sustain communities. These songs showed how "linguistic form, cultural significance, textual tradition and social interaction become one in performance" (Briggs

1988, xvi). Instead of offering clues about origins, then, the songs offer insights into richly complex, heterogeneous, and densely textured, gendered worlds. They afford one a glimpse into how women's cultural traditions are continually being invented, constructed, and improvised (Niranjana et al. 1993, 6). If, in a reflexive manner, performances comment on the situations in which they emerged, the very interpretative exercise this book undertakes implicates us equally in the process of producing meaning.

One aspect of life that remains considerably under-researched is that of conjugality. As this volume demonstrates, however, women's songs have effectively unearthed this dimension. Many songs appear to reinforce dominant values and reiterate the auspiciousness and prosperity of the family. Familial life emerged as the site for both worldly and spiritual fulfillment, so that women's aspirations appeared circumscribed by such concerns. Often, the nurturing aspects of the songs and the human bonds, relationships, and sense of community they underscore appear to cancel out the problematic aspects of the gender stereotypes they transmit (Katyal and Chanda 1998, 178). Sita songs, ranging from the intensely private to those that knit together small collectivities of women, offer rich commentaries on the social condition of women in the countryside. I found that these songs' appeal to women's potentialities resonated deeply among peasant women and also across caste and class. Thus, "women's affinity with Sita may be in response to her enormous tragedy yet it is widely believed that the raw deal meted out to her in the Ramāyanā has the power to move not just women, but everyone 'to the depths of one's being'" (Iyengar in Hess 1988, 24).

While self-effacing devotion is Sita's hallmark, her capacity to also inspire awe and reverence prompts women to try to shape themselves in her mold, so that even if they are ill-treated, they will ultimately hold enormous clout and power over their husbands and families (Kishwar 1999). Moreover, as some of the grinding songs showed, women appear to understand that the only way they are likely to get relatives to act in their favor is by seeming to be above reproach. However, despite the numerous images of conformity in Sita songs, they also provide a space for alternate voices and visions.

In this context, the question that needs addressing is, do the songs have an alternative or oppositional relation to dominant culture? For instance, songs that catalogue the ways in which women retain close ties with their brothers, thus defying the expectations of the marital home, could be interpreted as expressions of opposition to normative ideals. As women are the most disadvantaged by and stand to gain the least from the system as it is currently structured, it is hardly surprising that women's songs are so diverse in range and genre. The songs therefore reveal women as sometimes conforming, often interrogative, but also occasionally defiant and subversive.

Yet, despite such variations and multivocality, how are we to read the songs' overarching theme of gender discrimination? During fieldwork I often heard that having a son was necessary for the appropriate performance of rituals, and yet ironically parents reported enjoying their closest emotional bonds with their daughters, not their sons. If the preference for sons arises from the belief that sons will provide their parents with security in their old age, I found this belief repeatedly belied by the evidence in the field. Disputes brought before caste *pancāyats* (caste councils) for adjudication were good indicators of the tensions caused from the current costs of living, chronic job insecurities, and societal expectations.

For instance, in 2003 in Sadiapur village, which borders the town of Allahabad, when the father of Mahesh and Naresh Nishad died, the brothers sought the intervention of the Nishad caste's pancāyat, asking him to divide their father's assets equitably between them. The caste council divided the assets, but at the end of the proceedings, its flamboyant headman, Avinash Choudhary, made a caustic remark that created a stir. Choudhary suggested to the brothers that as their biggest asset had still not been divided, this also should be done. Pointing to their mother, he said, "after all, your mother is also alive, why not cut her up and also share her fifty-fifty?" Choudhary explained that he intended his remark "to bring home the point that while the entire wealth should have gone to the widow, the brothers had hastily dispossessed her and delinked her from it." After first embarrassing them publicly, the caste pancāyat delineated which of the brothers would be responsible for her shelter, food, and clothing and which would arrange for her medical treatment.

In a similar case, a woman approached her caste pancāyat with the grievance that while she had four sons, she was herself on the verge of starvation and destitution. The pancāyat convened to rebuke the sons and passed the decision that since they were all earning their livelihoods, they would have to either agree upon a pooling of resources for her monthly upkeep or take turns in shouldering this responsibility. Avinash Choudhary describes how the pancāyat staged a dramatic and public showdown in order to drive his point home: "The pancāyat decided, let's take a large sheet and collect alms. Let's put out this sheet in front of her dead husband's home and let's put up a board asking for alms, a paisa or so for the widow's upkeep. This proved embarrassing enough for the sons and they accepted the pancāyat's decision about their shared responsibility for the widow's maintenance" (fieldnotes, Sadiapur 2003).

Such accounts, which I heard in many of the villages where I conducted my fieldwork, suggest that sons do not always provide security to parents in their old age, and the situation is worse for widowed mothers. Examples of destitute widows who had been abandoned by their adult sons were commonplace and never failed to expose the hollowness of the ideology that assumed sons would provide eldercare. Among my singers for instance, Munraji of village Barsara, handicapped by blindness and the mother of two adult sons, lived independently, largely because she was made to feel a burden by her married sons. Some widows, whose songs are cited in the preceding pages, even asked me to intervene on their behalf and ask the government pension office to release the *vriddhā* (widow) pension to which they were entitled. It is no wonder that women's songs not only reflected this reality of gender disparity but also enabled women to imagine the limits of their conditions as well as the tensions of working within the constraints posed by complex patriarchal arrangements.

Through the songs in this book, I have sought to provide a key to unlocking the many layers constituting this gendered social universe, wherein such paradoxes are part of the complex everyday reality. In the process of shining light on how daily concerns are articulated and expressed in song, then, I managed to unearth the social construction of gender.

The cautionary tales of the jatsār of chapter 1, for instance, while issuing their notes of warning and setting out the limits of transgression also appeared to celebrate women's ingenuity. The ambivalence in the messages of these songs came through clearly. Hence, while seeming to endorse the trial by fire, the same songs also spelled out the attractions, even the irresistibility, of lower-caste men, thus exposing the conceit of upper-caste masculinities. While the work songs of chapter 2 questioned the social order more directly, their predominant notes being ones of negotiation and bargaining for greater freedoms within this order's confines, they invariably did so in ways that combined this questioning with acquiescence and conformity.In chapter 3, songs as discourses of emotion facilitated the unearthing of myriad emotions and anxieties at the core of women's transitions from natal to conjugal homes, both at the level of the collective and of the individual. It is in the Sita songs of chapter 4 that the varied experiences, voices, approaches, solutions, and messages covered the vastest spectrum, as Sita herself became a potent figure through which to discuss peasant women's own struggles. Chapter 5's inquiry into the gender dimensions of the Lorikāyan made it possible to trace how the passivity signified by Sita's upper-caste persona came to be valorized. In this masculine ballad, the role women played in forging of caste identities was fleshed out. The chapter traced the decline in values of independence and ingenuity as women's submissiveness and passivity were endorsed. The multiple renditions of Holi songs presented in chapter 6 reveal how technologies contributed to the transformation of women's songs and the ongoing displacement of women's voices as a consequence of modernity. Fighting the eclipse of traditional forms, then, is not the only reason to document the songs.

Nevertheless, my fieldwork did highlight the gradual decline of this rich oral tradition in the cultural milieu that once nourished and nurtured it. This decline, set in motion by increasing literacy and the primacy accorded to the written rather than the oral word in terms of authenticating factual information, has translated into the emergence of a significantly narrower and more restricted imagination of reality. Quite apart from the circulation of songs through the recordings discussed in chapter 6, the circulation of songs in print through chapbooks or journals further decreases community production and improvisation and, therefore, contributes to the gradual decline in the rich contextual variations. The community, instead of participating in the creation of the songs, as in the case of the Telugu catus, "is reduced to the role of their consumer" (Rao and Shulman 1998, 197). Even if some versions of the songs survive in print, they are now devoid of meter and melody. Further, rising literacy means the singing of songs is being supplanted by the reading of newspapers or the watching of television, activities increasingly antagonistic to the genres we have been discussing. Nevertheless, the fact that new songs do get produced is a reflection of the resilience and flexibility of the oral tradition.

As I finished writing this book, the landmark Women's Reservation Bill, which called for reserving 33 percent of the seats in Parliament for women, was put to vote in Parliament. Even during the years of my fieldwork, however, the movement for women's representation at the local level, in the pancāyats and village councils, had inspired a number of songs in favor of women political leaders and village heads:

Jab gaunvā ke mahilā pradhān hoyī,
Tab gaunvā ke hamro bikās hoyī

When the women of our village become pradhans
That's when development will reach our village.

Here we see cultural forms in the making. With NGOs in the countryside recognizing the pedagogical power of folksongs, just as Sufi mystics or caste reformers such as Phule[1] had done, messages of development are constantly being expressed through existing forms, such as songs, to make the new models more accessible. Consider the song below, which couches the message of an NGO in a motif that recurs in a number of folksongs—that of the garden and the maiden tending it:

Na bāte der bhaiyā na bāte der
Hamnī ki camkaī anganvā nū ho bhaiyā na bāte der
Ujaral bagiyā ki bilkhai maliniyā
Panapai me sāthi sapanvā nū bhaiyā na bāte der

It won't be long, brother, not too long
Our courtyard will shine again, brother it won't be long.
In her uprooted garden, weeps the maiden who tends it.
But for the new dream to flower, friend, it won't be too long.

Or, this one, which I heard sung at the Jan Sewa Ashram, an NGO in Badalpur, Jaunpur, emphasizing education:

Shikshā ke leke roshaniyā, kalamiyā me diyā na jalaibo

With the flame of education, we'll ignite our pens.

This book has been concerned with the countryside and the rural milieu. However, among the growing middle classes in India's towns and cities, it is common to find at least one or two lead singers who bring out their notebooks of the family's song repertoires, at least for wedding celebrations. Perhaps with the shift to literacy and people's increasing distance from contexts wherein oral traditions might be reaffirmed, the maintenance of notebooks for preserving the songs of grandmothers is a natural progression. In Israel, for instance, in recent years Cochin women's songs are undergoing an important revival as women are reclaiming and actively remembering and performing Jewish Malayalam songs from the notebooks of their grandmothers who first made *aliya* (or immigration to Israel as a religious duty) in the 1950s soon after the Jewish state was formed. This revival in Israel has triggered similar revivals within Muslim, Christian, and Hindu communities in Kerala, India. Similar processes are evident in other parts of India where women, distanced from their rural roots, revive their family and community traditions and in the process recover the voices and celebrations of past generations, particularly those of weddings. It is also worth noting the phenomenal success of several Bollywood films that attempt to show how a middle-class wedding celebration *ought* to be carried out by blending traditional elements with the thoroughly modern concerns and consumerist aspirations of the upwardly mobile. Yet, despite such pockets of revival, the question remains, what creative ways of remembering will the changing, transforming communities of the future adopt?

1. Vermilion (*sindūr*) is the auspicious orange and red powder in a woman's hair part that symbolizes her married status. The groom's ritual application of this powder in the bride's hair part marks the conclusion of the marriage ceremony.

2. A Launda-nach (*nāc*) is a male-only company of itinerant singers, percussionists, and performers that entertains rural audiences with skits, plays, dancing, and music. Cross-dressing is a key feature of these performances as men perform female roles.

3. In this nirgun song, Sakhī (women's female friend) could just as well refer to a male worshipper who has assumed the identity of one of Sita's girlfriends, the persona adopted by the Rasik branch of the Ramnandi sect to serve Ram and Sita. Van der Veer writes that in an attempt to bring about a radical transformation of their masculinity in the ritual theatre of temple worship, Rasiks dress as women (Van der Veer 1987, 691).

NOTES TO CHAPTER 1: THE DAILY GRIND

1. Another example is the ropni songs. See chapter 2.

2. Vaughan (1987, 119) notes that in Malawi "the distinctive feature of women's songs and stories about the 1949 famine is the emphasis they place on the role of marital relations in shaping the pattern of suffering. When asked about fam-

ine, women tell about family, marriage, divorce and children. In their pounding songs they sing about the role of husbands in famine—either praising them for their exemplary behaviour or (much more frequently) berating them for their neglect." As in the Bhojpuri songs, in Malawi "pounding songs composed and sung in normal times are frequently critical of men and deeply concerned with family and marital relations. Sung by one or more women as they pound maize in the courtyards of hut complexes, they can be timed to provoke the maximum amount of embarassment to the passing male villager, whose misdemeanours or inadequacies sound out across the village to the rhythm of the pestle" (Vaughan 1987, 121).

3. As in Malawi, there are songs in rural India that describe the impact of famine. Verrier Elwin (1946, 167), who collected folksongs in the Chhattisgarh region of the Central provinces between 1932 and 1944, recorded one about the collapse of a "subsistence gurantee" during the famine of 1886, a situation not unlike the one Vaughan outlined for the Malawi famine of 1949.

4. In this region the cadence with which jatsārs are sung makes them easily recognizable, even to the untrained listener. In the songs sung by the women in Chhattisgarh during the 1930s (Elwin 1946, 119), the grinding action of the two millstones on the grain caught between them symbolized the plight of the daughter-in-law caught between her affinal and consanguineal kin ("Grindstone is my mother-in-law/grinding peg my brother"). Like the corn, therefore, the daughter-in-law is trapped between the proverbial rock and a hard place, the two sources of intrakin group social control, and gradually ground down.

5. The tension between affines is a constant theme in Indian rural folklore. Numerous stories collected by ethnographers at the start of the twentieth century from the Santal Parganas, a large ethnic group in Bihar, for example, recount how a family fortune is saved or restored by the timely and wise actions of a daughter-in-law, and how a female—also a daughter-in-law—died for grieving the death of a Chamar, thereby breaking caste rules (Bompas 1909, 39–40, 194–96). The subtext to such folkloric accounts appears to be that daughters-in-law ought to be cherished, either because of their contributions to the well-being of the family into which they marry or because of their humanity, a discourse that hints at underlying tensions between affines in this context.

6. It is easy to forget the violence that can be inflicted on transgressors of existing social boundaries. Gough (1981, 322–23), for example, describes a case in south India of a cowherd who had sexual relations with the wife of an elderly bedridden Brahmin. The cowherd, as a consequence, was beaten, castrated, and murdered by other Brahmins in the village, his mutilated body left to hang from the rafters of a house as a warning to others. In many respects, both the discourse about purity and the symbolic murder of the

transgressor in this example mirror those involved in the lynchings of blacks by whites in the U.S. South.

7. Netua and Netuin refer, respectively, to the males and females of the caste of performers and acrobats.

8. Such nonviolent solutions in fact reinforce the role of violent sanctions, an everpresent threat.

9. The Saur is an expensive variety of fish.

10. A Bengalin is a female inhabitant of Bengal.

11. A kos is a measure of distance equal to approximately two miles.

12. Derived from the loaded concept of "sat" as a married woman's virtue, chastity and single-minded devotion to her husband (discussed in chapter 5) as well as evocative of the mythic goddess Sati, who committed suicide by immolating herself on her father, Daksha's, sacrificial fire to assuage an insult to her husband Shiva, (see chapter 4) "sati" has several layered connotations. The term implies the religiously sanctioned practice of widow immolation at the funeral pyres of their husbands. The voluntary as well as coercive nature of this controversial practice has generated immense debate, besides being on the agenda of social reformers through the ages, as well as contemporary feminists, especially since it signifies the cessation of a woman's social persona at the death of her husband. The practice, particularly associated with upper-caste pretensions, came to symbolize one of the hallmarks of upper caste "purity"and status. For a comprehensive discussion of the theme, see Courtright 2007.

13. Dom is a caste of funerary ritualists, an occupation regarded as low in the caste hierarchy because of the pollution associated with death. However, in many regions, particularly Benaras, the caste is known to be very wealthy because of the high fees they charge for their ritual services as well as the propensity of people to donate large sums to these specialists on the occasion of a funeral.

NOTES TO CHAPTER 2: SINGING BARGAINS

1. For debates on the voice of the subaltern, see Spivak 1993.

2. While on the surface male songs about migration tend to celebrate the heroism of the migrating men, they also reflect a deep anxiety about the uncontrolled sexuality of the women they left behind. The folk bard Bhikhari Thakur, for instance, engages the theme of migration in his popular musical Bidesiya. See Kumar 2001. Songs about migration sung by men and composed by male bards tend to differ in focus and mood from songs sung and composed by women.

3. *Meherin* meaning "householder."

4. "Status production," a term used by Hanna Papanek (1989, 97–116), refers to

the tendency among upwardly mobile castes to withdraw their women from working in the fields for the purpose of indicating the group's higher status. This is a form of Sanskritization, a phenomenon first theorized by M. N. Srinivas as the attempt of upwardly mobile castes to emulate the practices and norms of the upper castes, and refers to the process by which castes low in the caste hierarchy seek to emulate the practices of the higher castes and thus claim a higher status. This form of upward mobility is the feature of entire subcaste groups, rather than individuals, and is ongoing. As upper-caste women do not work in the fields but rather hire in labor for agricultural tasks, rural communities and castes that withdraw their women from agricultural work do so to assert their higher social status and engage in "status production."

NOTES TO CHAPTER 3: EMOTIONS IN A RITE OF PASSAGE

1. The words *Biyāh* and *Birahā* share etymological roots with the Sanskrit words *Vivaha* (marriage or unity) and *Viraha* (separation).

2. Kanyadān is the ritual gifting of a virgin daughter by the parents to her husband

3. The giving of these gifts serves as a ritual of appeasement for restoring the cosmic order and returning peace to the heavens and purity to the earth. This ritual prescribes the giving of alms to outcastes such as Doms and Bhangis, who are seen as mediators with the power to induce the demons to release the moon. Through their gifts, the upper castes effectively bribe the ritually polluting lowest castes to worship the demons and thereby restore order. Since such gifts represent the conversion of material into spiritual wealth, upper-caste patrons are doing themselves a favor. By responding charitably to the outcaste beggars, upper-caste patrons "managed thereby to sidestep the sin of interrupting the reciprocal flow of asking and receiving which is what constitutes dana" (Guha 1985, 17), that is, the reciprocal act in which asking must be matched by giving (18).

4. See song 8 below, sung by Bhagirathi Devi, wherein the human soul's final journey to meet the Creator is likened to the bride's ritual send off. Thus, in folk registers, the poignancy of a bride's departure also evokes the soul's final journey, contributing an additional element of pathos to the bride's ritual leave-taking.

5. Oldenburg shows that in Punjab, the growth of private property in land eroded women's economic power and social worth. However, it was women's wealth and dowry, that is, women's safety nets, that could be deployed to restore the failing fortunes of entire families in the nineteenth century. High demands for revenue and chronic indebtedness appear to have necessitated the conversion of women's resources and jewelry into cash for the purchase of land and other items (Oldenburg 2002, 47). Historically, therefore, the new

perception of land as property radically altered woman's rights. Land went up in value, as did other kinds of property, and the bride's dowry was no longer the equivalent of receiving a fair share in her natal family's holdings. Further, as ownership rights over landed property were definitively placed in the names of sons of the patrilineage, brothers came to view the return of an unhappily married sister to her natal home as "an unrightful" one (171).

6. The song refers to the erection of a leafy canopy, supported by four bamboo poles and decorated with leaves of the auspicious green mango, in the courtyard of the bride's house where the wedding rites are to be performed.

7. "Head ornament" is the literal translation, but what is suggested is something with which to hold the head high—an ornament or even a state of mind—so that the bride would not have to bow her head in submission or hang her head in shame.

8. Dumont drew attention to this term of abuse when applied to a person other than the speaker's wife's brother. Along with the term *mama* for mother's brother or maternal uncle, which also has abusive connotations, these two terms belong to the category of affines (Dumont 1966, 102). As in many other parts of north India, wife-givers and wife-takers, whose relationship is inherently asymmetrical and nonreciprocal, must be kept apart, a norm accomplished structurally through village exogamy (102).

9. In Agrahari's printed version of the love story, Gobind visits Maina and their meeting is reported to Maina's husband who kills her with his sword. It is the husband's sister who is the spy. Gobind takes Maina's body for cremation but on the way offers prayers to Shiva who, impressed with Gobind's devotion, revives Maina. Gobind returns to his home with Maina and asks his mother to shower her blessings on his bride.

10. The magic number seven also appears in Western fairytales such as "Snow White and the Seven Dwarfs."

11. On 17 August 2005 *The Hindustan Times* reported that on 16 August 2005, the Rajya Sabha passed the Hindu Succession (Amendment) Bill of 2004, granting Hindu, Jain, Sikh, and Buddhist women equal rights in property inheritance. According to this bill:

    i. Daughters have share by virtue of birth
    ii. Daughters will now get coequal share with sons
    iii. Daughters will now be subject to all liabilities and disabilities, including debt, mortgage, etc.
    iv. Since they have a share, daughters can dispose of their share
    v. Daughters can press for partition.

NOTES TO CHAPTER 4: SITA'S TRIALS

1. About the Ramnagar Ramlila, Linda Hess writes, "using a grand and varied outdoor environment that includes town, village, buildings, lakes and

groves, it sets up a microcosm of the sacred Rāmāyanā geography in an area of fifteen or twenty square miles. Actors and audience move together from place to place, often walking several miles in an evening to get from one scene to another. Even on the least popular nights it is common for more than 5,000 people to assemble for the event. An average audience might be 20,000, while on the most spectacular nights the crowds approach 10,000" (Hess 1988, 237).

2. Paul Courtright writes: "Pativratadharma may be interpretively translated as those morally significant actions, duties, and attitudes that are appropriate to the status of a married woman, the central focus of which is the welfare of her husband and all that adheres to him: household, reputation, kin, ancestors, descendants, deities, and life circumstances. Etymologically, the term means moral action (*dharma*) that is rooted in vows (*vrata*, from the Sanskrit *vr*, 'turn') undertaken for the protection and well-being of the husband or lord (*pati*). These duties, and orientations that frame them, are presented formally in classical treatises on morality (*dharmashastras*) and informally through patterns of behavior and expectations regarding married life passed through generations, encoded in rituals, and celebrated in mythology and folklore" (2007, 185–87).

    Usha Zacharias defines a *pativrata* as a woman selflessly dedicated to her husband to the point of ascetic renunciation (2001) while Uma Chakravarti lists the patrivrata's virtues as feminine self-sacrifice, virtue, fidelity, and chastity (1990). In nationalist discourse, through these very qualities "Sita embodies the purity, power of sacrifice, and spiritual authority of the upper-caste Hindu woman who can form the well-spring of sustenance for the Kashtriya Brhamanical male's battle against Ravana-like invaders, British or Muslim" (Zacharias 2001).

3. *Kaliyuga* refers to the present age of degeneration and corruption within the cyclical four consecutive ages.

4. In the folk imaginary, Sita embodies the generic but ideal peasant woman.

NOTES TO CHAPTER 5: WHEN MARRIAGE IS WAR

1. Caste census data is not available for post-independence India due to a policy adopted by the post-Independence state of not collecting data on any but Dalit (scheduled castes), which was needed for the implementation of affirmative action programs. Thus, one must refer back to the colonial census of 1931, the last time when such information was gathered, and seek to project current figures based on population increases. Over the past decade, state efforts to collect census data on caste remain mired in controversy.

2. Srinivas first identified the nature of caste dominance in his seminal work on the village Rampura in Mysore. Oliver Mendelsohn has refined the concept in recent years.

3. The newspaper reported that Dadan Yadav, a local Patna *pehalvān* (champion wrestler) and minister in the Rabri Devi government, had entered the political fray and sought to win votes by invoking the caste icon Vir Lorik through the installation of a gigantic statue of the hero Mahabali Vir Lorik Ahir (Powerful Brave Lorik, the Ahir). Given that, in the 1970s a private militia was also established in Lorik's name, the ruling party in Bihar was reluctant to broaden the party's caste base by means of this invocation. The brass statue, the paper reported, was massive, weighing 50,000 kilograms and reaching twenty-one meters, and would occupy 1,000 feet of the park in which it was slated to be installed. Rs.3 crores had already been spent on it and, if installed, its dimensions would have assured it a place in the *Guinness Book of World Records*. The report quoted Dadan Yadav as saying that the country needs a pehalvān like Vir (brave) Lorik to protect the poor and backward castes from the wily, exploitative feudalists (*The Telegraph*, 2 October 2002, Patna).

4. "Sanskritization" is a term coined by the sociologist M. N. Srinivas. See chapter 2 for further discussion.

5. *Biraha* (separation) is a song genre associated with the caste of Yadavas. Cattle herders and milk vendors are said to have developed the genre while minding their cattle. Biraha concerts by specialist biraha singers associated with distinct teachers (gurus) are popular in the region. Each Biraha singer claims the lineage of a particular guru.

6. Another version is that of Dadai Kewat, a farmer belonging to the riverfaring caste who claims to have learned it from an Ahir (now Yadava) guru over three years while grazing cattle. The latter text comprises approximately 14,000 lines and a Hindi translation of a summary of the text alone runs 120 pages. Despite the fact that enormous variations exist in oral renderings of the ballad across north India, I rely on these versions largely because of their accessibility to the reading public.

7. As an aside, the banquet occasions an expiatory feast given by Chanaini's father to publically redress his daughter's association with a Chamar, the breaking of an intercaste commensal taboo against interaction with a lower-caste male. The tenor of the episode suggests the caste's displeasure with Chanaini's action. The scene is therefore set for the forbidden love between Chanaini and Lorik, for whom the only solution appears to be elopement.

8. The anthropological literature on caste endogamy and village exogamy is pertinent here. For example, in Sherupur, Harold Gould found that upper castes such as Brahmins and Rajputs tend to marry their daughters into villages far from Sherupur. The intermediate castes such as Murao, Kurmi, and Ahir, on the other hand, tend to marry within close range of their villages. The lowest castes occupy an intermediate position between these two groups. With regard to the Brahmin and Kshatriya, Gould finds that only 12 percent of marriages were held within their own pargana (i.e., a

group of proximate districts lumped together for administrative purposes), here Haveli-Awadh, whereas 65 percent of marriages were held outside the three parganas west of Awadh, namely, Haveli-Awadh, Pacchimrath, and Amsin. In case of the intermediate castes, 72 percent of marriages were held within their own pargana and only 2 percent were held outside western Faizabad. The lowest castes held 59 percent of marriages within pargana Haveli-Awadh and only 1 percent outside western Faizabad (Gould 1960).

9. This episode also evokes Gandhi's use of fasting as a political tool and more recently, in 2011, the fasts undertaken by Anna Hazare and Baba Ramdev for the introduction of the Lokpal Bill received immense media coverage. It is worth remembering that Gandhi himself acknowledged having learned the political uses of fasting from the women in his family, who went on hunger strikes to make visible their sense of grievance within the family circle. The wide symbolic appeal of fasting and the presence of this motif in a prominent masculine ballad of the region underlines Gandhi's genius in adapting political tools and symbols that the masses would immediately recognize and resonate with.

10. Shahid Amin, in his fascinating introduction to the reprinted *Concise Encyclopedia of North Indian Peasant Life*, prepared by the late-nineteenth-century British officials Crooke, Reid, and Grierson, draws attention to the series of terms that describe women's experiences out of wedlock. *Dolkarhi* refers to a woman who had been taken to a bridegroom who did not take her a barat. *Gharkaili, Dhenmani*, and *Urhari* all refer to a woman who lives with a man outside of marriage (Amin 2005, 47). In a footnote, Urhari is further defined as "one for whom it would be foolish for a 'man' to shed tears"! Its occurrence in a proverb attributed to the legendary peasant poet Ghagh, suggests that losing one's "stri to a parpurush" (wife to another) was not all that uncommon. Crooke, in his printed alphabetical Glossary (1888), quotes the following proverb, "Urar" or "Urhari": *Mue cham pe cham katave / Bhuin pe sakra sove, / Ghagh kahen ye teeno bhakuwa, / Urar gayi ko rove* (Ghagh says there are three fools in the world: / he who lets the skin of his feet be cut by hard shoes; / he who sleeps curled up on the ground; and / he who weeps for his wife when she has "bolted") (Amin 2005, 47).

11. The immediate provocation for the BIA pledge was provided by the lavish expenditure of the landlord of the large Dera estate of Awadh on the wedding of his niece, where he fed thirty-five thousand people for six days. The colonial account delineates a four-pronged resolution adopted by the BIA in February 1864. This resolution allows me to assess the extent to which upper-caste marriage practices were causing anxiety within the administration. The association resolved the following:

    i. That no Kshatriya would borrow superfluous paraphernalia such as camels, elephants, horses for the marriage ceremony.

ii. That the bridegroom's father should take no more money from the bride's father than that required to entertain the wedding guests.

iii. That Kshatriyas would marry their daughters to none but men of equal rank.

iv. That the marriage expenses should not exceed half the individual's annual income.

Interestingly, the landowners of Awadh were seldom able to abide by these rules because marriages in taluqdari families were arranged in neighboring North West Provinces and Rajputana, where the writ of the BIA did not run (Jassal 1989, unpublished).

NOTES TO CHAPTER 6: TAKING LIBERTIES

1. Satua is a nourishing mixture of food ground into a paste for easy traveling, consumed by dissolving it in water.

2. Rasiya is also associated with the dance form 'Rās, popular in the region of Krishna's birthplace.

NOTES TO CONCLUSION: COMMUNITY HARMONIES

1. Jyotiba Phule (1827–1890), one of most influential social reformers of Maharashtra, founded the Satyashodhak Samaj to liberate lower caste shudras and dalits from exploitation by Brahmins. Phule worked tirelessly for social reform, women's education, and against the evils of the caste system. He is known as Mahatma or great soul.

Ādarsh gīt: idealistic song

Advaita: nondualism

Agni-parīkshā: trial by fire

Ajgar sāp: huge snake

Akharā: an affiliation with the distinctive teachings or
  "school" of an expert teacher or guru; also, wrestling arena

Anuloma: hypergamy, a socially accepted union wherein the
  wife-givers (the family of the bride) are typically inferior to
  the wife-takers (the family of the groom).

Arhar: a popular variety of yellow lentil or pulse, toor dal

Ashlīl: obscene

Bajār: a permanent market where one can buy general
  merchandise

Barāt: the bridegroom's party or marriage procession

Bhadralok: Bengalis with wealth, status, and a genteel
  aspirational lifestyle under colonial rule

Bhadramahilā: upper-caste or upper-class woman in Bengal

Bhaiyā: brother

Bhajan: spiritual song

Bhābhī or *Bhaujī*: wife of an elder brother

Bindī: forehead decoration or dot symbolizing
  auspiciousness, matrimony

Birahā: separation, longing; a genre of folksong highlighting
  the agony of separation

Biyāh: marriage

Burī: bad, vulgar

Cait: March–April

Carvāha: cattle herder

Chakkī: stone grinding mill

Charkhā: spinning-wheel

Chillum: a conical pipe for smoking tobacco and intoxicants like hashish

Cumāvan: a ritual blessing for the bride or groom involving the kissing of joints and limbs

Cunarī: a wrap or stole draped on the upper body of a woman

Cungī: a small token as additional free gift or favor from a vendor upon a purchase

Devar: the younger brother of one's husband

Dhamār: melodic style with distinct beat

Dhobī: caste of washermen

Dhol: barrel-shaped cylindrical drum with skin stretched on both sides

Dīdī: sister

Drsti: gaze, evil eye

Dub: a type of grass sprouted especially for ritual use

Duirāngi: two-timer or tease

Dusshera: an autumn festival symbolizing the victory of good over evil, associated with the victory of Ramayana over the demon Ravana

Ek-patnīvrat: pledged to a single wife

Gāthā: ballad

Gālī or *gārī*: abuse; insulting wedding songs

Ganj: a wholesale market for bulk goods

Ghāts: river banks; stone steps for bathing at rivers

Gopīs: female cowherders

Gurubhaī: one who shares the same guru or teacher

Haldī: turmeric

Janeu: a sacred thread worn across the body by "twice-born" caste males signifying high status and post-puberty initiation rites

Jarīb: a long wooden measuring scale used in agriculture

Jāta: a grinding stone, or two circular stones placed atop each other, operated by circular movements to grind the grain and spices placed therebetween

Jati sabhā: caste council

Jatsār: a genre of song sung at the grinding stone

Jeth: the elder brother of one's husband

Jobanā: breasts

Jogīra: tuneful mimicry and clowning at Holi festival

Kacnār: flowering tree

Kahrauā: a song genre associated with the caste of Kahars or water carriers

Kajlī: a song genre associated with the rainy season in north India

Kaliyuga: an era of degeneration and moral decline within the four cyclical ages; also, the era associated with the present

Kanyadān: an upper-caste marriage practice involving the ritual gifting of a virgin daughter by her father to the bridegroom

Kathākatās: performers or reciters of religious tales and stories

Karevā: a widow's remarriage to her deceased husband's younger brother

Keluwa: a ritual gift from a woman's natal home brought to her by her brother

Kharīf: the autumn harvest of crops sown at the start of the monsoon in July

Kodon: an inferior grain

Koel: cuckoo

Kos: an ancient measure of distance; two miles, the distance across which a shout can be heard

Krishna Lila: a performance depicting the glorious deeds of Lord Krishna

Lakh: one hundred thousand

Lāthi: a staff or stave

Launda-nāch: a company of itinerant male performers that performs for rural audiences, the actors who perform both men's and women's roles

Lava parachanā or *lava*: the scattering of parched rice, a key ritual in weddings

Lehanā: the practice of allowing a laborer to take home from the field the amount of harvested grain they can carry with both hands

Lila: the accounts of glorious deeds based on the hagiographies of deities

Maharaj: the head of a household, a king or lord

Mahuā: a variety of flowering tree whose flowers are distilled for liquor

Majīrās: hand-held cymbals

Mātā: chickenpox; also the goddess of chickenpox

Meherin: woman householder

Melā: fair

Mofussil: provincial town

Musarvā: pestle

Nautankī: a form of folk drama

Neem: a species of tree whose leaves and bark have medicinal and curative properties

Nirgun: the formless divine

Oel: a fruit used for pickles

Pakhawaj: a form of drum; the north Indian version of mridang, a drum the musician holds in front of himself

Pān: a fragrant postmeal digestive and mouth freshener; a key ingredient in ritual and ceremonial offerings, the leaf symbolizing fertility and auspiciousness

Pancāyat: an administrative, judicial, and decision-making body at the local level

Pāpī: sinner

Patīvratā: an ideal wife

Paramparā: tradition

Patīvratādharma: the actions, duties, and attitudes expected from the ideal wife that in turn ensure the well-being and prosperity of the husband and his household

Pehalvān: a champion wrestler

Phāgun: early spring, denoting the months of February and March

Phuhar: sloppy or vulgar

Pīr: Sufi mystic, saint

Piyarī: a ritual and auspicious yellow sari

Pradhan: a leader or administrative head at the local level

Rabī: a winter crop or spring harvest

Rang dālo: to smear color

Rasik: the feminizing of the human soul in relation to the divine; the ritual adoption of female attire by men seeking to transform their masculinity, associated with certain Krishna temples

Rasiya: a song based on the motif of yearning between Radha and Krishna, also associated with the dance form Rās, which is popular near Krishna's birthplace

Sādhu: a Hindu religious ascetic and seeker

Sagun: the divine embodied

Samskārās: rituals of the life cycle

Sar, sālā, sarau: the brother of one's wife

Sarpat: the long grass found on riverbanks, used in rope and basket weaving

Sasurāl: a woman's marital household

Sat: superhuman feminine strength derived from the quality of wifely chastity

Satī: a formidably chaste woman who sacrifices herself upon the death of husband; the practice of women immolating themselves on the funeral pyre of their husbands

Satitvā: the state of being imbued with sat

Satyāgraha: nonviolent protest

Savā lākh: one hundred and twenty-five thousand

Shringār: love; forms of adornment

Sindur: an auspicious vermilion powder applied in the part of married women's hair, symbolizing matrimony

Strīdhan: property and wealth comprising cash, goods, and jewelry that women receive as gifts both from natal and conjugal homes upon marriage

Stri-shakti: women's superior strength

Svayamvar: the exercise of a woman's choice of marriage partner

Tapas: heat generated from asceticism and yogic austerities

Tehsīl: an administrative subdivision comprising a number of villages; block

Tej: an inner fire associated with spiritual strength

U.P. Bhūmi Sudhār aur Shyam Adhikāri Abhiyān Samitī: Movement for Land Reforms and Labor Rights in Uttar Pradesh

Uraharī: an eloping woman or one who has been enticed away

Urs: the anniversary marking the day of a Sufi saint's departure from the mundane world and reunion with the Creator, also celebrated as the saint's wedding

Virah (also *birah*): yearning and pain of separation

Vivāha: marriage

Abu-Lughod, Lila. 1998. "Feminist Longings and Postcolonial Conditions." In *Remaking Women: Feminism and Modernity in the Middle East*, edited by Lila Abu-Lughod, 3–31. Princeton: Princeton University Press.

——. 1990a. "The Romance of Resistance: Tracing Transformations of Power through Bedouin Women." *American Ethnologist* 17, no. 1, 41–55.

——. 1990b. "Shifting Politics in Bedouin Love Poetry." In *Language and the Politics of Emotion*, edited by Lila Abu-Lughod and Catherine A. Lutz, 24–25. Cambridge: Cambridge University Press.

Abu-Lughod, Lila, and Catherine Lutz. 1990. *Language and the Politics of Emotion*. Cambridge: Cambridge University Press.

Agarwal, Bina. 1997. "'Bargaining' and Gender Relations: Within and Beyond the Household." *Feminist Economics* 3, no. 1, 1–51.

——. 1995. *A Field of One's Own*. Cambridge: Cambridge University Press.

Agnihotri, Indu, and Vina Mazumdar. 1995. "Changing Terms of Political Discourse: Women's Movement in India, 1970s–1990s." *Economic and Political Weekly* 30, no. 29, 1869–78.

Agrahari, Baldevji. n.d. *Jatsaari: Prem Govind Maina Ka*. Chhapra: Agrahari Brahman Pustakalaya.

Ahearn, Laura. 2001. "Language and Agency." *Annual Review of Anthropology* 30, 109–137.

——. 2000. "Agency." *Journal of Linguistic Anthropology* 9, nos. 1–2, 12–15.

Amin, Shahid, ed. 2005. *A Concise Encyclopedia of North Indian Peasant Life: Being a Compilation of the Writings of William Crooke, J. R. Reid, G. A. Grierson*. New Delhi: Manohar.

Bakhtin, Mikhail. 1984. *Rabelais and His World*. Bloomington: University of Indiana Press.

Banerjee, Sumanta. 1989. *The Parlour and the Streets: Elite and Popular Culture in Nineteenth Century Calcutta*. Calcutta: Seagull Books.

Basu, Srimati. 1999. *She Comes to Take Her Rights: Indian Women, Property, and Propriety*. Albany: State University of New York Press.

Beth, Sarah. 2005. "Taking to the Streets: Dalit *Mela* and the Public Performance of Dalit Cultural Identity." *Contemporary South Asia* 14, no. 4, 397–410.

Bergson, H. 1956. "Laughter." In *Comedy*, edited by Wylie Sypher, 61–190. New York: Doubleday Anchor Books.

Berreman, Gerald. 1993. "Sanskritization as female oppression in India." In *Sex and Gender Hierarchies*, edited by Barbara Miller, 366–92. Cambridge: Cambridge University Press.

Bhargava, Meena. 1996. "Landed Property Rights in Transition: A Note on Cultivators and Agricultural Laborers in Gorakhpur in the late 18th and 19th Century." *Studies in History* 12, no. 2, 223–41.

Blackburn, Stuart H., Peter J. Claus, Joyce B. Fleuckiger, and Susan S. Wadley, eds. 1989. *Oral Epics in India*. Berkeley: University of California Press.

Blackburn, Stuart, and A. K. Ramanujan, eds. 1986. *Another Harmony: New Essays on the Folklore of India*. Berkeley: University of California Press.

Bompas, Cecil Henry. 1909. *Folklore of the Santal Parganas*. London: David Nutt.

Boserup, Ester. 1970. *Women's Role in Economic Development*. New York: St. Martins' Press.

Brass, Paul. 2003. *The Production of Hindu Muslim Violence in Contemporary India*. New Delhi: Oxford University Press.

Briggs, Charles L. 1988. *Competence in Performance: The Creativity of Tradition in Mexicano Verbal Art*. Philadelphia: University of Pennsylvania Press.

Caldwell, Sarah. 1999. *Oh Terrifying Mother: Sexuality, Violence and Worship of the Goddess Kali*. New Delhi: Oxford University Press.

Chakravarti, Uma. 2006. *Everyday Lives, Everyday Histories*. New Delhi: Tulika.

Chatterjee, Partha. [1989] 1990. "The Nationalist Resolution of the Woman's Question." In *Recasting Women, Essays in Indian Colonial History*, edited by Kumkum Sangari and Sudesh Vaid, 233–53. New Jersey: Rutgers University Press.

Chowdhry, Prem. 2005. "Imagined Lovers: Ideology, Practice and Social Hierarchies." In *Women of India: Colonial and Post-Colonial Periods*, vol. 9, part 3, edited by Bharati Ray, 110–38. New Delhi: Sage Publications.

——. 2001. "Lustful Women, Elusive Lovers: Identifying Males as Objects of Female Desire." Indian Journal of Gender Studies 8, no. 1, 23–50.

——. 1994. *The Veiled Women: Shifting Gender Equations in Rural Haryana, 1880–1990*. Delhi: Oxford University Press.

Chowdhury, Prem. 1990. "An Alternative to the Sati Model: Perceptions of a Social Reality in Folklore." *Asian Folklore Studies* 49, no. 2, 259–74.

Courtright, Paul. 2007. "Sati, Sacrifice, and Marriage: The Modernity of Tradition." In *Women's Lives, Women's Rituals in the Hindu Tradition*, edited by Tracy Pintchman, 184–203. New York: Oxford University Press.

Crooke, William. 1907. *Natives of Northern India.* London: Archibald Constable & Co., Ltd.

——. 1894. *An Introduction to the Popular Religion and Folklore of Northern India.* Allahabad: Government Press.

Crooke, William, G. A. Grierson, and J. R. Reid, eds. 2005. *A Concise Encyclopaedia of North Indian Peasant Life.* Introduction by Shahid Amin. New Delhi: Manohar.

Deitrich, Gabriele. 1983. "Women and Household Labour." *Social Scientist* 11, no. 2.

Derne, Steve. 2000. "Culture, Family Structure, and Psyche In Hindu India: The 'Fit' and the 'Inconsistencies." *International Journal of Group Tensions* 29, nos. 3–4, 323–48.

——. 1994. "Hindu Men Talk about Controlling Women: Cultural Ideas as a Tool of the Powerful." *Sociological Perspectives* 37, no. 2, 203–27.

Dirks, Nicholas. 2001. *Castes of Mind: Colonialism and the Making of Modern India.* Princeton: Princeton University Press

Doniger, Wendy. 2000. *The Bedtrick: Tales of Sex and Masquerade.* Chicago: University of Chicago Press.

——. 1995. "Fluid and Fixed Texts in India." In *Michigan Papers on South and Southeast Asia*, 31–41. Ann Arbor, Michigan: The University of Michigan, Center for South and Southeast Asian Studies.

Douglas, Mary. 1968. "The Social Control of Cognition: Some Factors in Joke Perception." *Man* 3, 361–76.

Dube, Leela. 2001. *Anthropological Explorations in Gender: Intersecting Fields.* New Delhi: Sage.

Dube, Saurabh. 1998. *Untouchable Pasts: Religion, Identity, and Power among a Central Indian Community, 1780–1950.* Albany: State University of New York Press.

Dumont, Louis. 1970. *Homo Hierarchicus: The Caste System and Its Implications.* Complete English edition, revised, 1980 Series: (NHS) Nature of Human Society.

——. 1966. "Marriage in India: The Present State of the Question." *Contributions to Indian Sociology* 9, 90–144.

Eaton, Richard M. 2002. *Essays on Islam and Indian History.* New Delhi: Oxford University Press.

Elwin, Verrier. 1946. *Folksongs of Chhattisgarh (Central Provinces).* Madras: Oxford University Press.

Emerson, Joan P. 1969. "Negotiating the Serious Import of Humor." *Sociometry* 32, 169–81.

Ernst, Carl W., and Bruce B. Lawrence. 2002. *Sufi Martyrs of Love: The Chishti Order in South Asia and Beyond.* New York: Palgrave Macmillan.

Feld, Steven. 1987. "Dialogic Editing: Interpreting How Kaluli Read Sound and Sentiment." *Cultural Anthropology* 2, no. 2, 190–210.

Flueckiger, Joyce Burkhalter. 1996. *Gender and Genre in the Folklore of Middle India.* Ithaca: Cornell University Press.

———. 1989a. "Caste and Regional Variants in an Oral Epic Tradition." In *Oral Epics in India,* edited by Stuart H. Blackburn and Peter J. Claus. Berkeley: University of California Press.

———. 1989b. "The Hindi Oral Epic: Lorikayan (the tale of Lorik and Chanda) by Shyam Manohar Pandey. Allahabad: Sahitya Bhawan private, 1987 book review, *The Journal of Asian Studies* 48, no. 2, 427–29.

Foucault, Michel. 1978. *The History of Sexuality.* Vol.1, *An Introduction.* New York: Random House.

Frankel, Francine. 1989. "Caste, Land and Dominance in Bihar." In *Dominance and State Power in Modern India: Decline of a Social Order,* edited by M. S. A. Rao and Francine Frankel, vol.1. New Delhi: Oxford University Press.

Friedrich, Paul. 1996. "The Culture in Poetry and the Poetry in Culture." In *Culture/Contexture. Explorations in Anthropology and Literary Studies,* edited by Jeffrey M. Peck and Daniel E. Valentine. Berkeley: University of California Press.

Gait, E. A. 1913. *Census of India,* 1911. Vol. I, Part 1, Report. Calcutta.

Gal, Susan. 1991. "Between Speech and Silence: The Problematics of Research on Language and Gender." In *Gender at the Crossroads of Knowledge: Feminist Anthropology in the Post-modern Era,* edited by Micaela di Leonardo, 175–203. Berkeley: University of California Press.

Gandhi, Ramchandra. 1992. *Sita's Kitchen: A Testimony of Faith and Enquiry.* Albany: State University of New York Press.

Gardner, Katy, and Filippo Osella. 2003. "Migration, Modernity and Social Transformation in South Asia: An Overview." *Contributions to Indian Sociology* 37, nos. 1 and 2, v.

Gluckman, Max. 1965. *Politics, Law and Ritual in Tribal Society.* Cambridge: Cambridge University Press.

Gold, Ann Grodzins. 2000. "From Demon Aunt to Gorgeous Bride: Women Portray Female Power in a North Indian Festival Cycle." In *Invented Identities: The Interplay of Gender, Religion and Politics in India,* edited by Julia Leslie and Mary McGee, 203–30. New Delhi: Oxford University Press.

———. 1994. "Gender, Violence and Power: Rajasthani Stories of Shakti." In *Women as Subjects: South Asian Histories,* edited by Nita Kumar, 26–48. Calcutta: Stree.

———. 1992. *A Carnival of Parting.* Berkeley: University of California Press.

——. 1988. *Fruitful Journeys: The Ways of Rajasthani Pilgrims.* Berkeley: University of California Press.

Gold, Ann Grodzins, and Gloria Raheja. 1994. *Listen to the Heron's Words: Reimagining Gender and Kinship in North India.* Berkeley: University of California Press.

Goody, Jack, and S. J. Tambiah. 1973. *Bridewealth and Dowry.* Cambridge: Cambridge University Press.

Gore, Madhav. 1961. "The Husband-Wife and Mother-Son Relationship." *Sociological Bulletin* 11, 91–102.

Gough, Kathleen. 1981. *Rural Society in Southeast India.* Cambridge: Cambridge University Press.

Gould, Harold. 1960. "The Micro-demography of Marriages in a North Indian Area." *South Western Journal of Anthropology* 16, 476–91.

Government of India. 1974. *Towards Equality,* Report of the Committee on the Status of Women in India, Government of India.

Guha, Ranajit. 1985. "The Career of an Anti-God in Heaven and on Earth." In *The Truth Unites: Essays in Tribute to Samar Sen,* edited by Ashok Mitra. Calcutta: Subarnarekha.

——. 1983. *Elementary Aspects of Peasant Insurgency in Colonial India.* New Delhi: Oxford University Press.

Gupta, Charu. 2001. *Sexuality, Obscenity, Community: Women, Muslims, and the Hindu Public in Colonial India.* New Delhi: Permanent Black.

——. 2000. "Hindu Women, Muslim Men: Cleavages in Shared Spaces of Everyday Life, United Provinces, c. 1890–1930." *The Indian Economic and Social History Review* 37, 2.

——. 1998. "Articulating Hindu Masculinity and Femininity: Shuddhi and Sangathan Movements in UP in the 1920s." *Economic and Political Weekly* 33, no. 13, 727–35.

Guru, Gopal. 2000. "Dalits in Pursuit of Modernity." In *India: Another Millennium,* edited by Romila Thapar, 123–37. New Delhi: Viking.

Hall, Perry A. 1997. "African American Music: Dynamics of Appropriation and Innovation." In *Borrowed Power: Essays on Cultural Appropriation,* edited by Pratima Rao and Bruce Ziff, 31–51. New Brunswick, N. J.: Rutgers University Press.

Handelman, Don. 1996. "Traps of Trans-formation: Theoretical Convergences between Riddle and Ritual." In *Untying the Knot: On Riddles and Other Enigmatic Modes,* edited by Galit Hasan-Rokem and David Shulman. New York: Oxford University Press.

Hansen, Kathryn. 1992. *Grounds for Play: The Nautanki Theatre of North India.* Berkeley: University of California Press.

Hardiman, David. 1995. *The Coming of the Devi: Adivasi Assertion in Western India.* Delhi: Oxford University Press.

Hart, G. 1991. "Engendering Everyday Resistance: Gender, Patronage and Production Politics in Rural Malaysia." *Journal of Peasant Studies* 19, no. 1, 93–121.

Hasan-Rokem, Galit, and David Shulman, eds. 1996. *Untying the Knot: On Riddles and Other Enigmatic Modes.* New York: Oxford University Press.

Hershman, Paul. 1981. *Punjabi Kinship and Marriage.* Delhi: Hindustan Publishing Corporation.

Hess, Linda. 1999. "Rejecting Sita: Indian Responses to the Ideal Man's Cruel Treatment of His Ideal Wife." *Journal of the American Academy of Religion* 67, no. 1, 1–32.

——. 1988. "The Poet, the People and the Western Scholar: Influence of a Sacred Drama and Text on Social Values in North India." *Theatre Journal* 40, no. 2, 236–53.

Hiltbeitel, Alf, and Kathleen M. Erndl, eds. 2000. *Is The Goddess a Feminist?: The Politics of South Asian Goddesses.* Sheffield: Academic Press.

Hines, Naseem. 2007. *Maulana Daud's Candayan: A Critical Study.* New Delhi: Manohar.

Holland, Dorothy, and Margaret Eisenhart. 1990. *Educated in Romance: Women, Achievement and College Culture.* Chicago: University of Chicago Press.

Huizinga, J. 1955. *Homo Ludens: A Study of the Play Element in Culture.* Boston: Beacon Press.

Humes, Cynthia Ann. 2000. "Is the Devi Mahatmya a Feminist Scripture?" In *Is The Goddess a Feminist?: The Politics of South Asian Goddesses,* edited by Alf Hiltbeitel and Kathleen M. Erndl, 123–50. Sheffield: Academic Press.

Inden, Ronald B., and Ralph W. Nicholas. 1977. *Kinship in Bengali Culture.* Chicago: University of Chicago Press.

Jaffrelot, Christophe. 2003. *India's Silent Revolution: The Rise of the Low Castes in North Indian Politics.* New Delhi: Permanent Black.

Jafri, S. N. A. [1931] 1985. *The History and Status of Landlord and Tenant in the United Provinces.* Delhi: Usha.

Jassal, Smita T. 2006. "Migration and Song." In *Men of the Global South: A Reader,* edited by Adam Jones, 306–11. New York: Zed Books.

——. 2005. "Gendering Agrarian Issues: The Uttar Pradesh Experience." In *Women of India: Colonial and Post-Colonial Periods,* edited by Ray Bharati, 259–82. Vol. 9, Part 3. Project of History of Indian Science, Philosophy and Culture. New Delhi: Sage Publications.

——. 2003. "Whither Women's Empowerment: Mallahin Fishponds in Madhubani, Bihar." In *Livelihood and Gender: Equity In Community Resource Management,* edited by Sumi Krishna, 412–24. New Delhi: Sage.

——. 2001. *Daughters of the Earth: Women and Land In Uttar Pradesh.* New Delhi: Manohar.

———. 1989. "Agrarian Structure: A Study of the Faizabad District." PhD diss., Delhi University.

Jeffrey, Robin, Patricia Jeffrey, and Andrew Lyon. 1986. *Labour Pains and Labour Power: Women and Childbearing in India.* London: Zed Books.

John, Mary, and Janaki Nair. 1998. "Introduction." In *A Question of Silence? The Sexual Economies of Modern India,* 1–51. New Delhi: Kali for Women.

Kakar, Sudhir. 2001. "The Maternal Feminine in Indian Psychoanalysis." In *The Essential Writings of Sudhir Kakar,* with an Introduction by T. G. Vaidyanathan, 197–220. New Delhi: Oxford University Press.

———. 1988. "Feminine Identity in India." In *Women in Indian Society: A Reader,* edited by Rehana Ghadially, 44–69. New Delhi: Sage Publications.

———. [1978] 1981. *The Inner World: A Psycho-analytic Study of Childhood and Society in India.* 2nd ed. Delhi: Oxford University Press.

Kalpagam, U. 1986. "Gender in Economics: The Indian Experience." *Economic and Political Weekly* 21, no. 43, WS 59–66.

Kandiyoti, Deniz. 1998. "Gender, Power and Contestation: Rethinking Bargaining with Patriarchy." In *Feminist Visions of Development,* edited by Cecile Jackson and Ruth Pearson, 135–51. London: Routledge.

———. 1988. "Bargaining with Patriarchy." *Gender and Society* 2, 274–89.

Katyal, Anjum, and Ipsita Chanda. 1998. "How to Be a Good Woman: The Playway Method." *Indian Journal of Gender Studies* 5, no. 2, 165–83.

Kesari, Arjun Das. 1996. *Jhajhare Gendulwa Gangajal Pani.* Lokvarta Shodh Sansthan: Robertsganj, Sonebhadra.

Kishwar, Madhu. 1999. "Yes to Sita, No to Ram." In *Off the Beaten Track: Rethinking Gender Justice for Indian Women,* 234–34. New Delhi: Oxford University Press.

Kosambi, D. D. 1975. *The Culture and Civilization of Ancient India in Historical Outline.* New Delhi: Vikas Publishing House.

Kumar, Arun. 2006. "Culture, Development and the Cultural Capital of Farce: The Musahar Community in Bihar." *Economic and Political Weekly,* October 7, 4281–91.

———. 2001. *Rewriting the Language of Politics: Kisans in Colonial Bihar.* New Delhi: Manohar.

Lamb, Sarah. 2000. *White Saris and Sweet Mangoes: Aging, Gender and Body in North India.* Berkeley: University of California Press.

Leavitt, John. 1996. "Meaning and Feeling in the Anthropology of Emotions." *American Ethnologist* 23, no. 3, 514–39.

Lerche, Jens. 1997. "Politics of the Poor: Agricultural Labourers and Political Transformations in Uttar Pradesh." In *Rural Labour Relations in India,* edited by Byres Kapadia and Jens Lerche, 182–238. New Delhi: India Research Press.

Lutz, Catherine, and Geoffrey M. White. 1986. "The Anthropology of Emotion." *Annual Reviews in Anthropology* 15, 405–36.

Lyman, Peter. 1987. "The Fraternal Bond as a Joking Relationship: A Case Study of the Role of Sexist Jokes in Male Group Bonding." In *Changing Men: New Directions in Research on Men and Masculinity*, edited by S. Kimmel, 131–47. Newbury Park: Sage.

Macwan, Jyotsna, Fernando Franco, and Suguna Ramanathan, eds. 2000. *The Silken Swing: The Cultural Universe of Dalit Women*. Calcutta: Stree.

Mahmood, Saba. 2005. *The Politics of Piety: The Islamic Revival and the Feminist Subject*. Princeton: Princeton University Press.

Manuel, Peter. 1993. *Cassette Culture: Popular Music and Technology in North India*. Chicago: University of Chicago Press.

Marcus, Scott L. 1989. "The Rise of a Folk Music Genre: Biraha." In *Culture and Power in Benaras: Community, Performance and Environment, 1800–1980*, edited by Sandria Freitag, 93–113. Berkeley: University of California Press.

Mishra, Vidyaniwas. 2002. *Lok aur Lok ka Swar*. Delhi: Prabhat Prakashan.

Mitchell, Michele. 1999. "Silence Broken, Silences Kept: Gender and Sexuality." In *Gender and History: Retrospect and Prospect*, edited by Leonore Davidoff, Keith McClelland, and Eleni Varikas, 15–26. London: Blackwell.

Mohapatra, Prabhu. 1995. "Restoring the Family: Wife Murders and the Making of a Sexual Contract for Indian Immigrant Labour in the British Caribbean Colonies, 1860–1920." *Studies in History* 11, no. 2, 225–60.

Moore, Henrietta. 1994. *A Passion For Difference*. Cambridge: Polity Press.

Narayan, Badri. 2001. *Documenting Dissent: Contesting Fables, Contested Memories and Dalit Political Discourse*. Shimla: Sage.

Narayan, Kirin. 1995. "The Practice of Oral Literary Criticism: Women's Songs in Kangra, India." *The Journal of American Folklore* 108, no. 429, 243–64.

———. 1993. "Banana Republics and V. I. Degrees: Rethinking Indian Folklore in a Postcolonial World." *Asian Folklore Studies* 52, no. 1, 177–204.

———. 1986. "Birds on a Branch: Girlfriends and Wedding Songs in Kangra." *Ethnos* 14, 47–75.

Nilsson, Usha. 2001. "Grinding Millet but Singing of Sita: Power and Domination in Awadhi and Bhojpuri Women's Songs." In *Questioning Ramayanas: A South Asian Tradition*, edited by Paula Richman, 137–58. Berkeley: University of California Press.

Niranjana, Tejaswini. 1998. "'Left to the Imagination': Indian Nationalisms and Female Sexuality in Trinidad." In *A Question of Silence? The Sexual Economies of Modern India*, edited by Mary John and Janaki Nair, 111–38. New Delhi: Kali for Women.

———. 1993. "Colonialism and the Aesthetics of Translation." In *Interrogating Modernity: Culture and Colonialism in India*, edited by Sudhir P. Niranjana and Vivek Dhareshwar, 319–33. Calcutta: Seagull.

O'Hanlon, Rosalind. 1997. "Issues of Masculinity in North Indian History:

The Bangash Nawabs of Farrukhabad." *Indian Journal of Gender Studies* 4, no. I, I–19.

———. 1985. *Caste Conflict and Ideology Mahatma Jotirao Phule and Low Caste Protest in Nineteenth Century Western India.* Cambridge: Cambridge University Press.

Oldenburg, Veena Talwar. 2002. *Dowry Murder: The Imperial Origins of a Cultural Crime.* New York: Oxford University Press.

Ortner, S., and Harriet Whitehead. 1981. *Sexual Meanings: The Cultural Construction of Gender and Sexuality.* Cambridge: Cambridge University Press.

Osella, F., and K. Gardner, eds. 2003. *Migration, Modernity, and Social Transformation in South Asia.* New Delhi: Sage.

Pandey, Gyanendra. 2000. "Voices from the Edge: The Struggle to Write Subaltern Histories." In *Mapping Subaltern Studies and the Postcolonial,* edited by Chaturvedi Vinayak, 281–99. London: Verso.

Pandey, Shyam Manohar. 1987. *The Hindi Oral Epic Lorikayan.* Allahabad: Sahitya Bhavan.

Papanek, Hanna. 1989. "Family Status-production Work: Women's Contribution to Social Mobility and Class Differentiation." In *Gender and the Household Domain: Social and Cultural Dimensions,* edited by M. Krishnaraj and Karuna Chanana, 97–116. New Delhi: Sage.

Pinch, William. 1996. *Peasants and Monks in British India.* New Delhi: Oxford University Press.

Radcliffe-Brown, A. R. 1959. *Structure and Function in Primitive Society.* Glencoe, Ill.: Free Press.

Raheja, Gloria Goodwin, ed. 2003. *Songs, Stories, Lives: Gendered Dialogues and Cultural Critique.* New Delhi: Kali For Women.

———. 1996. "Caste, Colonialism, and the Speech of the Colonized: Entextualization and Disciplinary Control in India." *American Ethnologist* 23, no. 3, 494–513.

———. 1995. "'Crying When She's Born, and Crying When She Goes Away': Marriage and the Idiom of the Gift in Pahansu Song Performance." In *From The Margins of Hindu Marriage,* edited by Harlan Lindsey and Paul B. Courtright, 21–59. New York: Oxford University Press.

———. 1994. "Women's Speech Genres, Kinship and Contradiction." In *Women as Subjects,* edited by Nita Kumar, 49–76. Calcutta: Stree.

———. 1988. *The Poison in the Gift: Ritual, Prestation and the Dominant Caste in a North Indian Village.* Chicago: University of Chicago Press.

Rajan, Rajeshwari Sunder. 1998. "Is the Hindu Goddess a Feminist?" *Economic and Political Weekly,* 31 October, WS 34.

Ramanujan, A. K., and Stuart Blackburn, eds. 1986. *Another Harmony: New Essays on the Folklore of India.* Berkeley: University of California Press.

Rao, Anupama, ed. 2003. *Gender and Caste*. New Delhi: Kali for Women.

Rao, M. S. A. 1979. *Social Movements and Social Transformation: A Study of Two Backward Classes Movements in India*. New Delhi: Macmillan Company of India.

Rao, Velcheru Narayana. 1991. "A Ramayana of Their Own: Women's Oral Tradition in Telugu." In *Many Ramayanas*, edited by Paula Richman, 114–36. Berkeley: University of California Press.

Rao, Velcheru Narayana, and David Shulman. 1998. *A Poem at the Right Moment: Remembered Verses from Premodern South India*. New Delhi: Oxford University Press.

Rao, Vijayendra, and Michael Walton. 2004. "Culture and Public Action: Relationality, Equality of Agency and Development." In *Culture and Public Action*, edited by Rao and Walton. New Delhi: Permanent Black.

Rege, Sharmila. 1995. "The Hegemonic Appropriation of Sexuality: The Case of the Lavani Performers of Maharashtra." *Contributions to Indian Sociology* 29, nos. 1–2, 25–37.

Richman, Paula, ed. 1991. *Many Ramayanas: The Diversity of Narrative Tradition in South Asia*. Berkeley: University of California Press.

Rosaldo, Michelle. 1984. "Toward an Anthropology of Self and Feeling." In *Culture Theory: Essays on Mind, Self and Emotion*, edited by Richard Sweder and Robert A. LeVine, 137–57. Cambridge: Cambridge University Press.

Roy, Sureshvrat. 2056 Vikrami (Gregorian 2000). *Namami Ramam*. Kanpur: Manas Sangam.

Sarkar, Tanika. 1997. "Scandal in High Places: Discourses on the Chaste Hindu Woman in Late 19th Century Bengal." In *Embodiment: Essays on Gender and Identity*, edited by Thapan Meenakshi, 35–73. Delhi: Oxford University Press.

Sax, William S. 2002. *Dancing the Self: Personhood and Performance in the Pandav Lila of Garhwal*. New York: Oxford University Press.

Schechner, Richard. 1993. "Striding through the Cosmos: Movement, Belief, Politics, and Place in the Ramlila of Ramnagar." In *The Future of Ritual: Writings on Culture and Performance*, edited by Richard Schechner, 131–89. London: Routledge.

1977. *Essays on Performance Theory, 1970–1976*. New York: Drama Book Specialists.

Scott, James. 1985. *Weapons of the Weak: Everyday Forms of Peasant Resistance*. New Haven: Yale University Press.

Sen, Samita. 1999. *Women and Labour in Late Colonial India: The Bengal Jute Industry*. Cambridge: Cambridge University Press.

Servan-Schreiber, C. 2001. "The Transmission of Bhojpuri Epics towards Nepal and Bengal." In *Chanted Narratives: The Living Katha-vachana Tradition*, edited by Molly Kaushal, 43–60. New Delhi: Indira Gandhi National Center For Arts and D.K. Printworld.

Sharma, Ursula. 1993. "Dowry in North India: Its Consequences for Women."
In *Family, Kinship and Marriage in India*, edited by Patricia Uberoi, 341–56.
Delhi: Oxford University Press.

Shrivastav, Shyamkumari. 1982. *Bhojpuri lok geeton mein Sanskritic Tatva.*
Allhabad: Bharati Press.

Shramshakti. 1988. *Report of the National Commission on Self-Employed Women
and Women in the Informal Sector*, Chairperson Ela Bhatt, June, New Delhi.

Shulman, David. 1986. "Battle as Metaphor in Tamil, Folk and Classical
Traditions." In *Another Harmony: New Essays on the Folklore of India*, edited
by Stuart Blackburn and A. K. Ramanujan, 105–30. Berkeley: University of
California Press.

——. 1985. *The King and the Clown in South Indian Myth and Poetry.* New
Jersey: Princeton University Press.

Spivak, Gayatri Chakravarti. 1993. "Can the Subaltern Speak?" In *Colonial
Discourse and Post-Colonial Theory: A Reader*, edited by Patrick Williams and
Laura Chrisman, 66–111. New York: Columbia University Press.

Srinivas, M. N. 1995. *Social Change in Modern India.* New Delhi: Orient
Blackswan.

——. 1962. *Caste In Modern India and Other Essays.* Bombay: Popular
Prakashan.

——. 1952. *Religion and Society among the Coorgs of South India.* New Delhi:
Oxford University Press.

Srivastava, I. 1991. "Woman as Portrayed in Women's Folk songs of North
India." *Asian Folklore Studies* L-2, 270–310.

Stoller, Paul. 1984. "Sound in Songhay Cultural Experience." *American
Ethnologist* 11, no. 3, 559–70.

Tambiah, Stanley, and Jack Goody. 1973. *Bridewealth and Dowry.* Cambridge:
Cambridge University Press.

Tewari, Hanskumar, and Radahvallabh Sharma. 2000. *Bhojpuri Sanskar Geet.*
Patna: Bihar Rashtrabhasha Parishad.

Thapar, Romila. 2000. "The Ramayana Syndrome." In *Cultural Pasts: Essays in
Early Indian History, 1079–1090.* Oxford: Oxford University Press.

Tinker, Irene, ed. 1990. *Persistent Inequalities: Women and World Development.*
New York: Oxford University Press.

Trautmann, Thomas R. 1982. *Dravidian Kinship.* Cambridge: Cambridge
University Press.

Trawick, Margaret. 1990. *Notes on Love in a Tamil Family.* Berkeley: University
of California Press.

——. 1986. "Internal Iconicity in Paraiyar Crying Songs." In *Another Harmony:
New Essays on the Folklore of India*, edited by Stuart Blackburn and A. K.
Ramanujan, 294–344. Berkeley: University of California Press.

Upadhyaya, Krishnadev. 1991. *Bhojpuri Lok-sanskriti.* Prayag: Hindi Sahitya
Sammelan.

——. 1990a. *Hindi Pradesh ke Lok geet.* Lok Sanskriti Shodh Sansthan, Allahabad: Sahitya Bhavan.

——. 1990b. *Bhojpuri Lokgeet Bhag 1.* Allahabad: Hindi Sahitya Sammelan.

Urban, Hugh. 2001. "The Marketplace and the Temple: Economic Metaphors and Religious Meanings in the Folksongs of Colonial Bengal." *The Journal of Asian Studies* 60, no. 4, 1085–1114.

Van der Veer, Peter. 1987. "Taming the Ascetic: Devotionalism in a Hindu Monastic Order." *Man* 22, no. 4, 680–95.

Van Gennep, Arnold. 1960. *The Rites of Passage.* Chicago: University of Chicago Press.

Vatuk, Sylvia. 1975. "Gifts and Affines in North India." *Contributions to Indian Sociology* 9, 155–96.

Vaughan, Megan. 1987. *The Story of an African Famine: Gender and Famine in Twentieth-Century Malawi.* Cambridge: Cambridge University Press.

Wadley, Susan S. 1975. *Shakti: Power in the Conceptual Structure of Karimpur Religion.* Chicago: University of Chicago Studies in Anthropology, Series in Social, Cultural and Linguistic Anthropology 2.

——. 1976. "Brothers, Husbands and Sometimes Sons: Kinsmen in North Indian Ritual." *Eastern Anthropologist* 29, 149–70.

Zacharias, Usha. 2001. "Trial By Fire: Gender, Power, and Citizenship in Narratives of the Nation." *Social Text* 19, no. 4, 29–51.

Zijderveld, Anton C. 1983. "Humour and Laughter in the Social Fabric." *Current Sociology* 31, no. 3, 37–57.

SMITA TEWARI JASSAL is an associate professor of anthropology at the Middle East Technical University in, Ankara, Turkey, and a visiting fellow at the Centre for the Study of Developing Societies, Delhi, India. She has taught anthropology at Columbia University and was the Madeleine Haas Russell Visiting Professor of Anthropology at Brandeis University (2008–2009). She is the author of *Daughters of the Earth: Women and Land in Uttar Pradesh* (2001) and the editor, with Eyal Ben-Ari, of *The Partition Motif in Contemporary Conflicts* (2007).

Library of Congress Cataloging-in-Publication Data

Jassal, Smita Tewari.
Unearthing gender : folksongs of North India / Smita Tewari Jassal.
p. cm.
Includes bibliographical references and index.
ISBN 978-0-8223-5119-1 (cloth : alk. paper)
ISBN 978-0-8223-5130-6 (pbk. : alk. paper)
1. Folk songs, Bhojpuri—India, North—History and criticism.
2. Music—Social aspects—India, North.
3. India, North—Social life and customs.
I. Title.
PK1827.5.J37 2012
782.42162'914110542—dc23   2011027455